MORE PRAISE FOR
VITAL FACTORS

"When I first picked up *Vital Factors,* I thought it was going to be just another business book, with the usual pep talk mentality. However, I couldn't put it down. The case histories, with real people from all walks of life, were not only compelling and stimulating, they were enlightening and applicable to all readers. For those of us trying to 'make it' in the business world or even in our day-to-day struggles, this book gives us new tools, hones old ones, and makes it an enjoyable process. From someone who straddles the medical profession and the corporate world—and who read the book three separate times—I say 'thank you!'"
> —James M. Fox, orthopedic surgeon, medical director
> of Synergy Performance Health Fitness Centers, and author, *Save Your Knees*

"Change is the staple of the twenty-first century, but so is each individual's hope to make a difference. Lee and Paul provide a philosophy and a road map to not only embrace change on a continuous basis but to do so by finding a purpose, a mission with a truly global perspective. This book is a quick read that will have lasting impact."
> —Joseph A. Stanislaw, president, The J. A. Stanislaw Group,
> senior adviser to Deloitte&Touche USA, and
> coauthor of the book and PBS series *The Commanding Heights*

"A great practical book. Contains real-life stories about successful people, their struggles and achievements in their business and personal lives. It would help readers in designing their careers, and business and personal relationships."
> —Murli Tolaney, chairman, MWH Global, Inc.

"MAP has provided a methodology to measure every aspect of our business and accountability, measures which were missing from our previous management trainings. These two missing pieces are enabling Orange Line Oil to consistently grow in volume, gross sales, and profit margins in a challenging and declining market."
> —Scott Tredinnick, president, Orange Line Oil Company

Fall seven times. Stand up eight.
—*Japanese proverb*

JB JOSSEY-BASS

VITAL FACTORS

The Secret to Transforming Your Business—And Your Life

Lee Froschheiser

Paul Chutkow

Foreword by Barry Kemp

John Wiley & Sons, Inc.

Published by Jossey-Bass
A Wiley Imprint
989 Market Street, San Francisco, CA 94103-1741   www.josseybass.com

Jossey-Bass books and products are available through most bookstores. To contact Jossey-Bass directly
call our Customer Care Department within the U.S. at 800-956-7739, outside the U.S. at 317-572-3986,
or fax 317-572-4002.

Jossey-Bass also publishes its books in a variety of electronic formats. Some content that appears in
print may not be available in electronic books.

Library of Congress Cataloging-in-Publication Data

Froschheiser, Lee.
   Vital factors : the secret to transforming your business and your life / by Lee Froschheiser and
Paul Chutkow ; foreword by Barry Kemp.—1st ed.
       p. cm.
   Includes bibliographical references and index.
   ISBN-13: 978-0-7879-8447-2 (cloth)
   ISBN-10: 0-7879-8447-7 (cloth)
   1. Personnel management.   2. Organizational effectiveness.   3. Leadership.   4. Employee
motivation.   5. Success.   I. Chutkow, Paul.   II. Title.
   HF5549.F753   2007
   658.3'01—dc22   2006026758

Printed in the United States of America
FIRST EDITION
HB Printing   10 9 8 7 6 5 4 3 2 1

Contents

To past, present,
and future MAP employees,
who continue to help clients
like those in this book

FOREWORD

Barry Kemp

I do not come from the world of business. I write and produce television shows and movies for a living. So why am I writing the Foreword to a book that proposes to hold the secret to transforming your business and possibly even your life? Because I had an experience with MAP that may prove enlightening.

Some years ago—at my urging—my wife and I purchased a minor league hockey team that was in financial distress. I knew nothing about running a hockey team, yet I confidently put myself in charge of turning it around. When the turnaround didn't happen in a few years, I turned to MAP. I enrolled myself and some key team executives in a weekend seminar. You will read that MAP does not promise miracles. But that must have been what I expected because after using MAP to identify the problems in our operation and the Vital Factors that would correct them, I did nothing more. Somehow I expected our results to change without any further investment of time on my part. Not surprisingly, the team did not turn around, and eventually we sold it at a significant loss.

Several years later, my wife and I acquired another distressed business. (Same wife, by the way. Maggie. No wonder I love her.) This time it was a chain of four restaurants that had steadily and increasingly been losing money for a period of years. As with the hockey team, we knew nothing about the restaurant business, but this time we were smarter. This time Maggie, albeit reluctantly, took

---

Barry Kemp created and produced the TV series *Newhart* and *Coach* and produced the motion pictures *Romy and Michelle's High School Reunion, Patch Adams,* and *Catch Me If You Can.* He has received multiple Emmy, Golden Globe, and People's Choice nominations for his work

on the role of CEO. She, too, turned to MAP, but rather than expecting a miracle, Maggie knew precisely what she wanted MAP to help her accomplish. Over a two-year period, she took part in every monthly MAP meeting, expecting of herself what she expected of her employees. She followed up with her managers on a daily basis, insisting on seeing detailed daily reports that broke the business down into key Vital Factors and allowed every store manager to understand how they fit into the whole. The goals became clear. The path to achieving those goals became clear, and the restaurants became profitable in her first year of operation. They've become increasingly more profitable every year since.

I share this with you for one reason. As you will discover, MAP is an astonishingly logical, easy-to-follow, *proven* vehicle for managing your business and your life, BUT YOU HAVE TO WORK IT!

The stories in this book are inspiring, but best of all, they are stories that you yourself can duplicate if you're willing to use the MAP system and stick with it. I didn't. Maggie did. And the results were irrefutable.

Our Mission

This book can change your life.

We are going to introduce you to MAP, a powerful system of business management and personal growth. The MAP system works. Thousands of companies and individuals have already used it to transform their businesses and their lives.

We are going to show you how to make the MAP system work for you. We are not promising miracles. But we are going to tell you some amazing stories, true stories of men and women in business today. At a critical juncture in their lives, each of them came to a moment of truth. To achieve their goals in business and life, they realized that they had to make fundamental changes and they had to grow as individuals, managers, and leaders. But they had no idea how to begin the process of change. They had no focus, no winning strategy, no blueprint for success. Then they discovered the genius of MAP and its Vital Factor tools.

Through the MAP process these men and women learned an entirely new way of managing their businesses and their lives, and with MAP each of them was able to achieve lasting success and deep personal fulfillment. Listen to their stories. And as you do, we hope that one message comes through loud and strong: if they can do it, so can you.

Our mission is to show you how.

Lee Froschheiser
Paul Chutkow

A Little Taste
of What's Ahead

- Debra Paterson was eager to fly. She was working as an upper-level manager for a small banking group, and she was doing well. But Debra wanted more: she wanted to reach the top. To do that, Debra knew she had to grow as a leader and learn how to better manage her team. But where to start? And who could help her grow as a person and as a business leader?

- Michael Caito was a born entrepreneur: smart, gutsy, and hungry for success. A restaurant delivery company that he launched with two partners grew rapidly in the start-up phase, but then it hit a wall. Sales flattened. Profits fell. Morale plummeted. Michael was wracked with stress and a growing feeling of desperation. Who could help him and his partners manage the crisis? Where could they learn the secrets of sustained business success?

- Bill de la Viña needed help—desperately. To serve the Latino community he had a created a small money-transfer business, but soon it was growing faster than he could handle. What to do? Bill had no formal business training and no time for school. Who could teach him business fundamentals? And who could teach him how to successfully grow a business from the ground up?

- Ted Price faced one of the toughest challenges in business: managing highly creative people. As president of a hot video games company, Ted ran a staff of 150 people, most of them young techies with a passion for video games and computer programming. His people worked long hours, kept crazy schedules, and their burnout rate was disastrously high. Worse, they detested the necessary basics of business: controlling costs, measuring performance, and holding people accountable. Ted was stumped. Was there some surefire system of management that his people would embrace? Was there some proven path he could follow to take his young company from good to great?

• Katherine Le fled Vietnam in a rickety boat. Through grit and courage she made her way to California, learned English, put herself through college, and landed good jobs in banking and finance. Her formula for success was always the same: Self-reliance. Do it yourself. Work harder than everyone else. As she climbed the corporate ladder that formula served her well. But when she reached the top, Katherine ran out of answers. She worked to exhaustion, and when her people let her down, she did their work as well. Inevitably, her health suffered and so did her family life. Katherine needed help. But where could she learn the secrets of effective leadership? And who could teach her how to better manage her time—and her team?

• Andy Cohn's marriage was in turmoil. He was running a hard-charging manufacturing firm and his wife was keeping the books. Their business lives and personal lives were totally intertwined, and they were rubbing each other raw. Then one day his wife up and quit the business. Andy was overstressed, overweight, and now his marriage was in trouble. What should he do? How could he get his life and his marriage back on track?

• Christi Wilkins had a dream. As a child she had gone to school in Iran, and when she came to America her new school was a shock. Everything was different: the way the kids behaved, what the teachers expected, even the way kids took tests. Christi pulled through and decided to devote her life to helping other immigrant kids adjust to American schools. Too many of them were failing for reasons that Christi knew she could fix. Hers was a noble mission, but when Christi's nonprofit organization ran into trouble, where could she turn for help and guidance? Who could help her save those kids?

• Ray Thurston had it all. Through energy and innovation—and a little help from MAP—Ray had made a fortune in business. But now he wanted to do more; he wanted to give something back. So Ray forged a new mission for his life: saving endangered species and finding a cure for breast cancer. But Ray had no experience in science or medical research. What tools could he use to achieve those goals? And where could he turn for guidance and inspiration?

CHAPTER ONE

THE GENIUS OF MAP

I'm passionate about MAP.

I'm passionate about business.

And I'm passionate about helping people change and grow.

What I do, almost every single working day, is show people how to use the MAP system to transform their businesses and their lives. Use the MAP system and its Vital Factor tools, I tell them, and you can set into motion powerful changes that will dramatically improve every aspect of your business. Every single one. And guess what? You can then take these same tools home and use them to improve your relationships, your finances, your parenting, your retirement planning, even how you manage your weight, cholesterol, and stress. And if you share these tools with your kids, it will help them perform better at school and do better at sports, music, or art. In sum, it will help them achieve their goals in any field they choose.

At the outset I always hear skeptics. "Come on now, Lee," they say, "you're the CEO of MAP. You're just blowing smoke! MAP can't do all that!"

Well, I'm here to tell you it can. And MAP has the track record to prove it. MAP stands for Management Action Programs, and for forty-six years MAP has been transforming businesses—and lives. The MAP system is amazingly flexible. It works well inside big, brand-name corporations like Wells Fargo & Company, Marriott Hotels, SBC Communications, Trader Joe's, Cold Stone Creamery, Stewart Title, and Countrywide Credit. It also works well inside small businesses, creative start-ups, and nonprofit organizations, even city governments. Today the MAP system helps run construction companies, engineering firms, advertising agencies, restaurant chains, doctors' offices, fruit farms, and high-tech companies specializing in everything from biotechnology to computer gaming. MAP takes start-up companies and helps them grow, and it takes mature companies and helps them improve their performance. That's what my colleagues and I do, day in, day out, and at MAP we love every minute of our work.

Do you know why we are so passionate about what we do? It is because every day we get to work side by side with so many dynamic and fascinating business leaders. You'll meet many of them: Debra Paterson, Bill de la Viña, Michael Caito, Katherine Le, Ted Price, Christi Wilkins, Ray Thurston, and many more. These are men and women of extraordinary intelligence and accomplishment, coming from a rich array of backgrounds, and we feel privileged to guide them along the road to business success. But it goes much deeper than that. We are helping them grow as individuals, and we are helping them fulfill their highest goals and ambitions. Every day at MAP we feel blessed, for we have front-row seats at the American Dream.

The purpose of this book is simple and clear: we are going to show you, step by step, how you can use the MAP system to transform your own business and your own life. We are going to show you how to set goals and meet them every single time. The secret is an ingenious MAP concept called Vital Factors, and we're going to show you how you can use the Vital Factor process to dramatically improve your company's performance and profitability. We will also give you a set of simple, easy-to-implement Vital Factor tools that will help you and your team understand and master the execution of the six basic functions of management:

- Leading
- Communicating
- Planning
- Organizing
- Staffing
- Controlling

Everything begins with effective leadership, and we are going to share with you some very surprising ideas about what it takes to be an effective leader and motivator. As you will discover, the MAP ideas don't come out of any fancy MBA study or trendy new management fad. They come directly from decades of hands-on, real-world, in-the-trenches business experience. And here's the real beauty of it: the Vital Factor process itself helps organizations groom effective managers and leaders. In the pages ahead, dozens of men and women will tell you in detail how they have grown and matured as managers and leaders, just by learning the MAP system and implementing it throughout their companies and organizations.

Now, let's get right down to the marrow of it: What is the MAP system? How did it get started? How does it work? How, specifically, can the MAP system help you transform your business and your life? And how can MAP help you fulfill your highest dreams and ambitions?

The answers all trace back to a man named Eric Gillberg. I want to take a moment or two to tell you about Eric. He's a brilliant, inventive, no-nonsense man, and as you will see, MAP is his baby, his brainchild, the crowning achievement of his remarkable life. Hearing about Eric will help you understand the MAP system and how unique it is in its approach to management and leadership. Also, I want you to see what kind of life experiences shaped Eric's vision and what specific goals and values led him to the creation of MAP. Then everything will begin to fall into place, and you will better understand how the MAP system can work for you.

Eric Gillberg was born in Detroit some ninety years ago, near the end of World War I. His father was an immigrant from Sweden; his mother came from a family in Ohio. Eric's early life was not easy. His parents divorced when he was a young boy, and they sent him off to a boarding school in Kalamazoo. Later he returned to Detroit to live with his mother. Early on Eric realized that he had to fend for himself and be practical and self-reliant. At the same time, though, he saw that to succeed in life you have to learn how to live and work harmoniously with other people and how to serve their needs as well as your own.

During the terrible Depression years, Eric juggled school and several different jobs. First, he worked in the stockroom of the Henry Ford Hospital in Detroit. Then he went to work as a troubleshooter for Briggs Manufacturing, a company that was manufacturing wings for fighter aircraft. Though he was still very young,

Eric was given a big responsibility at Briggs: quality control. He had to make sure that every step in the production process was running perfectly and that every wing emerged without a single flaw. This was a critical, high-stakes mission: even a tiny mistake in manufacturing could result in the pilot and many other people losing their lives.

At Briggs, Eric showed that he had the makings of a first-class engineer: his mind was disciplined and precise but also supple and creative. Still, Eric wasn't yet sure what path he wanted to follow. When he entered Wayne University in Detroit, he started out with coursework in English and psychology. Then came Pearl Harbor and World War II. Right away Eric quit school and joined the U.S. Navy. It was in the Navy that Eric discovered he had a special gift: he was a born trainer and coach. Soon he was training top Navy pilots and getting them ready for combat. One of his toughest assignments was the *Dumpster*. In this exercise, pilots were dumped into frigid water, and in the water Eric taught them the skills to survive. Again, there was no margin for error: one mistake on a combat mission and the pilot could die.

When the war ended, Eric left the Navy and went into business. He bought a small franchise in California and quickly turned it into a moneymaker. Then Eric got a dream call. A man who knew of his special gifts and experience asked him to develop a series of innovative training programs to teach companies the secrets of leadership, management, and business success. Eric jumped at the opportunity. It was a perfect fit: it combined his passion for business with his natural gifts as a trainer. Right away Eric knew this was his true calling, what he was born to do.

Throughout the next several years Eric ran management training programs for AT&T and other highly successful companies. He groomed their leadership teams, drilling them on management fundamentals, and he worked hand in glove with men and women up and down their organizations. Eric learned that promoting lasting change was always a process, never a single event. You had to work with companies over the long haul, to mentor their people and guide the process every step of the way. Along with corporate giants like AT&T, Eric worked with many smaller businesses and creative start-ups, digging into their internal workings, pinpointing problems, and teaching their people how to solve them. In companies small and large Eric found that grooming top business leaders was like grooming Top Gun pilots for the Navy: you had to start out with people with the Right Stuff, give them first-class training, and every so often you had to throw them into some business equivalent of the Dumpster, so they could learn how to survive and manage a crisis—and feel their skills and confidence grow in the process.

By 1960, Eric was ready to go out on his own. He left the training program group and created his own business training and consulting company, with headquarters in Pasadena, California. As in any start-up venture, Eric's first concern was survival: bringing in enough business to pay the rent and his skeleton staff. Quickly, though, Eric developed strong relationships with leading engineering and construction firms in the LA area and with a top airline manufacturer. These industries were a good fit for Eric's expertise: he knew their challenges intimately, from his years in the Navy and from his early days inspecting airplane wings for Briggs Manufacturing.

In the early stages Eric's seminars focused on helping leaders and managers sharpen their interpersonal skills and their ability to communicate. That was a good start, but Eric wanted to innovate, he wanted to develop new ways to help his clients improve their production lines and their bottom-line business performance. To do that, he put together a team of highly experienced business executives and coaches. The team members were not academics or theoreticians. They were passionate, committed business professionals with long experience in the trenches of business. They knew how to run companies, recruit the best people, meet budgets, control costs, promote growth and profitability, and nurture creativity and innovation. By any standard this was an "A team," and it was also the foundation of MAP. Eric, now, was ready to go.

Once he had his team in place, Eric gave its members a very specific task. Many of Eric's early clients were project driven: they had to design and develop a product by a specific date, on a fixed budget, and then they had to manufacture it, inspect it, test it, and deliver it—on time, on budget, and with zero mistakes. Eric knew they needed a system to do that, a system of management that could set goals, fix budgets and deadlines, control quality, ensure accountability, and instill the discipline necessary to meet all the project's goals on time and on budget. What would such a system look like? And how would it work?

To answer those questions, Eric and his team studied the thinking and the management practices of several highly successful companies. More precisely, they drew together what they already knew from their own wealth of experience. What they saw was remarkably clear. Highly successful companies have the basic components that you would expect: strong financial foundations and the usual sturdy pillars: Effective leaders. Competent managers. A motivated staff. Clear plans and strategies. Concrete goals. Quality control. Attractive, reliable goods or services. And solid financial management. No surprises there.

But Eric's team found something else: these highly successful companies had not unearthed any magic formulas for success. To the contrary, they simply focused tightly on their business fundamentals, not only mastering them but also weaving them deeply into their daily operations. They did the big things well and they did the little things well. Day in, day out. Year in, year out.

The results were plain to see. The best-run companies, no matter what their field of endeavor, usually displayed a common set of attributes and virtues:

- Their business goals were clear, specific, and measurable.
- Their supporting values were clear, written down—and unbendable.
- Internal communication was clear, up and down the company.
- There was alignment: everyone understood and supported the company's mission, vision, values, and strategic objectives.
- Roles were clear: everyone had a written job description, with precisely defined duties and responsibilities.
- Individual goals were clear: each person had specific goals to meet, including measurable benchmarks for evaluating performance.
- There were controls: everyone's performance was measured and evaluated on a consistent basis—managers and executives included.
- There were incentives: people who consistently met their goals were properly rewarded and groomed for greater responsibility.

- There were consequences: people who consistently failed to meet their goals were given training, a different assignment, or if all else failed, they were given an honest appraisal and asked to leave.
- There was candor: it served no one's purposes to hide the truth or shy away from confrontation. In matters small and large, people in highly successful companies worked hard to uphold the highest standards of openness, honesty, and fairness.
- And their No. 1 priority, always? People. The best-run companies understood, deep in their marrow, that their most important resource was not new technology, clever marketing, canny pricing strategies, or astute financial planning. No. Their most important resource, what made them winners, was people. First and always and never any confusion about it.
- Training and personal growth, therefore, were bedrock essentials. To succeed in business you had to recruit and hire the best people, train them, keep them motivated and challenged, give them the tools and incentives they needed to succeed, and do everything in your power to help them grow as individuals, managers, and leaders.

These findings ignited Eric and his team. These attributes and virtues, when set down in an orderly fashion, suggested to them a formula, a blueprint for success, a set of ideals and practices that could lead any company or organization to growth and prosperity. And to that blueprint Eric and his team then added something else, an insight that shed light deep into the crevices of what separates the top companies—the innovators and the market leaders—from all the others.

The team found that companies were like people: each was unique, each had its own distinctive DNA, each had its own particular set of defining strengths and weaknesses. Moreover, each company had its own unique—but often hidden—set of *Vital Factors*, the critical elements that would either hold that company back or propel it to success. This concept of Vital Factors did not spring forth in one Eureka! moment; it took months of sifting and analyzing. But the more deeply Eric and his team looked at Vital Factors, the more convinced they became that they had found their grail, the keys to the castle, the tickets to success.

What exactly is a Vital Factor? The realms of medicine and sport offer the clearest analogies. If you have a heart attack and wind up in the hospital, every day your doctor and nurses will monitor your vital signs: your temperature, pulse, blood pressure, and the like. By carefully measuring and monitoring these Vital Factors, your medical team can evaluate your progress, address root causes, and develop a concrete plan to put you on the road back to improved health and vitality.

Likewise, winning sports teams and athletes routinely break their performance down into its critical component parts, to examine each part and see which is working well and which is not. In baseball, for instance, you can learn a lot by looking at a pitcher's win-loss record for the season. But you can learn a lot more by measuring his pitch speed, calculating the ratio of strikes to balls pitched, and pinpointing how many pitches he can throw before his arm starts to tire. Each of these is a Vital Factor, a component that can be isolated, measured, worked on, and improved.

A first-class pitching coach, though, digs much deeper. What small steps influence these Vital Factors? To find out, he and the pitcher sit down together and examine every aspect of the pitcher's fundamentals. His preparation. His grip on the ball. His focus on the catcher's target. The position of his feet. The alignment of his shoulders to the target. His windup. His delivery. The height of his leg kick. The angle of his arm as it comes overhead. The speed at which his arm flings forward. How each finger works at the point of release. Each of these components is a deeper fundamental, and each one ultimately affects the pitcher's win-loss record, his personal bottom line. So a pitcher needs to master all his Vital Factors. Working with their coach, the best pitchers focus tightly on their most critical Vital Factors—at MAP we always say, "Focus on the Vital Few; ignore or delegate the trivial many"—and then they drill each one to perfection, until their minds and their bodies naturally and consistently execute each one. When a pitcher masters all his Vital Factors and then blends them into a seamless and efficient pitching system, he will become a consistent winner and maybe one of the very best in his league. Mastering these Vital Factors is the key to success, the ticket to glory.

Eric's team saw it clearly: Vital Factors play the same role in every business—including *your* business. To succeed, you have to study the mechanics of your business, you have to pinpoint the critical component parts, the hidden business drivers, and then you have to devise ways to focus constantly on your Vital Factors: measure them, manage them, improve them, and ultimately perfect them. Moreover, businesses, like baseball teams, need first-class coaches and an effective *system* for teaching and mastering the Vital Factor process. Eric's team recognized that Vital Factors would vary from industry to industry, from company to company, from department to department, even from job to job. For a delivery company one Vital Factor might be profit per delivery. For a winery one Vital Factor might be bottle yield per acre of grapes planted. For a mail-order company one Vital Factor might be the time the call center takes to answer the phone, take the order, and process the customer's credit card. But Eric's team also came to this stark realization:

Whatever your specific Vital Factors are, if you want to win consistently in your business, you have to pinpoint your Vital Factors, measure them consistently, and focus tightly on your Vital Few. Then you have to put into place a system that will help you master your Vital Factors, hone them, polish them, and finally perfect them. Mastering the Vital Factor process is the art of execution. And doing it better than your competitors, day in, day out, is your path to success, your ticket to glory.

For Eric and his team, seeing all this was illuminating—and sobering. In their view there was no escaping the truth: the best-run companies truly were in a class by themselves. They had mastered their fundamentals and had woven them tightly into the operations of their companies. And they had learned how to master the Vital Factor process. That was the good news. But here was the bad news: many, many companies, even ones that were doing well, had not mastered their business fundamentals. Many had not mastered even the basics of effective execution. And here was the worst news of all: as Eric and his team could see, few managers or business leaders understood the concept of Vital Factors, much less how to identify their own Vital Factors, focus on them, and manage them effectively. Put simply, most managers and leaders had no effective system of management and no blueprint for success.

What to do?

This is where the true genius of Eric and his team came shining through. What if they could create a complete management system and a set of tools that any business could use to pinpoint its Vital Factors and ensure their proper management and execution? And what if that same system could do even more? What if it could actually perform six critical missions simultaneously:

- *Teach* business fundamentals
- *Pinpoint* a company's Vital Factors
- *Ensure* proper measurement and management of these Vital Factors
- *Establish* a top-to-bottom system of goals and controls
- *Catalyze* positive, ongoing changes throughout the company
- *Instill* those virtues that turn good companies into market leaders

What an idea! A system like that could transform almost any business or organization. It could improve the performance of small, family-run businesses and also big corporations. It could put a strong business foundation under creative start-ups, and it could revitalize old-guard companies that were losing energy and market share. At a stroke it could solve endemic business problems and simplify most of the complexities of management. What a wonder tool that would be!

And so it was that the MAP system was born. MAP, as I said before, stands for Management Action Programs, and that perfectly describes what the MAP system is. It is a detailed, comprehensive plan of action, one designed to perform the six critical missions that I listed earlier. MAP is also a blueprint and an operations manual. It shows companies precisely how to run their businesses, day in, day out, for optimum performance and profit. The system also includes a set of effective, easy-to-use tools that any company or organization can use to solve problems and get almost any job done, on time and on budget. And the foundation of the MAP system? Vital Factors and business fundamentals, the daily blocking and tackling that winning companies do better than their competitors. MAP is an ongoing process that, when implemented well, produces all those attributes and virtues that Eric's team found in the best-run companies. The process produces compelling mission statements, clear, unbendable values, strong business plans, and well-defined job descriptions and lines of authority, plus an entire system of goals and controls and incentives and rewards. Eric and his team precision-engineered the MAP system to accomplish all these goals. And over the past forty-six years, it has done just that, often brilliantly so.

Being so big in scope the MAP system did not have an easy birth. Today Eric lives in quiet retirement in Washington State, with his beloved wife, Alice, but he still has vivid memories of the birth of the MAP system. He and his original team assembled the system piece by piece, and then they went through long, often frustrating phases of development, field-testing, refinement, and polish. At the outset Eric never dreamed that his little baby would grow so big or that it would wind up helping more than 12,000 companies. Eric's first goal was modest and nothing fancy: he simply wanted to create an effective, easy-to-implement system of management that his clients could use to manage their projects and meet their goals on a consistent basis. No muss, no frills, just get the job done.

Nonetheless, the MAP system quickly proved to be an ingenious tool. It functions like the operating system inside your computer or your car: you install it inside your company, and it makes the engine and all the vital parts run smoothly and efficiently. The MAP system is a model of simplicity, yet it produces changes that are deep, powerful, and lasting. MAP can take any company, organization, or team—any entity that needs to be managed—and make it perform better. You will see proof of that all the way through this book.

One cornerstone of our philosophy at MAP is this core belief: if you want to grow your business, you have to start by growing the people who run it. To that end Eric and his team developed a series of three-day workshops and follow-up sessions to teach people how to manage their Vital Factors, execute their fundamentals, and grow as managers and leaders and reach their full potential. Again, it took time, experimentation, and field-testing, but the resulting formula proved to be highly successful. Over the past forty-six years, more than 150,000 men and women have used the MAP workshop to improve their leadership and managerial skills and enhance their careers. They emerged from the workshops better equipped to manage their companies and better equipped to train the people around them and help them grow as managers and leaders. Typically, managers and leaders who participate in MAP workshops then send their teams to these workshops, in order to drive the MAP system and its Vital Factor tools all the way through their companies. This sets in motion powerful ongoing changes, as you will see for yourself in the pages ahead.

The workshops are just one step. On top of that foundation the consultants and coaches at MAP also provide on-site support and guidance for client companies, helping them tailor the MAP system to their specific needs. In keeping with Eric's original philosophy, the MAP team does not work like typical business consultants. Our first priority is to build a lasting relationship with our clients. As you will hear, some companies have been working with MAP coaches for fifteen or twenty years. By patiently focusing on the long term we can earn the trust and confidence of everyone in the company, and we often wind up functioning like doctors or trusted family advisers. We meet with our clients on a regular basis, at least once a month, and we help them improve the health of their companies. We also function as *life coaches*, working closely with men and women at every level of a company, helping them meet their personal goals and sharing with them the secrets of success in business—and in life. In times of crisis, of course, our MAP coaches are there to help.

Eric Gillberg and his original team set all this into motion. They pioneered the concept of Vital Factors, they constructed the MAP operating system, and they spent long years field-testing it, fine-tuning it, and adjusting it to suit the changing needs of their clients and the surrounding business environment. It is a testament to what they built that the MAP system and its guiding principles have withstood the test of time. Economies change, industries change, people change, and business fads come and go as capriciously as birds on a telephone wire. But the underlying truths that Eric and his team discovered remain solid and immutable. And they remain just as potent today as they were when Eric started MAP, over forty-six years ago.

MAP TODAY

When Eric started MAP I was just a schoolboy, living with my parents and my brother in Nebraska. We were typical Midwesterners. My folks were warm and caring, and we always laughed a lot around the family table. My parents were disciplined and hard working, and my brother and I learned from their example. For us, this was bedrock: nothing substantial can be built without hard work. For several generations, none of my family had been to college; there was too much other work to do. I made schooling a top priority, though, and I was determined to get a college education.

Football and other sports were among my early passions. I learned the fundamentals of football in high school and college. Nebraska always had one of the top football teams in the nation. Why? Because year in, year out, we had first-rate coaches and first-rate training that focused on fundamentals. Every day we drilled our fundamentals, the basic blocking and tackling of good football, and the results were plain to see: we did the big things well and we did the little things well. That was our blueprint for success, and we turned in winning seasons year after year.

I was lucky: I learned the importance of fundamentals early on. I remember my father breaking down the fundamentals of the simple process of mowing grass, and I remember my mom taking my brother and me into the kitchen and teaching us the fundamentals of washing dishes. Whether it was from my coaches or my parents it was always, "Lee, start with the fundamentals and learn it from the ground up. And if it's worth doing, do it right. Give it your all." Thanks to them and my own hard work, I learned that executing your fundamentals well was essential to success in whatever you chose to do. And for my future career in business, that was the best lesson that money could buy.

Now let me tell you a story. After I graduated from college, I went to work as a teacher in a small town in Nebraska, in a K–12 school with only 144 students. We were too small to field an eleven-man football team, but this was Nebraska and we had to have football. So in our conference we played eight boys to a side, and year after year our team absolutely stank. When I joined the school, the team had won only three games total over the past three seasons. We were just plain bad. Anyway, that summer, before school started, the head football coach came up to me and said, "Hey, Lee, you played football. Could you help out as an assistant coach?"

"Sure," I said.

"Great, because I sure could use some help. This year I think we can really turn things around." I then asked the coach if he had any tapes of games from the previous year. "Sure," he said. "We film a couple of games each year."

I took the films home—in those days it was 8 mm film—and I watched them carefully. The following week the coach stopped me in the hall all excited. Then he handed me a playbook that was about a half inch thick. "I've added in about fifteen new plays for this season and I'm really excited. These plays are really going to make a difference for us!"

I looked at the playbook and said to him, "You know, that's great. Really good." I wanted to be encouraging and supportive. But candor runs deep in the Froschheiser veins, and I said, "So, what you've done is you've added on fifteen new plays that our guys won't be able to run very well."

The coach looked at me with this kind of blank look and said, "What do you mean?"

"Well, you could add a hundred new plays to this playbook and you're just going to have one hundred more plays that you're not going to run well. The issue is not how many plays you have in your playbook. The issue is your fundamentals, your blocking and tackling. Our people miss blocks. And they don't know how to tackle correctly. These are kids who don't have a lot of experience. Sure, you get them to remember the plays, but they still don't execute the fundamentals. Football is more than just running plays; the real key is how well your guys execute the fundamentals behind those plays."

The coach raised his eyebrows. "You know, you're right, Lee. But I'm not sure we have enough time in practice to address those problems. We do our normal summer training, but I get them into running plays really early, and we work on getting the plays down so they can actually play a game." The coach paused for a moment and then said, "But I'm willing to try something else. What should we do?"

"I think we should hone our playbook down to about eight or ten plays, a few basic plays that we can run well and execute well. Maybe, after we've mastered those, we can add in one or two more."

And that's exactly what we did. We spent all of our summer practices focused on execution. How do you tackle? Well, when you go to tackle, you put your face guard right into the middle of that guy's chest; you don't just stick your arms out. How do you block?

Well, you square yourself up this way, and you position your feet like that. Now, let's move on to the fundamentals of blocking.

And guess what? The approach worked. We got our guys to a place where they were able to execute eight basic plays really, really well. We trained them so hard they could practically run those eight plays in their sleep. They knew exactly how to step, where to step. When we started the season, our approach quickly became kind of a joke: the other teams knew exactly which play we'd run even before we'd run it. But guess what? It didn't matter! Because we were able to execute those plays successfully. And in the end we had a winning season. We went five and four. This was a major triumph. It was like a town celebration; the school hadn't had a winning season for who knows how many years.

Now, what's the point of this story? On the football field, half a continent away from California, I had learned what Eric Gillberg and his original team had learned about business: you have to focus on your fundamentals, you have to pinpoint your Vital Factors and then focus on the Vital Few, the small number of core plays that you can master and that will carry you to victory. Mastering your Vital Factors is the key to successful execution, the ticket to glory. The problem is that few people realize the importance of the Vital Factors—even people who are in the roles of leaders and coaches!

With these lessons under my belt, I went into business and moved quickly up the ranks of management and into leadership positions. Then I helped run several major companies. As I went, I deepened my understanding of the fundamentals and the finer points of management. Still, I wanted to learn more, and I wanted to share with others everything that I had learned along the way. When MAP signed me on as a business coach, right away I knew this was my calling, what I was born to do.

What makes MAP different? It's that we focus on those six basic functions of management: Leading. Communicating. Planning. Organizing. Staffing. Controlling. Beyond that, we teach people how to master the Vital Factor process and execute their fundamentals. As you will see, for a business leader the MAP system can be a liberation. When you and your team master your business's fundamentals, you have more time at work to innovate and be creative—and you have more time to be at home with your family and to lead a more balanced life. I have seen it work over and over: the MAP system helps overworked, overstressed executives get their lives back, their fun back, their creativity back—and their spouses and families back too. As you will see over and over, MAP transforms businesses and it transforms lives.

NOW THE BOOK

I salute Eric and his original team. They did a marvelous job. And I know what it took to help 12,000 companies transform their operations, boost their performance, and adopt a whole new concept of leadership. But at MAP today we see that as only a good beginning. The MAP system is unique. As far as we can tell, there is no other business management system like it, and there is certainly none that pairs business management skills with personal growth and transformation. Still, for years MAP has been referred to as "the best-kept secret in business consulting." We were a quiet success and we were happy to keep it that way.

Now, though, we have decided to take our proprietary system of business management and personal growth and make it available to the general public. We want to share the MAP system and the secrets we have learned with companies and individuals across the United States and far beyond. We want the MAP system to be available to everyone, from a baker in Pennsylvania to a delivery company in Kansas, and from a software designer in Bangalore to every start-up venture from Cambridge to Palo Alto. MAP can work wonders for each of them—and for each of you as well. We know that's true; we see the proof of it every single day.

This book is MAP's chosen vehicle. In the early chapters, we will show you how you can use the MAP system and Vital Factors at work and at home. And in the later chapters, we will take you deep inside the MAP process and show you what it can do when implemented over the long term. All along the way we will tell you true stories of men and women who have used MAP to improve their businesses and their lives. Our ongoing message to you is clear and empowering: if they can do it, so can you. This book will show you how.

Clear language and clear communication are essential to the success of any business, and they are absolutely essential to the MAP process. So no one in this book will be talking in abstractions or jargon-laden theory. Likewise, we will stay focused on practical solutions, what works and what doesn't. Our bedrock will be business fundamentals: Leadership. Mission. Vision. Values. Strategy and the like. But we will also devote whole sections of this book to life planning, the most effective ways to groom your successor, and an essential element of business success that we at MAP feel is too often overlooked: passion and commitment.

Over the years we at MAP have developed a few terms and concepts that we hold dear: *Vital Factors*. The *Vital Few. Team Consulting. Goals and Controls.* The *Big Red "S."* And one of my favorites: the *Onboard Troublemaker.* As we go along, we'll explain those terms and how you can use them to sharpen your thinking and simplify complex business problems. Once that's done, it's often much easier to work out a solution.

As we present the MAP system and its Vital Factor tools, we will also share with you something much larger: the collective wisdom of the entire MAP team. One day at a meeting of our board of directors we added up our combined years of hands-on business experience. It was over 250 years of experience—and that was just on the board! This book is truly a collaborative effort, drawing together the collective experience and wisdom of our team of MAP consultants and coaches, plus the real-life experiences of dozens of our MAP clients. As you will see, as coaches we form very close bonds with our clients, and the richness of the stories in this book flows directly from those bonds and from the business lessons that we have all learned together. This book is a collaboration in another sense as well. For an outsider's perspective—and for help with the actual writing—we at MAP turned to Paul Chutkow, the author of several acclaimed books about business. We put Paul through the MAP workshop and then sent him out to talk at length with several MAP clients, to see up close and with a journalist's eye how the MAP system worked for a wide range of companies and organizations. It was an illuminating experience: Paul saw things in the MAP system that we, being so close to it, hadn't seen. And when it came to the actual writing of the book, Paul was able to meld his cool, objective outsider perspective with my passionate, committed insider perspective. To make matters simple for the reader, Paul and I narrate the book with a single first-person voice:

mine. Still, I want readers to know that behind my solo-sounding, narrating "I" there stands the experience of the entire MAP team and Paul's unique perspective as well.

As you will see, the overarching theme of this book is *change*, and that theme will carry us far beyond the confines of business. In the pages ahead you will hear a wide variety of business leaders explain how MAP helped them make far-reaching changes—in their companies, yes, but also in their personal lives. Andy Cohn will tell you how MAP helped him save his marriage. A hard-driving CEO named George Rogers will tell you how MAP helped him become a better parent and a more understanding husband. A Los Angeles advertising executive named Hector Orci will explain how MAP led him to business success and then to a second calling: creating charter schools to help Latino kids grow and reach their full potential.

Where does the MAP process ultimately lead? At the end of this book a Phoenix businessman named Ray Thurston will tell you how MAP helped him turn a small family-run messenger service into a giant of innovation, one coveted by UPS. Ray made a fortune in the process, and now he has moved on to new and exciting missions: protecting endangered species around the world and helping to pioneer a new generation of cures for breast cancer. As Ray will tell you, he is now fulfilling his highest dreams and ambitions, thanks in large measure to what he learned from MAP and to the deep and lasting changes that MAP set into motion.

MAP, as you are about to discover, is a journey of growth and transformation. It begins with a single step, a step that you can now take simply by turning the page. At MAP we refer to this first step as the *awakening*.

CHAPTER TWO

THE AWAKENING

Debra Paterson was determined to reach the top.

She grew up in a suburb of Chicago, did well in school, and then she moved out to Arizona and began a career in banking. Debra started at the bottom, as a teller in a branch of a small community banking group in Tucson. But no matter. She worked hard, mastered the basics of banking, and then she worked her way through every position in the branch. Soon Debra moved into management, with assignments in marketing and human resources for the entire group.

In 1989, after nine years of good experience in Tucson, Debra landed a wonderful opportunity in San Diego with a much bigger bank, First Interstate. Before long, she was working as district manager for First Interstate's expanding network of branches in San Bernardino and Riverside Counties. This was a big responsibility: Debra had twenty branches reporting directly to her. By now, she had mastered both the fundamentals and the finer points of retail and business banking; there was no problem there. Still, Debra began to feel anxious: she wasn't sure she had the management and leadership skills that she needed to get to the next level, to really spread her wings and fly. As Debra explains it, "I had hit that point where you really need a bit more help."

Then one day Debra received a telephone call from MAP. One of our consultants said that he wanted to introduce her to a unique system of business management and personal growth. It had helped many people advance their careers and grow as individuals and leaders; would she like to attend a three-day MAP workshop, to give the system a try? Debra politely said no. At that stage she knew absolutely nothing about Management Action Programs, and even though she was eager to make changes at work and at home, her schedule at the bank was just too tight. There was simply no way she could take three straight days away from work. So thanks, but no thanks. Her leadership training and personal growth would just have to wait.

A few years later, though, Debra was feeling restless. First Interstate Bank had been acquired by another banking group, Wells Fargo & Company, and she wasn't sure where her career was headed. But Debra was still determined to reach the top, and she was still eager to grow as a manager and leader. But where to turn for help and guidance? Debra had no clear idea.

Then one day in 1999, at a business forum in downtown Los Angeles, Debra happened to be seated at a table with Sylvia Lange, one of MAP's executive consultants. The two women clicked. They exchanged business cards, and a few days later Sylvia called and asked Debra if she wanted to attend a MAP workshop. This time Debra didn't hesitate to say yes. She wasn't doing this on behalf of the bank; she was doing this for herself, to develop further as a leader and as a person and to give herself an extra boost in her journey to the top. "I was looking for something that might help my career be a little more successful," she says. "I was looking for a competitive edge."

A short time later Debra went to Newport Beach, California, for a three-day immersion in MAP's system of management, leadership, and personal growth. Right from Day One the experience was both a shock and an awakening. On the first morning the workshop leader pinned twelve personal profiles on the wall, each in a large format and each describing, in capsule form, one of the twelve participants in the room. The MAP team members had created the profiles beforehand from feedback received from each participant's bosses, peers, and direct reports. At MAP we call this *360-degree feedback,* because it gives a fully rounded picture of the individual and his or her defining qualities. The twelve profiles set forth a series of management traits, some of them strengths, some of them areas needing improvement. However, there were no names attached to any of the profiles. Debra and her fellow participants had to study the profiles, figure out which one fit them best, and then say so out loud.

Right away the process proved disconcerting for several participants: they chose the wrong profile! At a single stroke their image of themselves as managers and leaders was shown to be off the mark. For two or three others the impact was even stronger: they saw, in black and white, that they had serious shortcomings as managers and leaders. In effect MAP had held a portrait in front of them—and some of the participants didn't like the image painted by their bosses and coworkers. Still, for everyone the experience was illuminating, including Debra. "Some big light bulbs went off," Debra says. "I realized, wow, I'm going to have to change the way I've behaved in the past with my team to get to the next level." Her process of awakening, self-discovery, and personal growth had already begun.

After that shock beginning, Debra's workshop leader introduced a set of management tools that Debra instantly knew she could use as a leader and also take back to her division at the bank. Right away she saw the value of the Vital Factor process; she knew it could really help her and her team pinpoint the elements of their business that were generating the most profit and where they should focus their attention. She also liked MAP's tools for managing Vital Factors: regular Vital Factor Meetings and *Goals and Controls,* a system that asks each person to write down his or her goals for the month, with precise, measurable benchmarks for achievement. If the person meets his or her goals for the month, that's great; then the question becomes, how does he or she improve that performance for next month? If, however, the goals are not met, the person has to set down the corrective action steps he or she will take to make sure the next goals are reached the following month. As Debra saw right away, Goals and Controls was a concrete and transparent system of accountability, one that would improve the performance of any organization.

Debra also appreciated one of MAP's favorite mantras: "Focus on the Vital Few; ignore or delegate the trivial many." That means isolate the small group of Vital Factors that really drive your business and focus closely on managing them. This same idea is often referred to in management circles as the *Pareto principle,* and let me take a moment to explain its background. Back in 1906, an Italian economist named Vilfredo Pareto studied the Italian economy and came up with an unsettling observation: 20 percent of the people owned 80 percent of the wealth. In the ensuing years specialists in other fields noticed similar 80/20 phenomena: 20 percent of possible factors often generated 80 percent of the results. Forty years later a management specialist named Joseph M. Juran documented the same phenomenon in business: 20 percent of the factors, a relatively small amount, often produce 80 percent of the results. Therefore, to manage a business well, Juran wrote, it is important to focus on "the vital few, not the trivial many." The connection was rather distant, but Juran chose to call that the *Pareto principle,* and we often cite that principle at MAP. We trust that Vilfredo Pareto and Joseph Juran will forgive us for borrowing their terms—and for taking these terms a few steps further. In our work at MAP we often find that 20 percent of a company's customers generate 80 percent of the company's revenue. We often find, too, that in a poorly performing company it is 20 percent of the people who generate 80 percent of the problems!

Debra also liked another MAP tool: *Team Consulting.* This is old-fashioned brainstorming but with several important modifications. It's done against the clock and in a tightly controlled format, so as to focus everyone's attention and achieve maximum results. As I will explain in a later chapter, important communication builders and team builders are embedded in the process. In the course of her workshop Debra gained hands-on experience with Team Consulting, and back at the bank it became one of her most effective leadership tools.

Debra was also impressed by two other tools that MAP uses: the FIRO-B assessment and the Behavioral Style Analysis. Like her colleagues in the workshop, Debra had taken these tests before the workshop began and she found them extremely helpful. They are designed to help people see hidden psychological and behavioral patterns—in themselves and in their colleagues. This helps them see their own strengths and vulnerabilities as leaders and managers. The Behavioral Style Analysis also helps people see and evaluate their effectiveness as communicators. They see how they think they are communicating and how they are actually being heard. Again, for some people in Debra's group this assessment produced a rude awakening: they had seen themselves as good communicators but suddenly they saw how wrong they had been. Over and over the people around them were failing to get the intended message. Again, Debra decided to use these same tests in her own managing practices back at the bank.

In later chapters I will explain in detail how these two assessments work and how you can use them at work and at home. The point here, though, is this: suddenly Debra had a whole set of new tools that she could use with her team members back at the bank to help them generate ideas, set strategy, align their goals, improve their communication and execution, and build team cohesion. For Debra, these were big positives, but learning about these tools was also part of her larger awakening: it showed her what she had been doing right as a manager—and doing wrong.

As the workshop unfolded, Debra realized something else: though the MAP process seemed simple on its face, it was actually catalyzing changes at many different levels beneath the surface. "The genius of the MAP process," she says, "is they give you one target, but actually they are hitting about four other targets without saying so."

How true that is—and we do it by design. One MAP target that we often leave unnamed is leadership. Each day the agenda of Debra's workshop included various exercises that the group performed, often by breaking down into smaller Team Consulting groups. As the groups perform these exercises the leadership skills of each person are thrown into a bright light—providing another effective way for every participant to evaluate his or her strengths and weaknesses as a leader. We also go further. Throughout the three days, the MAP workshop leader discusses the essentials of enlightened leadership. At MAP we often define leadership with three words: *empower your people.* We also urge managers and leaders to learn how to delegate effectively. As we put it, "You don't pay your people to bring you problems; you pay them to bring you solutions. Insist that they do."

Moreover, at MAP we don't just *discuss* the attributes of effective leaders; our workshop leaders are carefully trained to *model* an effective leadership style. To our minds, showing is always more effective than telling, especially when it comes to teaching such skills as leadership and communication. The modeling works, as Debra Paterson saw firsthand. Without even realizing it at first, she began changing her own leadership style, and by the end of the three days Debra could see that her leadership style had been totally transformed. "The change was profound," Debra says. "I'm not sure what my leadership style was before MAP. But it definitely developed my leadership style into what it is today."

Now, did this three-day workshop have a lasting impact on Debra and the way she managed her team at the bank? Yes. When she returned to work the following Monday, Debra initiated important changes. Right away she and her team began the process of pinpointing their Vital Factors—the specific components that really drove their bottom-line results. Next they instituted weekly Vital Factor Meetings to monitor and measure those Vital Factors. As part of the MAP process they also devised a Vital Factor Spreadsheet, a tool for regularly measuring their Vital Factors and holding specific people accountable for improving each one, with clear targets and benchmark dates to evaluate the results. As intended, this process broke the team's workload into visible and measurable pieces, and it started a complete transformation of the ways in which Debra and her team conducted their daily business.

Looking back now, Debra says the MAP system fit easily into the way she ran her division at the bank: "We basically have a Vital Factor Meeting every Monday, except we call it our Weekly Assessment, around our business priorities. The process is virtually the same. I think what's great about MAP is that they are taking very basic business processes that work, are effective, and using them to bring some discipline to the work environment. We just happen to have our own language about it at Wells Fargo, but the concepts that we use to run our business are the same."

Still, the MAP process enabled Debra to take her existing practices to a higher level. The result was improved discipline and performance throughout her retail banking group. "I love the Vital Factor process," Debra says, "and I still use it. The concept of the Vital Few was something that our company talks about still, but using a little different language. What I've done over the past eight, nine years, is I've taken that concept and combined it with my own concept of business priorities. As a result, we have been able to stay focused on the Vital Few factors that are going to make a big difference for the company. The MAP experience has added more depth to my execution."

Debra's new approach to leadership also paid big dividends. Before MAP her leadership style had been molded by the traditional, top-down hierarchy that so many banks and companies adhere to even today. Meetings were formal, hierarchical, and usually uninspiring. The boss generally came in; laid down the instructions; said, "Any questions?" and that was essentially it. From there the staff were expected to go out and execute her instructions. There was no dialogue, no buy-in from the staff, no team building— and no excitement. Thanks to MAP, though, Debra's approach became much more engaging. She didn't dictate policy or solutions; she acted as a facilitator and questioner, asking her staff what *they* thought were the best solutions. After all, they were on the front lines dealing with customers; they were better placed to provide good, workable solutions. In sum Debra had learned to *empower her people*. Happily, too, her new leadership style was nurtured by the Vital Factor process itself.

Here, though, Debra had a surprise: at first her new leadership style was unsettling to her team:

> My team members were used to a very rigid approach. Their old boss would say, in effect, "Here's the information. Now you guys go out and do it." The underlying message to them was this: "We don't want *you* to solve the problem. We just want you to implement what *we* see as the solution." The meetings were so weird at first. My staff were like, "Just tell us what to do. What are we supposed to do?" They simply weren't used to having their manager facilitate discussion in this way, in a roll-up-your-sleeves, hands-on kind of way. And I thought, "This is good. We're going to figure it all out together."

Debra stuck to her new leadership approach, and soon the chemistry of all the team meetings permanently changed. "Now it's just a part of the way that we have meetings. The meetings are not led by me; I don't just regurgitate information out to them. The meetings are a real discussion now and a kind of loosely defined Team Consult. If we have a specific problem to solve or someone in the group has a specific problem to solve, then we switch to a formalized Team Consulting."

Debra was amazed by this transformation. First, she saw how it empowered her team members and gave them confidence. Her underlying message, she says, was this: "'I'm not the person who has the answers; this is your problem too and you need to have answers for yourself.' And that's exactly the right approach. One, they are closer to the customer and typically they do have better answers. But, two, it's developing the critical thinking skills necessary for the future leadership of your company." It's also getting staff input and, critically, their individual buy-in and responsibility. As Debra explains, "If the team members come up with the decision, nobody can later say, 'Well, they told us, or Debra said . . .' No. This way, we develop it. And we own it."

As Debra now saw, when you empower your people, they have ownership of what they do, and they have a chance to grow as managers themselves. At the same time, you become free to better perform your vital tasks as a manager and leader: namely, keeping your eye on implementing your mission, vision, and business plan. When you delegate properly, you also become more productive at work, and you will have more time for your family and outside interests. You'll lead a happier, more balanced life.

Debra experienced all of this firsthand. And she was so impressed by the changes that MAP set into motion that she signed up for a second MAP leadership seminar, this one using the movie *Twelve O'Clock High* as a conduit into the finer points of effective leadership. This classic World War II movie tells the story of Brigadier General Frank Savage, played by Gregory Peck, and how he took charge of a poorly performing bomber group and transformed it into a highly effective fighting unit, one of the very best in the U.S. military. It is a fine movie and an excellent MAP teaching tool. Seen through the lens of the MAP system, the movie is a one-day PhD course in the art of leadership. Debra found the seminar very effective, and she had MAP organize a *Twelve O'Clock High* workshop for her management team, making it the highlight of an off-site leadership retreat.

As she moved up the ranks at Wells Fargo, Debra took on different jobs, and she found herself using her MAP principles and tools in different ways. For instance, at one stage she was put in charge of the bank's training programs for twenty-three states. "Training used to be decentralized within the organization," Debra explains. "But then we decided to restructure all of the staff, so I had a brand new team to run learning and development. Our task was to bring a new philosophy and a new policy to learning and development, not only in peer training, technical training, and sales training, but also in leadership development."

In the beginning Debra and her new group faced some complex challenges. The team members came in with different backgrounds, different levels of expertise, and in many cases, different agendas. Achieving consensus, even on how to begin the reexamination of the training process, was complicated. Debra's solution? Team Consulting.

"The Team Consulting process was something that we used quite a bit in the beginning," she says:

> Then once we got our framework, we used Team Consulting to continually assess our effectiveness about where we were going, how we were going to do things. During our first meeting we basically used the Team Consulting process to identify how we wanted to be structured, how we were going to deliver, what it was we wanted to deliver, who was our customer. The structure of the Team Consulting process allowed us to begin those conversations and to come up with action steps much quicker than if we had relied on standard brainstorming without any structure around it.

From then on the process went smoothly.

By now Debra's career was also in smooth ascension. Wells Fargo made her a regional president for one of the larger territories in its system, the Metro Minnesota market. Right away Debra set important changes into motion, many of them inspired by what she had learned at MAP:

> There were so many things we could focus on, and so we were trying to decide as a team where we were going to put a stake in the ground, what we were going to set as a business priority. Our team members were already very good at doing the basic things like unsecured loans, car loans, overdraft protection and credit cards, but now we decided to get our bankers to become experts in home equity loans and improve our production there. We thought that focusing on home equity loans would meet our customers' needs and it would also be a profitable product for the bank.

Once they set that goal Debra and her team began to formulate strategy. How, specifically, are we going to get that lift in home equity loans? What specific steps can we take? In search of answers Debra used the Team Consulting process, and though it was entirely new to this group, it worked like a charm. "It really helped them understand that my style was, 'You guys own the problem and you have to solve it. You've got to use critical business thinking skills and strategic thinking skills and then to come up with what you're going to do to implement the plan.'" Within a week, Debra's group had formulated a plan for building the bank's home equity business, complete with specific action steps and deadlines. Debra was thrilled: "Now everyone understands that home equity is one of our top priorities, and we're focusing in tight on making that a success."

The things that impressed Debra most were not the bottom-line results of the Vital Factor process, welcome though those were. What impressed her most were the deep and lasting changes that the Vital Factor process set into motion:

> People don't necessarily agree with the philosophy of having the team develop and solve the problem; many of them think that it takes too much time. They think it's easier if the boss just tells people what to do and have them do it. What I always say in response is this: "Maybe it takes more time, but in the long run the old top-down system is just not sustainable. In the short run you may have a lift in your business results with that system, but then at some point that lift is going to drop off and people are not going to know how to sustain it." Why? Because the team didn't go through the process of coming to a solution together.

In his insightful book *Winning*, Jack Welch puts it this way: when you're on the way up the corporate ladder, your job is to provide answers. But when you reach the top, your job is to ask questions. Through MAP, Debra learned that lesson well, and she realized that for her it was a double victory: it helped her put her own time to better use, and at the same time it empowered her team members and groomed them for greater responsibility and leadership down the road. Debra sees that as one of the most valuable management lessons she's ever learned.

In many companies top-level leaders and managers like Debra first go to a MAP workshop themselves, and then they send their colleagues and direct reports to MAP for the same workshop on management and personal growth. In that way they can drive the MAP philosophy and system through their company. That's fine, Debra says, but the key is getting buy-in at the top. If the boss doesn't personally embrace the MAP system, it is very hard to build support for that system and the process of change that it sets into motion.

Looking back now, what does Debra Paterson see as the most important aspect of her MAP experience? The awakening. The self-discovery. "It's that self-discovery piece that really forces you to change," she says. "If you're not happy with who you are and how you're doing, well, MAP shows you that you'd better darn well make changes. If you don't, you're just not going to be happy. I think that's the clear message that the self-discovery piece leads to. You are there to understand and be real and true to who you are, and then to realize that you have the power to change that situation and here's how you can do it."

Debra's personal awakening and the changes she made had an impact far beyond her work:

> The self-awareness things that I learned through MAP and that I continue to learn in my business life have absolutely helped me in my personal life. Changing that tendency I had—and still have at times—to tell people something rather than ask the questions and allow them to self-discover, well, in a personal relationship that works too. It has certainly worked with the man in my life. I tell you, it works much better if I ask him how he thinks something should be handled and letting him come up with the solution than by me telling him what to do.
>
> A lot of these leadership skills that you develop and learn, they're just good people skills. Team Consulting and Vital Factors can be applied to one's personal life. I don't have children, but if I did, I think these tools would be so useful. You have family decisions to be made, or you have a lot of chores that need to be done and you have a busy household, I think that the concepts of Vital Factors, the Vital Few, and Team Consulting would really help. The communication skills can help too in dealing with kids and spouses. So can simply being more aware of where you are in your life, looking at your goals, and saying to yourself, "Am I really on track here?" All that flows from the MAP process. At least it did for me.

In his fascinating book *Good to Great,* James C. Collins and his research team identified Wells Fargo as one of the eleven best-run companies in American business today. Wells Fargo, they found, was one of the rare few that had made that difficult transition from good to great. We at MAP were thrilled that Wells Fargo made this prestigious list. And we believe that with leaders like Debra Paterson onboard, Wells Fargo is destined to become even better still.

MAP OVERVIEW.

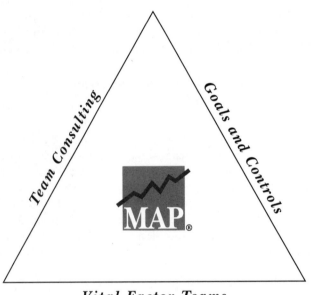

Vital Factor Teams

The Bottom Line

1. Know thyself. The first step in the *awakening* process is to see clearly your strengths and weaknesses as a leader and manager. Seek 360-degree feedback from the people around you.
2. Create a *Personal Development Plan* to maximize your strengths and overcome your weaknesses. Give yourself specific goals and deadlines and ways to measure your progress.
3. Learn to empower your people. That's the first step on the road to becoming an effective leader and manager.
4. Learn to listen. And learn to ask effective questions and to let others bring you their own solutions. They'll win and so will you.
5. Find yourself an experienced coach and mentor; this person can help you grow and guide you on your way.

CHAPTER THREE

MEANING AND PURPOSE

Do you ever feel that you're just drifting through life, with no clear direction and no ability to change course?

Do you ever wake up in the morning not wanting to get out of bed or with a knot in the pit of your stomach, simply dreading the idea of going into work?

Do you ever stop during the day and ask yourself, "How in the heck did I wind up in this job in the first place? This isn't what I want to do!"

Well, guess what? You're not alone. Debra Paterson was one of the lucky ones: she found her calling early on. So did I. That makes the process of change so much easier, because your goals and your direction are already clear. But all the time I see people who aren't sure if they are on the right path or even on the right playing field. And that makes the process of change much more difficult. Still, this is where the Management Action Programs process can really work wonders. Let me give you an example. One day in a MAP workshop I was coaching a young woman, and I said to her, "You know, you've got all the makings of a first-rate manager. You're talented, you're disciplined, and you've got great people skills. But tell me something. In your heart of hearts, if you really had your druthers, what would you truly want to do with your life?"

"That's easy," she said. "I'd like to be a graphic designer."

So I looked her right in the eye and said, "Then that's what you ought to do!" I waited for a moment, letting that sink in, and then I said, "Now, let's get down to the real question: What's holding you back?"

Together, we peeled that onion down until we came to the answer: fear. Fear of change. Fear of the unknown. Fear of failure. Fear that she didn't have what it takes to succeed as a graphic designer. Fear of not having a corporation there to support her. Whatever the overbrush, the core answer was fear.

I understand that. It's not easy to follow your dreams. And sometimes those dreams just aren't realistic to begin with. But living your life inside a box wrapped and sealed with fear is no answer either—and that is exactly what I told her. And from that point on the MAP process of awakening and self-discovery really began working for her. By studying the results of her FIRO-B and Behavioral Style Analysis tests, she came to see the full, accurate measure of her strengths and aptitudes, and from the 360-degree feedback she received in the workshop she gained confidence in her own abilities. I'm happy to report that ultimately she made the decision to go out on her own as a graphic designer and she's doing very well. She's much happier too. She doesn't have all the perks she had before, at least not yet, but she is finding much greater meaning and purpose in her life, every single day. Robert Mondavi, the celebrated Napa Valley vintner and pioneer, puts it well: "Find your passion, and you'll never have to work a day in your life!" That's beautiful advice—and very true.

In the chapters ahead I'm going to be talking a lot about alignment in the workplace, how to get your company and your team fully aligned behind a common mission, vision, and values. But alignment is just as important at the personal level. Are your dreams and ambitions properly aligned with your skills and talents? Is your job properly aligned with your goals for your life and your family? In a larger sense, do you find meaning and purpose in your job? Is your present career path truly aligned with your highest dreams and ambitions? If not, now—rather than later—is the time to begin the process of change. Let me put it this way: if step one in the MAP process is *awakening,* then step two is *meaning and purpose,* really stepping back and defining your purpose in life, what it is that will make you feel truly happy and fulfilled. Your personal alignment flows from that. Your vision and mission flow from that. Once your purpose is clear and well defined, it becomes much easier to develop an effective game plan to achieve your life goals and to find lasting happiness and fulfillment.

Now, in this context, I want to tell you about my friend Guillermo de la Viña, whom his friends call "Bill." I think you will find his story both helpful and inspiring. For Bill, everything good began when he found a deep and powerful sense of meaning and purpose in his life. That helped him define a new mission and vision for what he wanted to achieve. And once his mission and vision were clearly defined, Bill was able to develop a clear map of where he wanted to go and an action plan that would take him there. Life is a journey, and as Bill discovered, you'd better have a map.

Bill de la Viña was born in Cuba. His family came here forty years ago and settled down in Southern California, when Bill was fourteen years old. The early years here were rough for him. He had to help his family, learn English from scratch, adjust to a new culture, and find his way in school—and in life. As a young man, though, Bill had a stroke of good fortune. One day at a rodeo he happened to be sitting next to a man named Roger Vince Jessup, a true cowboy who had cattle and dairy ranches in Southern California. Vince took an immediate shine to young Bill and took him under his wing. "He became like a second father to me," Bill says. "He introduced me to American life and the American way. He also helped me smooth out some of my rough edges."

From the outset, Bill had big ambitions. "I'm a big thinker. I had a notion when I became an American that I wanted to create something. I asked myself, 'What am I good at?' The only way I could succeed was if I trusted my instincts. I became bilingual and after high school I was looking for a niche. Then I found a job that proved to be a great education."

That job was as a car salesman in the San Fernando Valley, and right away Bill learned an important lesson: build for the long term, not for the quick buck. "People would come in, we'd talk, and then they'd say, 'I want this car here,'" Bill recalls. "But I often would reply, 'OK. But for what your particular needs are, this car over here might be a better fit.' My goal was to make sure they'd be really happy for many years to come." Bill's candor and concern for his customer paid immediate dividends: he became the top salesman in the company. He also began collecting vintage cars, a passion that would one day serve him in a very unexpected way.

Bill spent four years in the auto business, gaining valuable experience in sales and business, and then he and his family decided to start something new. They created a company to manufacture women's clothing, and they made it a true family operation: his mother and father both helped out and so did other members of their extended family. The company did well, operating several different plants and selling to department stores like J. C. Penney. By now Bill had three young sons, and he felt he was really on his way in his adopted land. "We have this wonderful country where we have opportunity," Bill says. "I felt very blessed."

Then the family business turned sour, and a short time later one of his sons died an early and tragic death. Bill and his family were devastated. Their dream life seemed to vanish before their eyes. For months Bill was paralyzed with grief. The family garment business essentially disintegrated. Month after month, Bill was unable to recover his balance; with the death of his son, all the purpose and meaning seemed to have been sucked from his life. It took a long time, but one day Bill came to a stark realization: he had to get his head straight. He had to take care of his family and children. He had to start over, make a fresh beginning, and earn some money.

Looking for work, Bill answered a newspaper ad for a sales position in a young money-transfer company that was catering to the burgeoning Mexican community in Los Angeles. "I showed up one day, and the boss said, 'I'm looking for a guy to help me develop this business,' and he gave me the opportunity," Bill recalls. "I didn't care what they were paying me. I didn't care about anything. I took the job. My only goal was to get my feet back on the ground."

Bill threw himself into the task. At that time the only way for Mexican laborers to send money home was through Western Union. There were complicated forms to fill out, and many of the newcomers to the United States had trouble doing that. More often than not, the agents at Western Union didn't speak a word of Spanish, and they didn't know how to handle this new business. "They didn't understand their questions, they didn't understand their needs," Bill says. "They didn't understand their names, and they didn't know how to write them down." The result was often an escalating nightmare of errors, lost money, and family heartbreak. Bill found it agonizing to see. "I said, 'I'm going to clean this up. I'm going to talk to each one of them and help them solve their problems.'"

So Bill drew up a flyer and started knocking on doors. He went to mom-and-pop stores in Latino neighborhoods and enlisted their help. If they agreed to serve as his customer service points—his version of a Western Union office—he would pay them a percentage of every money transfer done through their shop, just as Visa and American Express pay shopkeepers a commission for handling a purchase via their credit cards. With the help of others Bill also simplified the transaction forms and printed them in Spanish, and he trained the staff at the mom-and-pop stores too. So when the Mexican laborers ran into problems, they had Spanish-speaking people right there to help. Bill was absolutely passionate about the work and the feeling it gave him. This was his calling, a job that once again filled his life with meaning and purpose. "It was a great feeling," Bill says, "helping these people out and meeting their needs. I did not go get the MBA. I didn't have all those schools, but I am going to create something. I am going to do something to help people."

Bill's approach produced rapid results. "Three months later, my boss called me and he says, 'Look, Bill, what you've done here, it's incredible. Now let's expand out and see what you can do.' He gave me an incredible challenge." Bill was up to it. For the next four years he helped build the business from the ground up, canvassing the farm communities and the back roads of Southern California, signing up shopkeepers and explaining to Mexican workers, oftentimes one by one, how they could solve their money-transfer issues with a single visit. By the mid-1990s, Bill had built a substantial network for the company, but he saw even greater potential still. "This job was the best thing that ever could have happened to me," Bill says now. "After working there for four years I knew I could build something bigger and better."

And so it was that in 1996 Bill launched his own money-transfer business, called Sigue Corporation (pronounced "see-gay"). As with any start-up the first weeks and months were difficult. Extremely difficult. "I remember when we first began," Bill recalls. "It was a Friday, and I had no money for payroll the following week. I was down to my last nickel, and I had people to pay. More than that, I had already developed a bond with my customers and to help them, I had risked everything. Well, back then I used to collect cars, and I had five or six cars that I really treasured. Nonetheless, that Friday I put an ad in the newspaper to sell one of my cars. I had no choice: I had to get some cash."

The following week, with payroll approaching, a man called about the car Bill had for sale. "It was a classic beauty, a 1964 Cadillac, in pristine condition," Bill says. "It had 20,000 miles on it, and the guy wanted to take it to Australia or somewhere. I loved that car and I hated to see it go. But we settled on a price, and I closed the deal. Sigue was saved: that money was going to carry me over. It was survival."

Now Bill set out to build his own money-transfer network from scratch. And he followed the same formula as before, this time putting a big yellow and red Sigue poster in his money-transfer agents' windows. The process went quickly; Bill had already developed solid working relationships with shops across the greater Los Angeles area. Then Bill and his small start-up team began building a similar network across Mexico, shops where families could go to receive the money being sent to them. "Now a worker's family can go almost anywhere in Mexico and pick up the money," he says. "They don't have to go to a bank."

Still, Bill's challenges were just beginning. As his business grew he came to a distressing realization: he was the leader of the company, yes, but he was flying totally blind. He had no formal business training, little understanding of business fundamentals, no time to go back to school, and no reliable system for running his company. "I had no idea how to run a company that was growing like that; I was just relying on my instincts," Bill admits. "I didn't have anyone to tell me when I was right and when I was wrong. I constantly felt like I was in a big fog, unable to see."

Then Bill found MAP. He was looking for some sort of management system that he could use to run Sigue, and he looked at several before finally deciding to take a MAP workshop to see if this was a system that he and his team could adopt. As it was for Debra Paterson, the workshop was both a shock and an awakening for Bill. "It was like getting an MBA in three days," Bill recalls. "In fact it was an incredible experience. It was very transformative for me. It was a very positive shock."

At the workshop Bill and his colleagues received a list of what we at MAP believe are the key attributes of a leader. The list is a valuable tool. It gives people clear criteria by which they can judge themselves and others as leaders. It's an evaluation tool that each of you can use right now.

The Attributes of a Leader

1. A clear vision
2. The ability to recognize the potential in others
3. The ability to develop trust
4. The ability to encourage excellence
5. Integrity
6. Empathy
7. Sense of humor
8. Humility
9. Passion
10. Confidence
11. Courage
12. Style

For Bill, this list threw into question his own leadership ability and style:

> Was I confident in my own leadership skills? No. Absolutely not. You have doubts. You have concerns. In any business you have paranoias. The sign of a great leader is that he openly shows vulnerability. As we started the process, there were two or three of us running the company. And we knew there were changes that needed to be made. We needed to do a lot of learning. We needed to develop our skills as leaders and managers. There was a hunger, a sense of need in the organization: how do we make all of our areas perform better?

In the workshop Bill decided that MAP might well be the solution he was looking for. But he still had one overriding concern: would his people embrace MAP as well? "You can have great skills and all the passion in the world, but you still have to go back and manage people. You have to go back, measure results, and hold people accountable. And you can't do it alone. You need support. You need buy-in. You need commitment—yes, that's the word: commitment."

LEADERSHIP

Despite his doubts Bill decided to give MAP a try. But he also decided to make some personal changes first. Using MAP's list of leadership criteria, Bill took a long, hard look in the mirror and evaluated his own qualities as a leader. He also identified specific areas he needed to work on, starting with having confidence and developing trust. But how could he improve in those areas? And how could he perform better as a leader when he returned to work?

Bill found guidance by working with a MAP coach. But another key turned out to be the Vital Factor process itself. Now, instead of having himself and two or three other executives sitting alone at the top, making all the decisions, Bill adopted the MAP leadership style, becoming a facilitator and going to great lengths to empower his people. The process deepened every time they sat down for their monthly Vital Factor Meeting. Bill and his team would focus on the MAP mantra: "Focus on the Vital Few; ignore or delegate the trivial many," and then they would zero in on the key factors that were driving the growth and profitability of their money-transfer business.

To manage those key business drivers Bill and his team put different people in charge of various Vital Factors and held them accountable for the results. At the same time, Bill sought input from everyone around the table, and sometimes they would tackle a specific problem using Team Consulting. At a single stroke, Bill's outreach and the MAP tools broke down most—but not all—of the social and corporate barriers that can paralyze any organization and disempower its staff. After those barriers started coming down Bill's team began sharing ideas and critiques in an open, supportive way. Now everyone was engaged and held openly accountable—including Bill. "The MAP system forces leaders to be humble and have humility," Bill says. "You have to be the first to say, 'I made a mistake.' Otherwise you'll never build a strong team."

Through the MAP process—and his own expanding leadership skills—Bill soon began to see profound changes throughout the company, far more than he expected to see. "MAP's genius is in its mix of simplicity and complexity," Bill says. "It's like an iceberg. What you see on the surface, the appearance, is very simple, but once you look underneath it's very complex, very in depth. It's like baseball. You can go to a game and say, what are we doing, watching grass grow? But there's a lot going on. MAP is like that. . . . The genius of the system, of Vital Factor Meetings, is it shows people how they're doing. There's nowhere to hide."

WRITE IT DOWN!

At this point I want to build on a few things that Bill said. I feel well placed to do so: I led Bill's introductory MAP workshop, and I worked as his personal coach, helping him implement the MAP system and grow as a leader. As both Bill de la Viña and Debra Paterson have described, the Vital Factor process does break down barriers and it does foster collaboration and a leadership style that is far more empowering for your team. But this process has many other dimensions as well. For one thing it promotes effective communication and alignment inside your team. Here, language is key. As Debra explained earlier, putting her staff into the MAP process gave them all a common language and common terms to use. This is important because having a common language helps the people in a team to frame their management process and set goals that are clearly understood, and it promotes the process of alignment throughout the team. I will build on this in Chapter Seven, "Clear Communication."

Good oral communication is not enough. In the Vital Factor process we insist that people *write down* such important things as their mission statement, their values statement, and their individual monthly goals. We don't want to say that all talk is cheap, but spoken goals are often only *intentions,* not the fixed, specific targets that are the lifeblood of the Vital Factor process. Writing it down makes a goal concrete and measurable. Writing it down increases accountability. And having your team members sit down and draft the primary documents of your company is an ideal way to promote collaboration and consensus building. Drafting those documents as a team helps ensure that everyone on that team becomes an owner of the outcome. And the process itself builds your team and grooms your people for greater responsibility and leadership.

At MAP we believe that every company or organization should have three documents: a mission statement, a values statement, and a business plan. And they should be clear, understandable, and compelling. All three are essential to business success. I always tell my clients that, but inevitably I run into a few skeptics. In fact, whenever I preach the virtues of clear communication and writing it down, someone steps forward and says, "Come on, Lee! Success in business is about holding down costs and generating growth and profit. It's about the bottom line. Now what the heck has clear communication got to do with the bottom line?"

Here I just sit back and smile. Mission statements define who you are and where you intend to go. Values statements are your compass, the needle that keeps you firmly on course. (If you don't believe in the importance of values, go have a chat with the boys from Enron!) And your business plan is the rudder that steers your ship. So when skeptics question the importance of those documents, here is what I tell them:

Think for a minute about Thomas Jefferson and the other framers of the Declaration of Independence and the U.S. Constitution. They sat down and drafted documents that not only defined America and its mission but also laid the foundation of ideals, principles, values, and laws on which the nation operates to this day. And guess what? They didn't just sit down one day and dictate it to a secretary. They worked the language and polished every word, over and over, and they used the process itself to promote alignment, consensus, and collective buy-in. With words and language and clear communication, they launched a revolution. And on the shared values of liberty, individual empowerment, and collective prosperity, they launched a nation that would grow into an enterprise of unparalleled wealth and economic gain. How's that for a bottom line?

At MAP we feel so strongly about the importance of writing it down that we have made it a cornerstone of the Vital Factor process, through the instrument of the monthly or weekly Vital Factor Meeting. Let me explain how it works. A company that has been *MAP-tized* will have broken the company's business process into its Vital Factors and organized a set of Vital Factor Teams to monitor and manage these factors. A money-transfer company like Bill's, for instance, might have a top-management Vital Factor Team overseeing the entire company, a marketing Vital Factor Team to manage the promotion of the product, an operations Vital Factor Team to manage the call center and the money-transfer process, and a financial Vital Factor Team to manage such areas as accounting, financial planning, taxes, monitoring exchange rates, and the like.

Each of these teams gathers monthly for a Vital Factor Meeting, and the first item on the agenda is always the Vital Factor Spreadsheet. At each meeting the team examines its particular set of Vital Factors, written down on the spreadsheet, and evaluates their health. Then the team focuses in on the tough questions. How do we improve our Vital Factors? How do we take areas that are doing well and make them even stronger? How do we fix any areas that are not performing well? Drawing on that discussion each team member writes down his or her individual goals and action steps for the following month and fixes target numbers to them, so they can be measured and evaluated at the next Vital Factor Meeting.

Let me give you a simple example. Let's say that Bill's sales team sets as its goal a 20 percent increase in new customers in the fall quarter. To meet that goal the salesforce agrees to increase the number of its sales calls by 30 percent during the month of October. That's the target—and it is *written down* by the manager in charge of making sure that the target is reached. At the following Vital Factor Meeting that manager comes in with the scoresheet indicating the result: Did his team increase its sales calls by 30 percent or not? If so, great. Can that success be repeated? And should we shoot even higher for next month? If the goal was not achieved, why? And what precise corrective actions is the sales team going to take to make sure it meets its new, compensatory target for November?

That's the process of Goals and Controls, and in the MAP system it opens every Vital Factor Meeting. And just as Bill said, there is nowhere to hide. Because the process is done out in the open, with each Vital Factor goal written down and defined in quantities that can be objectively measured, there can be no fudging, and no areas where people can obfuscate or say the dog ate their homework. It's all there in black and white. Results—and responsibility—are plain for everyone to see.

Now, how can MAP's insistence on writing it down be applied to your personal growth? Let me give you a specific example and a specific tool to use. Paul Chutkow, my coauthor in writing this book, went through the MAP workshop to see firsthand how it works. Paul has a diverse background as a foreign correspondent, author, and business writer, and I thought the workshop would help him draw his thinking together in preparation for writing this book with me. For help I turned to Craig McNey, one of our most gifted coaches and workshop leaders, and asked him to "take Paul into one of your workshops and really let him have it: the full MAP experience!" Well, Craig did just that. And on the third morning of the workshop, with the twelve participants grouped around the table, Craig turned to Paul and said, "You know, Paul, you're a very creative guy, and you have a fascinating array of things that you do. But I don't think you're properly focused. I don't think you've properly defined your Vital Few. I think you need a Life Plan."

Paul blanched. "A Life Plan?"

As Craig then explained to the group, at MAP we believe that companies have Vital Factors—and so do people. Companies need mission statements, and so do people. Companies need to spell out—and *write down*—their specific goals, with target dates for achieving them, and so do people. The Life Plan is the ideal tool for doing all of that. In Chapter Fourteen I'll tell you exactly how to do a Life Plan, but the point here is this: on Craig's advice Paul took some time to think deeply about the direction of his life, to define his guiding purpose and values, and then he set those down on paper, along with a set of specific goals he wanted to achieve during the coming quarter and the coming year. For Paul this process was both clarifying and empowering. With a few strokes of his pen his life and his work suddenly snapped into focus. And so did his plans and goals for the next several years. I urge you to begin the Life Plan process yourself, right now, and the perfect first step is to reflect awhile and then define what you see as your purpose in life, what will bring you lasting happiness and fulfillment. I will build on this theme in subsequent chapters. But right away this process will help you see how well your present job is aligned with your longer-term goals for yourself and your family. And you'll be amazed at the changes that the Life Plan process sets into motion.

ACCOUNTABILITY

Now I want to build further on that wonderful point that Bill de la Viña raised: that in the MAP process there's nowhere to hide. That is so true. Because each element in the process is open, transparent, and measurable, in very short order the process flushes out who's performing well and who is not. It tells you who are the doers and who are the slackers and excuse makers. The Vital Factor process also quickly flushes out those individuals who resist team building or who fail to move into full alignment with the team's or company's stated mission and goals. Every once in awhile the process will also flush out someone who is downright hostile to your goals or who is pursuing his or her own agenda. At MAP we have even given folks like that a name: *Onboard Troublemakers*. Bill de la Viña can tell you all about it. "In one of our early years our profits were very good, and I decided to create a bonus program to push our people a little and also to reward them for their hard work," Bill recalls. "I said to some of my top guys, 'I want you to come up with a bonus program.'"

As soon as the bonus planning began, however, it revealed a deep schism inside Bill's company. There was a top tier of managers who saw themselves as the kingpins; then there was the lower tier, the troops in the trenches, the people who manned the phones and did the daily grunt work of dealing with Sigue's customers and money-transfer centers. And here was the rub: it was the kingpins who were developing the bonus plan. When they presented their first draft, Bill was not pleased. "The top tier wanted to take the biggest piece of the pie for themselves," Bill says, "and there wasn't too much left over for anyone else." Bill demanded a better effort; he asked them to revise the plan and make it fair for everyone.

In their ensuing attempts the kingpins came forth with several different bonus formulas, but their goals were never clearly defined or written down, and each time Bill rejected their plans. In draft after draft the kingpins rewarded themselves with big bonuses, while the troops in the trenches were slated to get little more than token bonuses, in some cases no more than $20 for the entire year. The longer this process went on, the more frustrated Bill got. He saw it plainly: under these plans his frontline people were getting the shaft. "It's our phone operators who do a lot of the work," Bill says. "They're the ones who are sweating it out."

This process dragged on and on, and the kingpins seemed unable—or unwilling—to come up with an equitable bonus program. Finally, the end of the year was in sight and there was still no effective plan on the table. At this stage Bill was still learning the rudiments of the MAP system, and he was still feeling a bit tentative as a leader. But now he decided to bring into the mix four core tenets of the MAP philosophy: goals, controls, deadlines, and consequences. In a word, accountability. "I realized I had to set some sort of standard. So I told those guys, 'I'm setting a deadline. If you guys don't have a workable plan by that morning, there will be consequences.'" Specifically, Bill said that if they failed to come up with a suitable plan, he would give half of the money allocated for their bonuses to charity.

The deadline day arrived, and Bill knew in his gut that it wasn't going to go well. So as any experienced manager would, Bill developed a contingency plan. He telephoned the local branch of the Salvation Army and asked them to send an officer to Sigue headquarters that same afternoon. "I have the feeling," he told them, "that I'm going to give away a lot of money today."

Sure enough, at the appointed hour, his bonus planners sat down in a meeting with Bill and presented their latest draft. Little had changed: the kingpins were still giving themselves handsome bonuses and giving only a pittance to the troops. Now Bill was completely exasperated, but he gave them one final chance. "I told them, 'I'll give you one hour to come up with a solution and to tell me why you deserve this bonus.'"

An hour later Bill came back into the room and still nothing had changed. So later that same day an officer from the Salvation Army came to the offices of Sigue, and Bill presented the charity with a large check, on behalf of all of Sigue's executives. As Bill had promised, the check represented a portion of the money that the kingpins had allocated in bonuses for themselves. Now they got nothing, not a dime—and Bill made sure that each of his frontline people got a substantial bonus. The Salvation Army folks were delighted—and his bonus planners were held visibly accountable for their failure, just as Bill intended.

This was a watershed moment in the history of Sigue. Bill had created his company with one noble mission to fulfill: to help Latino workers get settled in America and send money to their families back home. Some of his cohorts hadn't gotten the message; they thought Sigue existed to make them rich. In MAP terms, their personal goals were simply not aligned with the goals of the business. And the kingpins were subverting Bill's entire mission. They had shown themselves—over and over and in front of everyone—that they were not team players. Just the opposite. Indeed, the entire episode laid bare deeper truths inside Sigue, and it helped Bill grow and mature as a leader:

"I finally saw it: they were Onboard Troublemakers," Bill says now. "But I would also add that it had become evident that we had a very dysfunctional team, a team that was lacking cohesiveness. The bonuses are what brought it out. So it's been a journey of discovery. When you clarify your mirrors and your lenses, then you can see things when they come up, and you can say OK, this is a symptom of a larger problem—I have to take action. I have to flush all these situations out."

Bill indeed took action. He eventually fired several of those errant kingpins; the rest finally got the message and left of their own accord. Then Bill took further steps to tear down any remaining walls dividing his staff. His message was loud, clear, and empowering: "We're all in this together. We all contribute to the success or failure of the company. We all have to pull hard—and together—as a team."

The results have been overwhelming. Today Sigue Corporation is one of the largest money-transfer companies in the United States and in many major markets across Latin America. It handles literally billions of dollars in transfers every year. Sigue also provides other services to the Latino community in the United States. Once Bill got rid of his Onboard Troublemakers, there was alignment throughout his organization and everyone supported his original purpose, mission, and values. These days, talking about his personal journey of discovery and the lessons he's learned puts Bill de la Viña in a very reflective frame of mind:

> Passion is essential and so is feeling like you're doing something important and meaningful. That's the key ingredient—for whatever you do in life. That's basically how you begin to define your niche. When you feel that you have found it—yes, this is what I want to do!—then that is where you must put your faith and start building on it. This is the way I look at it: everything else you have done up to then in your life is just preparation. No matter how many years you go to school, no matter how much training you get,

you're preparing for something in life, the purpose of why you're here on Earth. But you have to discover it—and know it when you see it. And when you fulfill your purpose in life, nothing is more beautiful. Every day is rich. Every day you touch life itself.

Need we say more?

The Bottom Line

1. Step back, and define what will give your life true *meaning and purpose*. Then create a mission and a vision for your business and your life. The mission is your purpose. The vision is where you intend to go.
2. Begin a Life Plan. Write down your purpose, mission, and vision. Then set down your personal Vital Factors. Work the language. Get it right. This can be the map that will guide you for years to come.
3. Create a Vital Factor Team to help you manage your life. These people will help you achieve your goals and give you guidance along the way.
4. Assign yourself measurable goals and deadlines. (I want to lose ten pounds over the next forty-five days. I want to lower my cholesterol by 20 points by July 1st, and so forth.)
5. Hold yourself accountable for the results. Welcome constructive criticism and advice; they're great tools for personal growth.
6. In sum, take charge of your life and run it like a business. It is! Set clear, concrete goals, and then hold regular meetings to assess how you're doing. Stay focused on what gives your life *meaning and purpose,* and watch how quickly everything else falls into place or melts away, leaving you feeling happy and free!

CHAPTER FOUR

VALUES

Michael Caito is a born entrepreneur.

He's smart, resourceful, and not afraid of risk. So are Michael's business partners: his younger brother, Anthony, and their childhood friend, Matt Martha. Today the three of them are running a very successful company, and they have matured into very capable and charismatic business leaders.

Like all entrepreneurs, though, Michael, Anthony, and Matt faced difficult challenges on their road to success, and I want to tell you their story in some detail because I think it holds out important lessons for other men and women who have the entrepreneurial spirit and a business idea that they are eager to develop. I also think their story is fascinating and inspiring, and it highlights one essential element of business success that is very dear to MAP and to my own heart: *values*.

As I tell their story I'm going to focus on Michael, because I have worked closely with him as a personal coach, and I know his motivations and feelings well. Anthony and Matt have been just as effective as Michael in building their business, and I admire them both. To simplify the storytelling, though, I'm going to tell it mostly from Michael's perspective, so you can follow this entrepreneurial story from a consistent point of view. Early on, Anthony and Matt put Michael in charge of executing the vision the three of them shared. Together, they have built an amazing business, one that I know will inspire other entrepreneurs.

Michael and Anthony grew up in Buffalo, New York, in a close-knit family with Italian roots. Michael had a typical American childhood, he did fairly well in school, goofed off a lot, and when he graduated from high school he felt a little restless. He had no clearly defined ambition and no particular direction he wanted to follow. College? A career? Michael wasn't sure. He needed to get out on his own, taste the world, and find his own path. And Michael knew exactly where he wanted to start: on the sunny shores of California.

When he was seventeen, Michael had taken a trip to Southern California to visit a cousin, and when he saw the palm trees and the beaches and all the pretty girls, Michael thought, "Wow, LA sure beats Buffalo!" A year later a girl he was dating moved to Southern California, and Michael decided it was time to shake up his life: "I convinced my dad I wasn't crazy, then I packed all my stuff in garbage bags, loaded them into my car, and drove out to California. I lived with my girlfriend and her mom. I was eighteen."

Michael still had no clue what path to follow, but he began taking classes at Saddleback College in Mission Viejo, south of Los Angeles, and to support himself he worked at a restaurant called Stix. Soon Anthony and Matt came west too, and they also went to work at Stix. The guys liked the work, especially when the restaurant launched something new and innovative: Pick Up Stix, a quick service take-out restaurant catering to local residents and business people. The new venture did well, and it gave Michael and Anthony a strong, healthy jolt: "We got a taste in our early twenties of what it felt like to see a business concept take off," Michael says. "It was exciting."

Soon an idea began percolating in Matt's head, the idea of creating a business that would deliver quality meals from local restaurants to homes and businesses. As Matt told Anthony, "Hey, if they can do it, we can do it too!" Anthony loved the idea. They then asked Michael to join in the venture. Michael readily agreed. The three of them had no business plan and no knowledge of how to run a business. Risk? Sure, but who cares? The idea was cool, and Matt, Anthony, and Michael figured they could have a lot of fun in the process and learn the ropes as they went along. So in 1993 the three musketeers decided to launch a restaurant delivery business of their own, called Restaurants on the Run.

The three partners started with little more than their can-do spirit and their defining idea. Their first "headquarters" was not the Taj Mahal. "We had a closet for an office, 110 square feet, triangular in shape," Michael laughs. "That was our call center. People called in, ordered food from the menus of a few local restaurants, and then we used our own cars to make the deliveries. We were tiny but people liked the concept."

Though they had no business training, the three partners had latched onto a winning concept. They did well, and within three years they had launched a sister business in San Diego. They saw the potential to open in several other cities as well. Soon, though, they ran into problems. Sales flattened. Profits sagged. And morale plummeted. "We had no structure. No president. No titles," Michael says. "And no system of accountability." Still, their little start-up venture continued to grow, year after year, and Michael, Anthony, and Matt struggled to keep up with their growing sales volume—and their mounting headaches. For a brief time they brought in a traditional consulting firm. Under its guidance, Michael was named CEO, and his top managers got fancy titles as well. But to Michael these felt like Band-Aids on the Titanic. Now everyone was working harder and harder, but profits were still stagnant, and with each passing day Michael felt more and more discouraged. But he had no idea where to turn for help.

Then along came MAP.

One day Michael was talking with a friend from the Entrepreneurs' Organization (EO), a global, nonprofit leadership organization for business owners. Michael told him about his growing problems with the business, and his friend told him about MAP. As he explained, MAP was a small, innovative, and highly regarded business consulting firm headquartered in the LA area, with satellite offices in several other West Coast cities. Michael's reaction was, "So what? I've had my fill of business consultants." His friend said MAP was different. MAP had developed and fine-tuned a practical, highly effective system for running any business, big or small. MAP also ran intensive workshops for people whose companies were either in trouble or just determined to improve their operations and performance. "Check 'em out," his friend told Michael. "Maybe MAP can help."

Michael did check out MAP, and then he decided to sign up for one of our three-day management workshops. Michael went through it and he was impressed—but he was not ready to embrace the MAP system. "No way," Michael recalls. "I wanted it, but I decided I'm not going to implement this." The problem was not just money; it was time and effort. To implement the MAP program he thought he would have to send his entire top management team through the MAP workshops, to show them what it was about, and then he would have to totally transform the way the company operated. He would also have to transform the way he operated as CEO, and he would have to figure out a way to convince his entire staff to buy into the MAP system. Too much time, too much hassle, Michael decided. And I've got too much else to do.

Still, inside the company, nothing changed. Everybody was working just as hard, but their results were no better than before. Sales were OK, but profits were flat. Throughout the company, stress was high and morale was low. Michael knew something was fundamentally wrong inside his company, but he had no idea how to pinpoint it—or fix it. He was becoming increasingly discouraged. In the start-up days he used to love to come to work; every day was a kick. No longer. The fun and excitement had been sucked away, and there were some mornings when Michael simply dreaded coming in and sitting at his desk. He also developed back problems. This went on for months. Finally, Michael made the call to MAP. And whom did he land on as a coach and mentor? Me. Lee Froschheiser. At that time I was one of MAP's senior consultants.

Michael and I liked each other right off. He was bright, energetic, and quick on his feet, and I could see that he was determined to succeed. What I also liked about Michael was that he challenged me; I like to surround myself with people who make me better, and I knew that Michael would do that. Also, though he had no idea about business fundamentals, I knew in my bones that Michael Caito was a natural-born entrepreneur and leader. He was the kind of clay that a coach loves to mold. Michael and I agreed that I would come in as a coach and help him, Anthony, and Matt tailor the MAP system to their specific needs and goals. Michael was still skeptical at the outset, but he was willing to give the MAP system a try.

"I brought in Lee in July of 2002, and he began pushing the MAP process throughout the company," Michael says now. Right away Michael, Anthony, and Matt put into place the cornerstone of the MAP system, Vital Factor Teams. To guide the company and set strategy they first set up a top-management Vital Factor Team. That team then began restructuring roles and responsibilities and pinpointing the Vital Few, the specific Vital Factors that were controlling costs, sales, and profitability. Then that team created more-specialized Vital Factor Teams to manage all the component parts of Restaurants on the Run: sales and marketing, planning, operations, finance, new technology, and the rest. Still, even as the top-management team put the MAP system into place, Michael remained unconvinced. In his eyes the MAP system was too simple and too basic to be effective. Then he began to see the results: "Suddenly, people were accountable. And they had specific criteria by which they could measure their own performance. We could all feel the change."

Within the first months Michael saw a whole range of surprising changes. The regular Vital Factor Team Meetings quickly improved communication among the top leaders and kept everyone aligned with the overall strategy and tightly focused on the Vital Few. Also, if anyone wanted to raise issues regarding policies or people, the monthly meetings offered an ideal setting in which to address them and clear the air. At these Vital Factor Meetings Michael, Anthony, and Matt sat around the table with their Vital Factor Team members, encouraging input from them, and for Michael this was especially welcome: the burdens of leadership seemed to lighten. An effective team was forming around him.

For my part, I liked what I was seeing, but I knew I had to coach Michael, Matt, and Anthony and help them grow as managers and leaders. This involved a lot of personal, one-on-one mentoring. We went over their FIRO-B and Behavioral Style Analysis assessments and discussed what they revealed about their leadership qualities and communication patterns. Our work extended beyond the office. For instance, when Anthony decided to get married, I put on my cap as "Uncle Lee" and had the bride and groom use the Behavioral Style Analysis to evaluate their different communication styles. Not surprisingly, the test showed important differences between them (think "women are from Venus, men are from Mars"). So one evening at dinner I sat the couple down, with the assessments in hand, and we discussed how they could best talk with each other in an effective and supportive way. Specifically, I said to the bride-to-be, "If you want to get Anthony's attention, here's how to talk with him." On the other side, I said, "Anthony, here is how your bride likes to be talked to and heard." My immediate goal, of course, was to help them sidestep some of the pitfalls of any relationship, but at the same time I was trying to show Anthony how he and his partners could use the same test to improve the company's hiring practices and deal more effectively with complex staffing issues.

With Michael I did something similar. In chairing some of his Vital Factor Meetings I never provided solutions. I just asked challenging questions and tried to facilitate dialogue, so that Michael and his team would come up with solutions on their own. That empowers the team and ensures their buy-in to the final plan. In sum, I was modeling the kind of facilitating leadership approach that Debra Paterson and Bill de la Viña have already discussed. Michael took to it like a fish to water, and very soon he was recasting his own leadership approach and style.

Early on in the Vital Factor process Michael and his team broke down their business into its key component parts and focused on these parts one at a time. Their immediate goal was simple: to diagnose the real reasons why sales and profits were below their targets—and fix the problems. To make that initial diagnosis Michael and his team zoomed in on some key business fundamentals.

VISION AND ALIGNMENT

In my first meetings with Michael, Anthony, and Matt, I quickly discerned a problem, and I told them so: "You three aren't on the same page. Michael has one vision for the company, and each of you has a vision of your own—and it's not the same vision. Unless you three agree where you're going to go with this company, this organization is going to be dysfunctional."

From there we discussed their differences in vision and pinpointed the core issue dividing them. It came down to this: Michael was eager to grow the business by buying other companies and expanding into new markets. His partners, in contrast, wanted to grow the business by finding ways to increase the profitability of their existing operation. I put it to them this way: "You've got to ask yourselves: 'What do we want this company to look like three to five years from now?' You two talk about profitability; Michael

talks about growth. You might have to have growth without profitability, but you guys have to decide." With that little nudge the
three of them thrashed through the problem openly and candidly,
came to a joint decision, and then aligned themselves behind a
common goal: maximize profitability. Needless to say, I was pleased
by both the process and the outcome.

LEADERSHIP AND COMMUNICATION

In talking with Michael I made no bones about it: if he wanted to
grow as a leader, he had to make some serious changes. At that time
Michael was running Restaurants on the Run like a big Monopoly
game: buying and selling businesses as part of an aggressive expansion strategy and trying in essence to own Boardwalk and Park
Place, with four hotels on each. Through their discussion process
the partners were able to constructively discuss Michael's approach
to spending money and his lack of focus on the profitability issue.
By the end Michael saw that he needed to provide a much clearer
focus and direction for the company—and rein in some of his plans
for rapid expansion.

Michael also came to understand a core truth: a leader can
have vision, sure, but he has to be able to articulate that vision in
a compelling and convincing way to the people in his organization. Only then can they embrace that vision and align themselves
behind it. Dialogue is essential. When people can truly understand the guiding vision, they can get behind it and make it their
own. And then they can work to build that vision with passion and
fervor. People who work inside the best-run companies often say
the same thing: you can feel the pride, you can feel the energy,
you can feel the passion, you can feel the commitment. Clear
vision, clear purpose, and clear communication help generate
those feelings.

HUMILITY

Bill de la Viña said it well: the most effective leaders show their vul-
nerability. Many of them radiate humility. That's why MAP includes
humility in its list of the twelve attributes of an effective leader. The

media may glorify a Donald Trump or a Lee Iacocca, but in our experience at MAP, the most effective and the most trusted presidents and CEOs operate in a quiet, self-effacing way. With them it's the company that is always most important, not the ego charge that the president gets from being at the helm. At the outset Michael did not understand, at a deep personal level, what it meant to be an effective CEO, and his learning process was by no means easy. But Michael is a very intelligent young man, and he soon came to understand the value of learning how to say, in effect, "I don't know it all. I'm open to changing. I'm open to learning. I'm open to trying something different."

VALUES

Early on I asked Michael, "Do you have a business plan?"

"Sure," he said, and from a bookshelf he pulled it down. But before he handed it to me he literally had to blow the dust off. It turned out to be a canned business plan, done by an outside consultant, for a handsome fee of course. And all it had done was sit on the shelf. So then we set in motion a serious planning process. Michael and I developed a questionnaire and sent it to the members of his Vital Factor management team. Some of the questions sought their input about the company's guiding vision, its business strategy, and the short-term and long-term goals that would be most effective in realizing the guiding vision.

That was pretty standard business fare. But we wanted to go much deeper. Accordingly, we built into the questionnaire a series of questions about a realm that many business consultants rarely approach: values. I asked Michael and his team: "What are your values regarding your customers?" "What are your values regarding your employees?" "What are your values in regard to accountability?" "What are your values in regard to decision making?"

At the next business planning session, with the full management team together, I asked these managers to tell me their responses to these value questions. And from there we got down to the nub of it: I said to them, "OK, what really are your core values?" And then they started debating these values and discussing them. The result? We ended up narrowing them down to six

important core values. Then Michael and I drilled deeper. We said
to the group, "Now, why are these important?"

Here we ran into some confusion. Not everyone was sure what
those values really meant in terms of the day-to-day operation of
Restaurants on the Run. It took awhile, but finally they understood
the point: those values weren't just some empty words to print out,
frame, and stick on the wall. No. Those values were both the foundation and the guiding principles of the company—the guide wires
that would hold the company on course every step of the way forward, through the good times but also through the almost
inevitable business downturns and crises. Those values were in
essence the ground rules of the company, the standards that all of
its employees and managers should uphold on a daily basis. From
there we turned to a core MAP principle (discussed in Chapter
Three): *write it down*. The managers wrote a formal *values statement*
for their company, and the process of drafting it was very healthy.
It engendered input from everyone, then open and constructive
discussion, then a formal drafting of words and language. The final
document produced consensus, alignment, and buy-in. Again, the
process proved even more important than the final outcome.

Then I asked the really tough question: Were Michael and his
partners upholding those values inside the company? Or were they
just paying lip service to them? To answer that, we looked at one of
the specific values that the team members had defined: grooming
their people for greater responsibility. I said to them, "Be honest
now. Are you really developing your people? If I went out and asked
your employees do you really develop them, what would they say?"

Michael's management team sheepishly admitted that the
response would be no. The result? We were able to pinpoint one
of the principal reasons why the company had hit a wall and sales
had stalled: company staff were both inexperienced and disheart-
ened. Staff development was a stated value inside the company, but
no one was honoring that value in practice. What did Michael and
his team have to do? In the MAP terminology the answer was simple: *corrective action*.

As soon as we had pinpointed the problem Michael moved
quickly, with the full approval of Matt and Anthony. He called a
general staff meeting, explained the guiding vision for the company, and opened a company-wide discussion of the values that

underpinned that vision. At the same time, he pledged to make staff training and development a high priority—in keeping with those stated values. That meeting—and the lines of communication that it helped open—did wonders for staff morale and of course for productivity. And Michael and his team had learned a valuable lesson: Define your values. Manage to your values. Uphold your values. That always keeps you on course, and in the end it improves your bottom line.

THE VITAL FEW

Many start-up companies in their first critical months are inclined to grab business from wherever they can find it. Many of them urgently need revenue just to stay afloat. Restaurants on the Run was no exception. In the early years its business relied on two basic sources of revenue: deliveries to individuals at home and multiple-meal deliveries to businesses. When I came in, Michael, Matt, and Anthony were putting equal focus on both revenue streams. Stop, I said. Let's pinpoint the Vital Few, the key drivers of the business. I knew there was a elephant in the room that they had to confront: should they really be focused on both target markets? The fact was that residential delivery was chewing up their resources at a monstrous rate. Each home delivery was eating up call-center time, meal preparation time, and driver time, not to mention piling up costs for gasoline and vehicle wear and tear. One typical business order—with one delivery—might be ten or fifteen lunches, with a bill of $250. One private individual's order—with one delivery, probably further away—might typically be a single lunch, with a bill of $20. Now, where should Michael and his team put their focus? Of course I knew that I couldn't answer the question for them. They had to examine their Vital Factors—specifically profit per delivery—and come to the answer for themselves. The process, as usual, was more important than the immediate result.

MEASUREMENT

In addition to our reminder to focus on the Vital Few, we at MAP have other mantra-like phrases we use to keep us tightly focused. Here's another: "What gets measured gets done." To help Michael and his team decide if it was wise to continue putting equal focus on residential and corporate deliveries, I had them start measuring their profitability per delivery. Up to then they had been evaluating their business strategy and performance only by revenue gained. However, once they examined their profit per delivery, all the fog melted away. They could see in black and white how they were misallocating their resources. Moving away from the residential side of their business was then a relatively easy decision. From that point forward the company's revenues and profitability radically improved—in line with the partners' earlier strategic decision to emphasize profitability over growth. The guiding lesson here was clear: by pinpointing their Vital Factors and measuring them, Michael and his team were able to readjust their focus and achieve the exact results they desired.

In the early stages Michael was baffled by the MAP approach. Values? Communication? Vital Factors? The Vital Few? This was *not* what he had expected when he had signed on with MAP. Still, once he got into the MAP routine—and saw the results—Michael became a true believer. He, Anthony, and Matt saw the results not just in their balance sheets but also in the way they and their management team grew, both professionally and personally.

"Executing the fundamentals in any company is difficult, and in this regard we were very fortunate to find MAP," Michael says. "We like to refer to MAP as 'meat and potatoes,' the fundamentals of any business. MAP has enabled us to create accountability throughout the organization for those fundamentals. We were able to identify the critical issues in the organization, put them on a scorecard, roll it out to every city, get agreed-upon standards and goals, and then execute against them. The definition of accountability is measuring performance and taking appropriate actions to get there, and that's what we do now on a month-to-month basis. It has really simplified the process."

Today, Restaurants on the Run, the little venture that Michael, Anthony, and Matt started from scratch, no longer suffers from overwork, low morale, and stagnant profits. The company is headed toward record annual sales. It has profitable branches in several cities across California and the West, and the three partners have plans to expand into other promising markets in the Midwest and beyond—and specific action steps to take the company there. In addition, the partners have launched a new company, based on another idea from Matt Martha. It brings together their expertise in restaurant takeout and forms a marketing and technology enterprise to help restaurants drive their profits, much in the same way as these partners learned to do from MAP. This time Matt will be CEO.

At the same time, Restaurants on the Run continues to prosper. "The results have been astounding," Michael says. "Our profits climbed 300 percent the first year, and they've climbed 500 percent since the pre-MAP days. MAP is not a little fix here, a little fix there. It's a whole way of running your company, a whole way of doing business. On a personal level I realized that my weakness was details. MAP helped me with that. Now I go home, I feel organized, and I don't feel like I have to work seventy hours a week. I have a life again."

There's more. Before he brought the MAP system into his business, Michael was suffering from severe back pain. Some days he literally could not get out of bed, and there were many days when sitting in his chair at the office was excruciating. As Michael discovered, some of his pain was caused by stress. As MAP helped him iron out the problems at work, he worked in parallel to address his back problems. With a few simple exercises to reduce stress and build flexibility, plus the progress he was making at work, Michael's back problems soon disappeared.

Now I'm a very positive guy and a true believer in the MAP system. But I am not going to say that MAP can solve each and every problem for you. However, the MAP system and its Vital Factor tools can give you inspiration and guidance, and those same tools can help you make deep and lasting changes in your life and work. And here is one of the things that makes me proud and happy: Michael is now a full-fledged coach in his own right, and he's actively helping his people use the MAP system, and he's also helping them grow as managers and leaders. Move over Bill Parcells. Watch out Bill Cowher. Michael, Matt, and Anthony are on the way!

The Bottom Line

1. Values matter. When properly defined they become the anchors of your business and the guiding principles for how your business behaves and how you treat your employees and customers.
2. So sit down with the people in your company—and your family—and discuss your values. Then draft a *values statement*. Make it a collective experience. Get input from your top people. Write it down. Use the process to forge a common vision, alignment, and consensus.
3. Always manage to your values. Hold people accountable to those values. Hire people who are in line with your values.
4. In times of crisis turn back to your values statement. Enduring values are always more important than today's profits. And you will be amazed at how firmly those values can lead you through a crisis.
5. Take a page from Michael and his team: clearly identify the profit centers that really drive your business. Then focus tightly on them. You will be amazed at the results.

CHAPTER FIVE

PASSION AND COMMITMENT

It is now time to meet Doug Ducey.

Doug is a gung ho, effervescent kind of guy; he radiates kinetic energy and boyish enthusiasm. In his time off he coaches his son's Little League baseball team, and as soon as you meet him you can easily picture Doug at the big game, pacing up and down the sidelines, clapping his hands, shouting encouragement, pumping his fist at good plays, and then consoling his young charges if they strike out or make an error in the field. And if they win the big game you know exactly what Doug Ducey will do: take the whole team out for ice cream!

Doug is now president, CEO, head coach, and team cheerleader for Cold Stone Creamery, a hot young franchise group with a giant ambition: become the ultimate ice cream experience and the No. 1 best-selling brand of ice cream in America. Cold Stone has its "world headquarters" in Scottsdale, Arizona, and everything about the place is positive and fun. And as you listen to Doug outline his ambitions for Cold Stone, you can almost hear him thinking, "There is no *bad* ice cream. But there is only *one* Cold Stone Creamery ice cream!"

Doug of course doesn't come right out and use words like those. He's far too shrewd for that. Instead he wraps Cold Stone's global ambitions in the sweetest of toppings: "Our mission," he says simply, "is to make people happy." Ice cream itself, he explains, is all about making people happy. Kids, adults, and grandparents of all ages love ice cream. Rich people, poor people, middle-class people—everyone loves ice cream. And ice cream, like coffee, knows no national or cultural boundaries. Americans love it; Europeans love it; Asians love it; Latinos adore it. And what does Doug see as one of Cold Stone's biggest potential growth markets? Why, Japan of course! All over the world, Doug says, ice cream and economic progress fit together like, well, like scoop to cone. And wherever there's ice cream, Cold Stone wants to supply the ice cream, the cones, and all the toppings as well.

To fulfill these global ambitions Doug infuses his team with a message that knows no national or cultural boundaries: he wants every aspect of the Cold Stone experience to be fun, happy, and uplifting. At Cold Stone's on-site training program, which the company calls Cold Stone University, what is the dominant feeling that trainers teach new franchisees to communicate? Passion! And also what Doug calls "an attitude of abundance." Ice cream, you see, chases away the blues. It makes you feel happy, satisfied, and full. A mouthful of Cold Stone is not just sweet to the tongue; it's nourishment for the heart and tonic for the soul. As Doug talks, radiating his own passion and attitude of abundance, you sit back and think, "Man, this guy's good. And what a gift for sales and marketing! I wonder where he learned it."

Well, thereon hangs quite a story. Doug grew up in the Midwest, but for college he was irresistibly drawn to the big skies and kick-back living of Arizona. He enrolled at Arizona State University, and soon his entrepreneurial instincts found a perfect home: he went to work part-time as a college sales rep for Anheuser-Busch. Talk about a natural fit and a ready-made market: college kids and Budweiser. They fit together as easily as, well, kids and ice cream. "I sold beer in college," Doug says now. "It was a great background to get into sales because everyone said, 'Yes!' It was a very easy sale."

After college Doug decided to go for a real-world PhD in what is probably the world's leading graduate program in sales and marketing: Procter & Gamble. Nobody knows how to build a brand like Procter & Gamble. Indeed, its product names are woven deep into the American consciousness: Tide, Charmin, Bounty, Pampers, Pringles, Iams, and now Gillette. And for a young man on the rise the opportunities at Procter & Gamble seemed limitless: the company had brands and offices all over the world. Doug was thrilled to be there, and right away he found his special niche: food.

"The brand I handled was Folgers Coffee, and my mission was to take Folgers from the grocery shelf to the restaurants," Doug says. "This was about fifteen years ago. If you remember, fifteen years ago people made coffee at home for a few cents a cup, and if they ordered it in a restaurant they just asked for coffee, not a particular brand." Doug and his team set out to change that. "Restaurateurs believe in brands: Heinz Tomato Ketchup, A1 Steak Sauce, so to take a brand as big and powerful as Folgers, with 51 percent of market share at that time, and say, 'Mr. Restaurateur, how would you like to serve a brand that over half your customers like enough to serve to their dinner guests at home?' 'Well, sure,' they'd say. 'We'll do that.' At age twenty-eight I had a sales force of twenty-eight guys. We had an objective of 40 accounts in the first quarter—and we actually sold 400 accounts for Folgers."

With those kind of results Doug was over the moon. He felt he had really found his calling. He was also deeply impressed by Procter & Gamble and the way it was run. And what a pedigree: a 150-year history, $30 billion in sales, and nary a layoff. "It was a great corporate culture, a traditional corporate culture, with great core values," Doug says. "I loved it. I thought it was awesome." Moreover, there was no guesswork at Procter & Gamble. Every decision was based on rock-solid market research, and the company rarely, if ever, wandered down blind alleys. "Going with your gut" was simply not in its ethos or in its operations manual, as Doug soon found out.

"We started to hear from the customers—'We would like gourmet coffee, cold bean coffee'—and I'd go back to headquarters and talk to the folks there," Doug says. Back then, though, the number of establishments asking for gourmet coffee was minuscule, and the supporting market research was mostly anecdotal. The powers that be at Procter & Gamble were not impressed. "When I would say, 'Customers are asking for fancy coffees,' they would say, 'That's a fad. This is Folgers, the red can, 51 percent market share. We know the brand. Shut up. Go.'"

Still, Doug's initial passion remained undimmed. At Procter & Gamble he was getting exactly the education he wanted: how to build and manage a brand, how to run his own business, how to build a winning corporate culture. And thanks to his success with Folgers, his star was on the rise. Soon, though, Doug began to get restless. For one thing he missed the big skies of Arizona. He didn't mind the white shirts and button-down collars of Procter & Gamble, but he sure did love the casual Southwest and his old haunts in Phoenix, Tucson, and Sedona. His wife loved Arizona too. And there was something else: the entrepreneurial bug was gnawing at his innards. Doug, in essence, had earned his PhD, and he was getting itchy to go out on his own, to put his education to work and build a brand of his own.

Franchises appealed to him, and for a time Doug flirted with the idea of joining Subway sandwich shops in some capacity, but when he studied the company up close he just didn't see the kind of growth opportunity he was looking for. Then he found a young start-up ice cream company called Cold Stone Creamery, and Doug just knew in his gut that this was it. The heck with market research! Everyone loves ice cream! Yes, Doug knew that here was a place where he could really make his mark. It was based in Arizona too! "I loved the idea of Cold Stone," Doug says. "The book hadn't been written. The future was wide open. And there seemed to be tremendous opportunity. I didn't see it at the time—I'd like to say I did see it, but I didn't—but a lot of what I had learned at Procter & Gamble could be applied to Cold Stone and building the brand."

Talk about getting in on the ground floor. "There were only four of us in the beginning," Doug says, "myself; Don Sutherland, the founder, who is my partner now; Kim Cramton, our first employee; and Ken Burke." Doug put some money into the company, in exchange for one of the first franchises, but beyond that Cold Stone's operating capital was close to zilch. What they did have, though, was passion and something new in the ice cream business: a spirit of innovation. "We had a good model and a few existing stores around Phoenix," Doug says. "What gave us confidence were the reactions of the customers and the emotional connections they had to our ice cream and brand." Those emotional connections were simple to trace: at Cold Stone everything was both fresh and fun. "We make our ice cream fresh on site. We bake our own brownies. We make our own waffle cones. And we offer a variety of candy, fruit, and other mix-ins that the customers can use to customize their ice cream. We encourage them to change their choice every time."

Cold Stone had another advantage: it was coming into an industry that had not changed much over the past thirty years. "We're innovative, but we're not *that* innovative," Doug says. The real truth, he says, is this: "No one was doing anything new, so we took advantage of a lot of decent, good American brands that were sitting on their laurels."

In the beginning Cold Stone had no major ambitions except one: survive. "We were an absolute start-up," Doug says. "We didn't know if the model really worked or if it would work outside of Phoenix. We certainly didn't know if it would work in Southern California or anywhere else. We simply didn't know the market." Imagine what his professors back at Procter & Gamble would say to that! "You get an F, kid. But nice try."

Starting your own business is not for the faint of heart. Just ask Doug Ducey, Michael Caito, Bill de la Viña, or Eric Gillberg. Or for that matter, Robert Mondavi, Bill Gates, or Steven Jobs. Or Howard Schultz of Starbucks fame. The plain truth is that when you break new ground there is rarely any reliable market research to guide your way. And if you're afraid of risk and afraid to trust your gut, well, then you'd better think twice about going out on your own. Still, as Doug learned, there is something liberating and exhilarating about daring to follow your passion. It is the ultimate form of taking charge of your life. And here is the best news: there is a proven system that can help you launch your own business and make it a success: Management Action Programs. Helping start-ups is a big part of what MAP does. Time and again, entrepreneurs like Doug or Michael Caito come up with a great concept, they have all the passion in the world, they get their baby born, and then, sooner or later, they say, "Uh-oh. We're out of the launch phase. Now what the heck are we going to do?" And that is exactly where MAP can come in and help.

Doug's uh-oh moment emerged from Cold Stone's early success. He and his partners didn't have the capital to go out and build a lot of stores. But as soon as people got a taste of the Cold Stone concept and the freshly made ice cream, many of them saw Cold Stone Creamery as a promising business opportunity. "People were literally knocking on the door," Doug recalls, "saying, 'Hey, I'd like to franchise this. Can I write you a check?'" From there, franchising the brand was an easy decision. The execution, though, was far more difficult.

In building Cold Stone's network of franchisees, there was no big boom period, only a steady, incremental expansion. Southern California was a big growth market early on: Cold Stone set up 70 shops there before it had a single shop in Northern California. But everywhere a shop opened, people liked the Cold Stone products and the company's spirit. "Cold Stone was authentic, genuine, and sustainable," Doug says, "and we had the fundamentals of quality, service, cleanliness, and experience. Each year we did better and better. In our first year we opened 14 stores, then 21, then 49, the next year 76, then 144. In 2004 we opened 362 stores. We basically doubled on top of ourselves, year by year."

But how do you manage that kind of growth? How do you keep bringing on new franchisees and get them trained and aligned behind a common mission and common goals and values? How do you instill discipline throughout a rapidly growing enterprise, without sacrificing the quality, passion and, excitement that are so key to success? In Doug's case, the answer to each of those questions was MAP. As with Michael Caito and Debra Paterson, though, for Doug MAP was not an instant sell.

"Stan Sipes from MAP must have called me over forty times before I returned his phone call," Doug laughs now. When he finally did return the call, Doug had specific business challenges he wanted to address, but his most pressing concern was personal: his life was spinning out of control. "Part of my thinking was, 'OK, I'm a businessperson, a husband, and I'm going to be a father,'" Doug recalls. "I thought, 'Something has to give.'" His life had become a monstrous juggling act, and Doug feared that he had little choice but to cut back on time with his family: "I thought, 'This is the life I've chosen, this entrepreneurial pursuit, and it's probably going to have to be my family where I cut back, because there's just too much to do—and I've got to do it.'"

THE AWAKENING

Doug went into the MAP workshop with low expectations; he figured that at Procter & Gamble he had already learned most of what he needed to know about the fundamentals and the nuances of management. At MAP, though, Doug had a rude awakening, beginning with the 360-degree feedback. "When you go into MAP, you feel like you're about seven foot nine. Then when they go around and read your strengths and weaknesses or opportunities, you feel like you're going to fall through the back crack of the chair! I immediately saw in the beginning exercises that this was something that could help. I think it was some of the best days of my business career. For me it was like a retreat just focusing on the business of Cold Stone Creamery."

LEADERSHIP

Right away Doug came face to face with a different style of leadership, one that he knew he could use to delegate authority, empower his team, and cut down on his personal workload. Using the MAP system, Doug saw that he could handle his obligations and still have more time at home with his family. "MAP helped me see that my initial fears were incorrect, that there was a way to get these things done without necessarily doing it all myself. It's very much the lessons I had learned at Procter & Gamble, but before MAP I didn't see how I could directly apply them to what I was doing at Cold Stone."

VITAL FACTORS

Beyond MAP's approach to leadership, Doug also embraced many other aspects of the MAP system, starting with the concept of Vital Factors. "I was hooked immediately," he says now.

> I began writing our vision statement while sitting in the three-day seminar. That was the beginning of our "Pyramid of Success," which is the guiding document in our organization. These are the things we always focus on: direct results, culture, values, development of people, and having people list the three or five quarterly goals they're going to achieve. All of this embryonically began at MAP. The idea of focusing on what is vital, the idea of setting goals, of holding folks accountable—it's hard to say I learned that at MAP because I knew that from Procter & Gamble. But we weren't doing it. MAP came in and said, "Hey, you've got a million things on your plate; here are the three that are important." As we

started to do that, it was like the fog lifted and we really began to gain momentum.

EMPOWER YOUR PEOPLE; HELP THEM GROW

After his own experience at the MAP workshop, Doug sent his top people through MAP training. "MAP appealed to me because we looked for people who had great energy, enthusiasm, and positive, can-do attitudes but who weren't necessarily traditionally trained in the Procter & Gamble sense," Doug says. "We had hired two wonderful people, and I wanted them to get a better understanding of traditional management techniques, so I put them through MAP." Once all the top people had common training, a common business vocabulary, and a common management system to use— all fruits of the Vital Factor process—Doug's Vital Factor Team examined the key drivers and accelerators of their company and began making fundamental changes. "MAP set a great foundation for what we call *brutal facts,* or *proof over harmony.* OK, here are our strengths, weaknesses, and opportunities, but let's put ourselves in a position where our strengths can be strong and our weaknesses can become obsolete."

ALIGNMENT

Today the MAP system is tightly woven into the fabric of Cold Stone Creamery. "We're a branded company so we've branded some of what we do," Doug says. "But we use Vital Factor Teams. Some of the other MAP tools we've customized, like we do with our ice cream. Still, you can see MAP running through our organization, a controlling thread from the leadership team through the franchise community, who are the end-using consumers in our system."

Doug has seen the impact firsthand. "In the beginning, we had twenty stores operating, we were in complete chaos, and we had three or four people doing a bit of everything. It didn't seem like anything I had learned before was applicable. MAP helped tie that together and say, yes, these lessons are applicable and here's how to do it. With organizations like Anheuser-Busch and Procter & Gamble the business is big, significant, and structured, versus Cold Stone where there was not much there. We had to create our structure from scratch."

ACCOUNTABILITY

With the franchisees one of the biggest issues is quality control and protecting the brand; one bad apple can damage the company's image and reputation as well as spoil things for all the good franchisees. What to do? Doug's answer was pure MAP: use the MAP system to manage your supply chain, from your vendors to your distributors. First, teach franchisees the importance of having Goals and Controls, accountability, and consequences. Then help them implement the MAP system to achieve those ends. Doug did just that. As a result each Cold Stone franchise now sets its own specific business goals, then monitors and measures them through performance indexes and Vital Factor Spreadsheets.

"I believe in local store ownership," Doug says, but he also knows he must maintain accountability and discipline right from the top, right from his own office. To underscore the point he points to a large stack of papers sitting on his desk:

> Those are customer complaints, the first thing I read each morning. They refer to individual stores, and it is up to those stores to fix those complaints. We have CEOs all over the country. If someone is a bad franchisee, we get them out. We have five lawyers on staff. It is my job to protect the brand and the good franchisees. If I keep seeing someone's name come up on these customer complaints or if they have bad operational indexes, it means they're not participating and engaged, and we get them out of the system in order to protect the brand and franchisees. My dad was a cop. I'm not a cop, but we do have rules.

TRAINING

The cornerstone of alignment for Cold Stone is training its staff and franchisees and steeping them in the philosophy and values of the company. This gets done on-site in Scottsdale, at the company's Cold Stone University. The training, Doug says, is rigorous:

> The franchisees come and live here for two weeks. We teach them everything we know about this business. Our mission is to make people happy, and we think that goes all the way up to our executive team and includes the crew members and the ice cream lovers

they serve. As a franchisor and leader of the organization, my job is to make people happy by enabling them to be in business for themselves and do meaningful, enjoyable, engaging work. We're in the ice cream business and by definition it's fun. It's our job to provide our franchisees with the knowledge and the tools they need to be successful and happy. We expect the franchisees to become passionate about their businesses and, in turn, their job is to impassion ice cream lovers across the world.

Speaking as a coach, I'd give Doug's approach to training an A plus. He's managing his franchisees as if they were his employees: he's taking MAP principles and tools and extending them to his supply chain and vendors. In other words he is driving his values and the process of alignment into every corner of the organization.

VISION AND MISSION

Doug's vision is to see Cold Stone Creamery expand around the world, driven by the passion and ingenuity of its franchisees and by the quality of its product line. He has looked at other business models, but franchising is the one that he and his partners prefer. Why? Local ownership and personal empowerment. "I think franchising for us is a great advantage, a great multiplier to what we're doing, because we're working with business owners who will put up their money for our idea and take ownership of it. I prefer this. If I could wave a magic wand, if I were bequeathed $50 million, I would not buy out our franchisees and own our own corporate stores. I would continue to support the franchise community."

Many entrepreneurs with a hot company might be tempted to launch an IPO and use the stock market to raise capital and fuel expansion. Not Doug. "There was a day when going public was attractive," he says. "We couldn't get those guys [outside investors] to return our phone calls. Now they call all the time. But we're over the capital crunch, and so I look at our franchisees as our stakeholders. I report to them; I am accountable to them. I don't need to announce to an analyst on Wall Street if we miss a goal. If we set a goal to be open 365 days and we're open 362, who knows? Who cares? Wall Street would say, 'You missed. You failed.' We don't need that."

On the international side the immediate platform for Cold Stone's growth is Asia. In 2005, the company announced that its first international pursuit would be a joint venture in Japan, and it already has a handful of stores open there. Doug also has dreams about China, starting in Shanghai. He recently visited China and was very excited by what he found. When Starbucks opened in China, it had to teach the Chinese about coffee; tea drinking was deeply engrained in Chinese culture but not coffee drinking. Doug saw that no such introductory phase was needed with ice cream. "We don't have to teach them to like ice cream," Doug says. "They love ice cream! So we think it's a great opportunity."

Specific Goals and Target Dates

Doug is impatient. He thinks big and wants to grow Cold Stone as fast as he can. And he has an ambitious plan to make that happen. In keeping with the MAP philosophy and process he and his partners have set down on paper—write it down!—their specific goals and target dates. And are they big! "If we wanted to go slowly and stabilize, we'd have an incredible amount of time to follow MAP principles to the letter," Doug says. "But we're trying to reinvent this entire category. We're trying to become a breakthrough brand. Our vision is that the world will know us as the ultimate ice cream experience by making us the No. 1 best-selling ice cream brand in America by December 31, 2009. That means overtaking Ben & Jerry's, Hagen Dazs, Baskin-Robbins, Dairy Queen, and so on. So we've got a lot to do."

Harmony and Balance

With such ambitious goals for the business can Doug really meet his goal of spending more quality time with his wife and children? By using the MAP system and leadership approach, Doug believes he can. "I think *balance* is a foolish thing to aspire to, if by that you mean work eight hours, sleep eight hours, play eight hours," he says. In this expansion phase of Cold Stone that's just not realistic. The key is time management, and in life as in business the key is fundamentals: Planning. Organizing. Prioritizing. Focusing on the Vital Few and ignoring the trivial many. At MAP we often say,

"Either you manage your time or it will manage you." Doug has learned that lesson well: "I now feel I'm able to carve out the time that I want to spend with my family," Doug says. "I'm the head coach of my son's baseball team and the third base coach. I may not make all the practices, but I do make all the games. Those sorts of things are ones that MAP helped me see can be done."

CREATIVITY AND INNOVATION

By managing his time well and by delegating the trivial many to other people, Doug has more time to be creative and innovative—and to seek creative juice from other companies and cultures. As a case in point, Doug went on an exploratory trip to Italy, looking at ice cream–making equipment, tasting Italian ice creams and gelatos, and examining Italy's fabled style and merchandising techniques. The trip was in many ways a revelation. "I looked at the stores in Italy and thought, 'Wow, what incredible merchandising! And I brought a lot of ideas home. How our stores look was largely a result of my trip to Italy. We think of ours as an experimental brand, and we want to really develop this idea of making people happy."

In Japan Doug also got an important lesson in hospitality and customer service. When he arrived in Tokyo his host was waiting for him at the airport, so he didn't have to worry about finding a taxi or renting a car and contending with hard-to-navigate maps and traffic. In some countries a business host might simply send a limo to the airport, but not in Japan. There, a proper personal welcome is a mark of honor and respect for the arriving guest. "Our host was waiting for us at the airport," Doug says. "It was such a great gesture. I think of us as a very service-oriented country, but in Japan I realized, 'We can do better.'"

SPIRIT

For anyone who believes that passion and spirit are *not* fundamental to business success, Doug Ducey has one word: "Hogwash!" Passion and spirit are the very essence of customer service and creating a pleasurable buying experience. In Doug's view, passion and spirit are also essential cornerstones of building a successful team and a successful brand. And here Doug and his top managers really walk the walk. If you call into the Cold Stone Creamery head offices, you are greeted by a warm, bouncy message—in a kick-back Arizona style that would make the white shirts back at Procter & Gamble lift an eyebrow in disdain. And when you make your way to Cold Stone's world headquarters outside Scottsdale, that same spirit greets you right at the door. There's a cart full of Cold Stone creations in the lobby. And what's that singing you hear? A bit of high spirits drifting over from Cold Stone University, in session down the hall.

As a last bit of topping on this unique corporate sundae, the walls are filled with cheerleading posters and rewards—mission statements, value statements, salesperson of the month, year-by-year growth of the franchisees—all done in bold, celebratory colors. At one level the messages are pure Cold Stone: fun, happiness, team spirit, success, and that "attitude of abundance." But to a trained MAP eye there is another layer of messages: Have a clear mission and vision. Manage to your values. Empower your people and help them grow. Set ambitious goals and reward your people for reaching them. And never underestimate the power of passion and spirit.

"When people come to our stores, we believe it is our job to make their day," Doug says.

> Our mission statement starts out, "We will make people happy." We have an opportunity to do that. Our customers are eating ice cream; it's fun. We try to give people peace of mind, security, joy, and hope in the future. If you're always struggling and running your business irresponsibly, you're killing the spirit. On the other hand, if you go out and achieve great success, then your people and your franchisees will have confidence and increased buying power and they'll invest more in their homes, their education, their children, and everything they're doing. All those ripples come from running a successful company.

Thanks, Doug. I couldn't say it better myself.

The Bottom Line

1. Whatever you do, do it with passion and commitment. Invest yourself totally. Be sure that where you are in life today is aligned with where you want to be in five years or ten years. If not, make changes! Get on track to fulfill your dreams and aspirations.
2. What's the goal? Whatever you're doing—a business, a project, or just a meeting—clearly define what the goal is. Alignment flows from that.
3. Goal alignment has to extend through your team and then through your entire supply chain (in Doug's case his franchisees). Manage your supply chain just as carefully as you manage your own people. It affects your Vital Factors too.
4. Remember: goals should not be general or vague. They have to be specific, and they have to be measurable.
5. And always remember the wise words of Robert Mondavi: "Find your passion, and you'll never have to work a day in your life!"

CHAPTER SIX

DISCIPLINE AND ACCOUNTABILITY

Passion is not enough. Just ask Steve Campbell.

Steve is a hands-on, hard-working guy, always has been. At the age of twelve he was pulling nails out of stakes for a buck an hour. By sixteen he was working in a grocery store—and absolutely loving it. He even thought, "OK, this is it, what I want to do with my life." But it didn't work out quite that way.

When he was eighteen, Steve went for a ride on his motorcycle and had a terrible crash. "I broke my neck," Steve recalls, "and that changed the course of my life." During his period of rehabilitation Steve became friends with a next-door neighbor named Pat Anthony. Pat owned a concrete company, and when Steve was back on his feet, Pat gave him a job pouring concrete on a few construction projects. Pat urged Steve to see the job as only a short-term solution. Concrete, Pat told him, was a brutal way to make a living; Steve really ought to find something else to do.

Fat chance. Steve loved the work, loved being out in the field managing projects, loved lining up new clients, loved the camaraderie of the construction crews, and he loved kicking back with them after work, maybe drink a few beers, go fishing together on the weekends. "We work hard, we play hard," Steve says, and he had a real feel for the job: soon he was a foreman running his own crews.

The next step was probably inevitable: a few years later Steve decided to go out on his own. Pat urged him not to, but Steve had made up his mind. And that was that. He had no college education, no business plan, no financial backers, and no prospective clients standing in line, promising him their business. The truth is, when he took the plunge and launched Campbell Concrete in Riverside, California, Steve had little more going for him than passion and a prayer. "I had $2,000 in the bank," Steve laughs now, "and I started out with myself and one laborer." The year was 1984, and Steve Campbell was all of twenty-six years old.

Still, Steve knew concrete, and just as important, he was one heck of a salesman. "I could sell an Eskimo an ice cream pie," Steve says:

> You know why I'm a good salesman? Because I believe in the product. I know what we can do. When we first started, I was typing up my proposals on a manual typewriter. I'd work up the bid, send the proposal out, get the job, do the contract, and then I'd do the scheduling, go out in the field, manage the men, and when the job was done, I'd type the bill up, send it out, collect it myself, and try to meet the deadline. I never missed a payroll my whole time in business. I'd make sure the guy was going to pay me and the bank was going to cover me. I did everything myself.

Steve focused his business goals on the area that he knew the best: pouring high-quality concrete for foundations, slabs, driveways, and sidewalks in residential communities across the Riverside area and beyond. He also focused on a goal that he hoped would separate him from his competitors in the construction industry: reliability. Get the job done on time, on budget, and always with top-quality materials and craftsmanship.

Steve's formula worked: before long his business was galloping forward. And that's where all his troubles began. "Before I knew it I had 100 guys doing a lot of work and it was totally out of control," Steve recalls. "I knew how to do the work, but I wasn't a businessman." Poor accounting and poor record keeping got Steve into some tax problems, and that was a major headache. And then it got even worse.

The economic downturn of 1993 and early 1994 punctured the construction boom in Southern California, and Campbell Concrete got whacked. Hard. "We were losing money and I didn't know what to do," Steve says now. "So finally we said, 'Let's go up to Vegas,' and we did." Steve opened an office in Las Vegas, where the construction market was continuing to boom, and week in, week out, he shuttled back and forth, trying to handle the increased workload and put out the inevitable fires. By now he was married, and with his wife staying back in Riverside, Steve was working as hard and as fast as he could just to keep going. He was also working hard to keep his team intact, and he felt a strong obligation to keep his people and their families on his payroll. Otherwise they could face financial ruin. To keep them afloat Steve took many of his best workers with him to Las Vegas.

"They were happy to go," Steve says. "They could make more money in Vegas, have a good opportunity, and live cheaper." But nothing got better back in Southern California. "My guys were having a hard time in the recession. Things were difficult and I lost a few key guys. I pretty much pulled my hair out."

By this point Steve knew he was in serious trouble and he needed help—desperately. But he had no idea where to turn. Then one day he talked with a pal in the plumbing business, and he told Steve about Management Action Programs. More specifically, he told Steve about Lew Herbst, one of MAP's top business coaches and mentors. Steve called Lew right away. They arranged a meeting, and straight off Steve put all his cards on the table, face up. "I sat down with Lew and said, 'I'm out of control; I need some help.' I told him the whole story, and Lew said he could help."

What was Lew's answer? The MAP system. And business fundamentals.

"As a first step," Steve recalls, "Lew came in and interviewed our people. Then he talked to me, got my input on where we were at and how it was going. Then he started preaching the MAP gospel. He gave us Vital Factors, Goals and Controls, and he set up monthly meetings where we would go over all the costs, all the financial statements, to figure out where we're at. At each meeting he set goals for everybody, and the following month he came back to see if we had met those goals. And if we didn't, we got the wrath of Lew."

Right away Lew had pinpointed one of Steve's most egregious problems: the total lack of accountability and discipline inside

Campbell Concrete. Worse, the problem started right at the top, with Steve's leadership style. Steve loved the operations side of the business, he loved working side by side with his men, but there was a price to pay for that approach: Steve was more buddy than boss. He had passion, he had spirit, and that helped him recruit good people and then mold them into a team. But when his people failed to toe the mark, Steve couldn't call them on it. The company motto is "We kick ass," but that was the one thing Steve was never able to do. When Lew started coming in as coach and mentor, that became his first job. He became the Enforcer.

"I'm more of a rah-rah leader, a we-can-do-it! guy," Steve says. "Lew established a game plan and rules and regulations. It took a coach who was not part of the daily camaraderie to come in and say, 'You guys have to perform for me once a month.'" That attitude was totally alien to Campbell personnel, and at the outset Steve's team didn't like Lew—or the MAP system—not one little bit. There was no surprise here: Steve's people were a bunch of tough, hard-working cowboys. They came to work at dawn in their pickup trucks, they did backbreaking construction work all day long under the hot California sun, and as a result they were a close-knit bunch. Lew was an outsider. From a very different world.

"When Lew first came in, people didn't like him. You couldn't mess with him—and they knew it," Steve says. Still, the problem ran far deeper than that. "They didn't want to be held accountable," Steve says. "And they didn't like this outsider coming in, holding meetings, and telling them what to do."

The MAP system, by its very nature, imposes discipline and accountability, whether people like it or not. The monthly Vital Factor Meetings, with their black-and-white spreadsheets and their clear, written-down Goals and Controls, give each person specific tasks and responsibilities to fulfill. Success is applauded, and failure is there for everyone to see. At each monthly Vital Factor Meeting each individual staffer is held accountable in a way that is totally clear and transparent. And month after month Steve's teams bristled at the entire Vital Factor process, especially when they failed to meet their goals.

"Our people hated those meetings to begin with," Steve says. "They'd wait till the day before the meeting to write down whether or not they had reached their goals. They were coming in unprepared, and Lew would call them on it. It's a big thing when you get held accountable in front of everybody and you didn't do the work; that's embarrassing."

Resistance to Lew and the Vital Factor process grew, but now Steve stuck to his guns: he was beginning to understand the demands of leadership. "They'd grouse about it, but I told them it's not going to change. That's the way it is. Lew is going to be here forever, so you'd better get used to it."

IMPLEMENTING GOALS AND CONTROLS

Now let's take a closer look at the system of Goals and Controls that Lew put into place at Campbell Concrete; it will show you how you can implement the same system inside your company or in your personal life. And Steve's experience will show you how the system of Goals and Controls, by its very nature, imposes discipline and accountability up and down any organization.

First of all, what does MAP mean by a goal? It's *not* a vague intention. It's not, "Next month I hope to do better in my sales position." In the MAP system you have to set very specific goals and ones that can be objectively measured. Goals should also be directly linked to a specific Vital Factor, one of the key components that drives your business, your department, or your project. To be effective, goals have to be set down—in writing!—with specific measurements and deadlines attached. Here are some examples from Steve's company. One of his salespeople set this goal: "I will close $3 million in jobs in the next 30 days." In the accounting department one monthly goal was this: "I will reduce accounts receivable over 60 days to under 10 percent of total receivables in the next 30 days." For field superintendents it is essential to hold actual costs well below estimates—that is key to profitability. So one typical monthly goal was, "I will achieve an 80 percent rate on all jobs that close at or below the estimated budget in the next 30 days." In each case these are concrete, specific, measurable goals that directly affect the company's Vital Factors and bottom-line profitability.

MAP gives managers a starting point for this approach, a thumbnail description of the Goals and Controls system to use as a guideline for implementation. Here it is:

I. Each person—manager or staffer—sets goals that meet these criteria:
   A. The goals are based on the Vital Factors you can affect in your job.
   B. The goals are measurable in regard to
      • Output (revenue, sales, profits, units, or donations)
      • Cost (profit margins, expenses, labor, cost of goods, accounts receivable)
      • Quality (errors, defects, customer/employee satisfaction, returns, waste)
      • Time (deadlines, cycle times)
   C. The goals are clearly stated, with the intended result spelled out.
   D. Accountability is crystal clear: you are responsible for the results.
   E. Those results contribute to concrete objectives, such as
      • Profit
      • Reserves
      • Service level
      • Not-for-profit donations
   F. The goals are challenging but realistic.
II. The next step is to negotiate agreement on those goals, usually within the framework of your Vital Factor Team.
III. Then make plans on how to best fulfill your goals.
IV. Set deadlines.
V. Take action. (This is Management *Action* Programs, after all.)
VI. Regularly compare performance to goals.
VII. Take corrective action as needed.

Here, for example, is a simple, generic goal statement, the kind that Lew insisted Steve's people set down, in writing, each month in their Vital Factor Meetings:

I will increase/decrease [*a specific Vital Factor*]
by [*an amount in dollars, percentages, or numbers*]
by [*a certain date*], which will result in
[*additional profit, contribution, reserves, or service level*].

At first, Steve's people found this system of Goals and Controls a little hard to understand—and very hard to swallow. Again, this was no surprise: most of Steve's people were construction guys with little or no experience in management. Still, Steve now realized there was no choice: he had to transform the operational style and culture of his company. "I treat my people very well and I always try to promote from the inside," Steve says. "Those guys in the Vital Factor Meetings are guys who came up from the field, so they didn't have basic skills. They knew how to run a big truck but not a big department." They had to learn—and grow.

Slowly, under Lew's relentless coaching and prodding, Steve's people got the hang of Vital Factors and Goals and Controls, and their entire attitude toward the process of management began to change. "They dreaded it," Steve says, "but each month Lew would come in and say, 'You guys need to be prepared.' Then I'd get upset and say, 'Guys, this isn't going to work. You need to be come prepared.' They don't like being on the hot seat. So they started getting into it more, coming in more prepared. And then they started seeing results."

One person who was held prominently accountable was Steve himself. Lew called him on his mistakes and there was nowhere to hide. As a result he had to stand back, look himself in the mirror, hard, and then make some fundamental changes. "I wasn't real good at accountability," Steve says. But now he realized he had to improve on that and set the right example for everyone else. "Every month I started reviewing the Vital Factor Spreadsheets, which give all the key indicators of the company on one single sheet of paper. You can go through it and analyze the company quickly. I saw that we were lacking some vital financial information, and Lew helped us figure out several areas that we had to monitor and measure."

In order to bring discipline to the financial side of Steve's operation, Lew set in motion a major overhaul of procedures and personnel. "I was an operations guy, but the accounting side—that's always been a problem with this company," Steve says. "Lew helped me hire better people and hold them accountable. He was always pushing me: Get more financial data. Get the financial reports out faster. Do them better. He made me see that the accounting side is at the core of the operation. There was no way to effectively plan unless we had a clear read on the financials."

A first step in the company's makeover was to create a Vital Factor Team that was solely responsible for the company's accounting and financial side. Then Lew and Steve put specific people in charge of different aspects of accounting and financial planning, and Lew coached them on how to get results. All this was classic MAP.

Lew also had to bring discipline to Steve's approach to staffing. "Hiring anybody is a fifty-fifty shot, no matter what you do," Steve says. But until Lew came on board, Steve's main hiring guide was his own gut—and that sometimes got him into trouble. "I've always believed in promoting from within," Steve says. "And a lot of times I got in trouble with that because I'd promote a guy who just wasn't ready."

Lew showed Steve how to improve his hiring and promoting skills, for starters by giving promising job applicants the FIRO-B and Behavioral Style Analysis tests. Lew showed Steve how to interpret the results of those tests and use them in the interviewing process. I'll show you that too, in a forthcoming chapter. To further help Steve with staffing, Lew would interview promising job applicants, to give Steve multiple points of view about a given candidate. All this helped Steve enormously. By watching how Lew handled the interviews and by using those test results himself, Steve became far more insightful about choosing the best people and working with them afterward. He was now taking his natural managerial and leadership skills and putting a solid, proven business foundation underneath them.

"I've always taken good care of my people," Steve says. "Without good people I wouldn't be in the position I'm in today. I was a foreman before I started my own company, and many of the guys who were on my first crew work for me today. I have many who have been with me for twenty years. These guys would walk through fire for me. I'm not trying to pat myself on the back, but that's true. They have pride."

As the months passed, and as the MAP system took hold inside Campbell Concrete, Steve saw that pride grow, in large measure because of the discipline and accountability imposed by MAP's system of Goals and Controls. In essence Steve's people were now passing Lew's strictest tests, and they were damn proud of it. "After awhile they understood the process," Steve explains, "and they felt better about it. Once they saw the system was not going to go away, and it was not there just to beat them down, they began to see what a benefit it is. It's good stuff. It makes them be better business-people. So now they appreciate it a lot more than they did three years ago." Again, this was classic MAP.

Nothing fuels pride like success in your chosen field. We at MAP tell business leaders that the top two motivators for their people are recognition and pride. That was certainly true at Campbell Concrete. With their growing pride, discipline, and professionalism, Steve's people began winning more bids and earning a highly respected reputation in the concrete industry: they got the job done on time and on budget, and their work was always top quality. One aspect of the Vital Factor process was key: job costing. That meant doing spot-on estimates and bids, and then in doing the project, effectively managing all costs, including time. Job costing went straight to the bottom line, and it was a process that Steve and his teams had never before mastered. "For a long time I had no job costing," Steve says. "We brought in job costing and we started making more money. Under the new system, estimates had to be right; our guys out in the field had to be right; our budgets had to be right. We had to look at everybody in the entire chain. We had a lot of huge projects for this company, and this made them work. And we started to make much more money."

Candor was the oil that greased this entire process. And by his own hard-nosed example, Lew impressed upon Steve the importance of preaching candor—and practicing it. "Lew has been around the block," Steve says. "He has helped improve many big companies and he's dealt with companies that had issues. I just always trusted his judgment. He's not a yes-man, and I respect that. I trusted Lew to give me open, honest opinions about people, decisions, and the direction of the company. Lots of people who worked for me would give me the answers that they thought I wanted to hear. Lew would be honest and open." Jack Welch, meet Steve Campbell.

Through the MAP system and through Lew's patient mentoring, Steve felt himself grow as a manager and as a business leader. Indeed, his entire approach to leadership was soon totally transformed. "I used to be wound pretty darn tight," Steve says. "I'd blow up in a second. Lew has taught me patience, and I've gotten older too. Nothing ruffles my feathers anymore. The biggest pieces, though, were accountability and Goals and Controls. They turned everything around."

Once the Campbell machine was working well and there was accountability and discipline up and down the system, Lew turned his attention to another MAP fundamental: incentives. Namely, a bonus plan for Steve's people. Before that Steve had used an informal system of bonuses, based on little more than his gut feeling about an employee come bonus time. Lew changed that. He built into the company a clearly structured bonus plan, based on Vital Factors such as revenue, profitability, gross margin, and accounts receivable. Again, performance in these areas was measurable, so there was a fair and transparent basis for handing out bonuses. Steve saw how that improved performance and staff morale. "We don't have profit-sharing," Steve says, "but now all the people who come in under me have a bonus plan. The better they do, the better their division does, the more money they make. There is fairness and honesty—the program works. Everyone can see the results."

Lew Herbst was pleased with the transformation at Campbell Concrete, but ever the Enforcer, he also drew out important lessons that were relevant for Steve's company and other businesses as well. Here are a few of those lessons:

- Gathering accurate and timely financial information is critical.
- Teaching all levels of staff to understand—and manage—their Vital Factor financial information is also critical.
- It is essential for key managers to agree on the financial Vital Factors to focus on and then to set monthly goals related to them.
- Holding monthly meetings to review the financial Vital Factors is also essential (although that is a discipline that many companies—including Steve's—fail to maintain).

Still, the transformation of Campbell Concrete produced amazing results. By the year 2000, Steve's firm was one very hot company, and it was one of the most respected in the LA and Las Vegas construction markets. Las Vegas, along with the Phoenix and

Scottsdale region, by then was the fastest-growing area in the entire United States, and Steve's team was one of its top performers. As the boom in construction continued, several big companies started gobbling up the smaller companies in an effort to boost their workloads, market share, and profits. Steve could see the handwriting on the wall: he had to partner up.

"I tried with a couple of guys here in Las Vegas, three big subcontractors," Steve says. "The idea was to make one big company and go out and sell together. It was a great concept, and it was working until one of the guys fell off the track. He didn't keep his side of the bargain, so the whole thing fell apart."

Nonetheless, the consolidation in the construction industry only continued to accelerate. When Steve started his company back in 1984, he had had to fight for each client just to survive. Now, even in a boom period, he was still fighting for survival, though on a much different scale. "I saw what happened when you combine a couple of big companies together," Steve says. "They're the big dogs, and they have a lot of buying power. If we didn't jump on, I thought we would probably dry up in Las Vegas or at least have a very hard time. The big dog can eat; the little dog is going to get eaten."

So Steve began talking with BMC Construction, one of the biggest firms in the region, about a merger or acquisition. "They were very interested," Steve says. When the big dog BMC examined Steve's books and did its due diligence, it found Campbell Concrete to be profitable and well managed, with exceptional discipline and accountability throughout the organization—very rare commodities in the construction business. "We ended up coming to terms," Steve says simply. The final sale price for Campbell Concrete? A paltry $85 million. Not bad, especially for a company that Steve had launched twenty years before with only $2,000 in the bank. It was also a fine reward for imposing discipline and accountability throughout his company. Bravo, Steve! Great job!

A FEW LESSONS FROM LEE

Like Lew, I look at the story of Campbell Concrete and I see valuable lessons that other companies would do well to learn. Here we go:

- On a winning football team there is a distinct line of demarcation between the coach and the team. It is a line that should not be crossed. It's the same in business. In his early years as a leader, Steve crossed that line. He wanted to be buddies with his employees. He worried about whether they liked him or not. That's only natural. But guess what? When you cross that line you get confused—and your people get confused. Discipline breaks down. Accountability breaks down. And the leader has a hard time restoring order and holding people accountable for their actions and performance. Steve was a classic case in point—until Lew set him straight.

- When it comes to measuring accountability, we at MAP use a little tool that we call the *Accountability Pendulum.* It's real simple. It is a 1-to-10 scale that describes how disciplined your company's corporate culture is. Figure 6.1 applies this scale to Steve's company.

  Now I'm going to ask you to use the scale shown in Figure 6.1 for a self-assessment: Where does your company stand in terms of discipline and accountability? And be honest; your future could depend on it.

- One of my favorite MAP tools is the *Empowerment Pendulum,* which lets you put a number on how tightly you control your

FIGURE 6.1. THE ACCOUNTABILITY PENDULUM: DOES THE COMPANY CULTURE MAKE EMPLOYEES FEEL THEY'RE IN JAIL OR AT A COUNTRY CLUB?

Steve's Company Before MAP

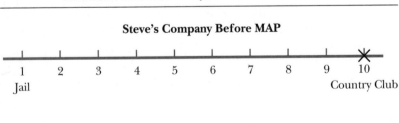

Steve's Company After MAP

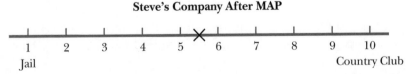

people compared to how much you empower them to succeed. This is the focus of another MAP mantra: "The more tightly you control your people, the more you sap their power to succeed." Well, you can graph that too for yourself and your company, using the scale shown in Figure 6.2.

Steve's case also clearly illustrates the three phases of MAP:

1. *The Mechanics Phase.* This is the *how* phase, when you and your team are just learning how to use the MAP system and tools. You are discovering the answers to questions like these: What is a Vital Factor? What is a goal and what is a corrective action? How do I prepare for my monthly Vital Factor Meeting? This phase is probably the most difficult, because everything is new, including MAP concepts and terminology.
2. *The Enlightenment Phase.* As you saw with Steve's team, this is when your people get the hang of the process and it all starts coming together. They no longer ask, "How do I do that?" Now they ask, "Why?" In this phase your people push the process themselves and ask, "Why don't we measure this Vital Factor or focus on that fundamental; it directly affects profitability."
3. *The Internalization Phase.* This is the fun part, the *who* phase. This occurs when your team has totally internalized the MAP philosophy and operating system. Monthly Vital Factor Meetings are accepted ritual, so is Team Consulting, Goals and Controls, accountability and discipline, strategic alignment, managing to your values, empowering your people, practicing candor, and instilling passion in your people. Remember back in Chapter One when I talked about how Eric Gillberg and his

Figure 6.2. The Empowerment Pendulum: Does the Company Favor Control or Empowerment?

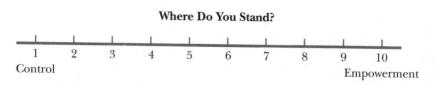

Where Do You Stand?

| 1 | 2 | 3 | 4 | 5 | 6 | 7 | 8 | 9 | 10 |

Control   Empowerment

team found that the best-run companies shared particular attributes and virtues? Well, MAP companies that successfully enter the Internalization Phase display many of those same attributes and virtues. They are on the road to success. And they are not asking how they do it, or why they do it, but who is going to do it—and who will take the responsibility and the credit.

This evolution is clearly visible in Steve Campbell's company. By the time he sold his company to BMC, Steve had matured as a leader, and his people had largely internalized the MAP process. We say that Campbell Concrete had evolved into a Phase Three MAP client. There is one more phase, Phase Four, when a company is so thoroughly adept at running the MAP system that it begins pushing it into its chain of suppliers and clients, as we already saw with Cold Stone Creamery. This is the ultimate win-win: you do better, your own people do better, and your suppliers and customers do better too.

With MAP, Steve Campbell was able to evolve personally right along with his company. Today, with his new financial freedom, he could easily retire. But Steve is too active for that, and awhile back he turned his natural entrepreneurial impulses to a new horizon: gas stations. "We started with one station and now we're launching our fifth," Steve says proudly, and this time he brought the MAP system in right from the beginning. And guess who is advising him every step of the way? That's right: our man Lew Herbst. As Yogi Berra might say, it's déjà vu all over again.

Right off, some of Steve's people in the new venture balked at Lew coming around, holding meetings, telling them what to do, and enforcing discipline and accountability. Who was this kick-ass guy anyway? Steve just laughed and told them, "Listen, you guys, Lew is going to be here forever. You better get used to it."

The Bottom Line

1. As a leader, understand where you are with your team members. Have you crossed the line or are you so close to it that you no longer keep your objectivity and hold them accountable? Do they see you as the boss or as just another member of the team?
2. Understand too where you stand on the Accountability Pendulum. Are you a jailer or a country clubber? If adjustments are needed, make them.
3. Entrepreneurs have to develop into real leaders. You have to manage, control, and hold people accountable.
4. You also have to actively empower your people and help them grow. If you're running a country club, your people will never grow.
5. If you have the entrepreneurial itch, remember Steve Campbell and how he started: with $2,000 and no formal business training. But he had plenty of passion and a readiness to learn and grow. If he can do it, so can you. With a little help from MAP of course.

CHAPTER SEVEN

CLEAR COMMUNICATION

Tammy Miller is one surprising woman.

If, from a distance, you saw Tammy at a business conference, in her beautifully tailored pin-striped suit, right away you might conclude that she ran a prominent design studio or was the editor-in-chief of a very successful magazine. She's trim and fit, and Tammy radiates a warm, engaging, can-do leadership style. She also has flair and sophistication, and you could easily imagine her dining with prospective clients in London, Paris, or Tokyo. But here's the fun part: none of those distant impressions comes even close to the truth.

Tammy Miller is CEO of Border States Electric Supply, a big-shoulders, hard-hat company that provides heavy-duty electrical supplies and other equipment to public utilities, industry, and construction companies across the western United States. In fact Border States is one of the largest electrical and communications distributors in the country. Tammy knows cable, she knows construction, she knows the name of every forklift driver at the Border States warehouse in Phoenix, Arizona, and forget London, Paris, and Tokyo: most of Tammy's off-site meetings happen in bedrock America, in places like Fargo and Grand Forks, North Dakota, and El Paso, Texas. In a male-dominated industry Tammy Miller has reached the top—and she's loving every minute of it.

"We are 100 percent employee owned, and we have forty-three branch locations in eleven different states and Mexico," Tammy says in a quiet moment in her office in Phoenix. "Every day is a challenge, and every day there's something new."

For Tammy it has been quite a journey. She was born and raised in North Dakota, and her early business experience was in public accounting. She found it dry, and she didn't like the spirit or atmosphere of the accounting firm where she was working. She needed a change; she needed to be in a company where she could grow, spread her wings, and become more entrepreneurial. Border States Electric, with its headquarters right there in Fargo, North Dakota, seemed worth a try. So in 1991, Tammy joined Border States in its accounting department. Being a fast study she picked up the electric cable business in short order, and then, to broaden her range of experience, the company expanded her duties to include operations and inventory management. In 2003, she was moved out to Phoenix to help manage the rapidly growing markets in the Southwest. Then, in 2006, Tammy was given the title and additional responsibilities of CEO for the entire company.

With such an impressive rise to the top you might imagine that Tammy Miller would have a little pomp and swagger and take a little credit for herself. But again, you'd be wrong. Tammy's style is self-effacing and totally down to earth. On MAP's list of the attributes of a leader, Tammy would score well on humility. As for her own success, she gives all the kudos to her mentors inside the company and to Border States's strong core values and its history of solid management practices. "Our stock value has increased every single year in the history of the company, except for one," she says. "And we have never lost money."

Looking back now, Tammy sees 2003 as an important turning point in her career. Her move to Phoenix gave her added responsibility and autonomy, and it put her in charge of a region of enormous growth and potential. But something else happened in 2003: Tammy Miller discovered MAP, Management Action Programs. At that time MAP was not entirely new to Border States Electric; two of Tammy's colleagues in Phoenix had been to MAP workshops before. The results, though, had not been dramatic or lasting. Nonetheless, after Tammy took the reins in Phoenix, Rodney Wacker from MAP's Phoenix office called and invited her to a *Twelve O'Clock High* workshop. She accepted. Jim Wichterman, one of MAP's most skillful coaches and mentors, led the workshop, and it gave Tammy some fresh ideas about leadership and management.

"At first I just sat back and enjoyed the movie," Tammy recalls. "Then Jim paused it and started asking questions about what to look for in the movie, and we began looking at all the different leadership styles and characteristics. Then it wasn't just watching a movie; you had to pay attention. It was a great way to learn, rather than being strictly in a lecture setting. In fact it was fabulous."

That experience was so positive that in 2004 Tammy decided to take the full plunge and attend a three-day immersion in the MAP system of management and personal growth. Again, Jim Wichterman was the workshop leader, and this time the impact was even more profound. Like Debra Paterson, Bill de la Viña, Michael Caito, Steve Campbell, and others, Tammy entered the MAP process with one approach to leadership and she came out with another. She also came away with a clearer understanding of her own strengths and challenges as a leader and manager. "It was really life-changing for me," Tammy says now. "It was the best, most effective, and most customized leadership program I had ever experienced."

The proof, though, has been in the pudding. According to Tammy she has now implemented the MAP system—Vital Factor Meetings, Goals and Controls, Team Consulting, and all the rest— throughout her top management team in the Southwest region. And the results have been very positive. Some long-festering problems have been solved, internal operations are smoother and faster, and there has been an impressive jump in regional revenues and profitability. For the company as a whole too, revenues have jumped. For fiscal 2007, total revenues were projected at $610 million, up from $475 million in 2006. Part of that rise came from a recent acquisition, but much of it resulted from improved performance throughout the company, due to improved discipline, accountability, coordination, cost management, and bottom-line profitability—all changes catalyzed by MAP.

Tammy says:

It's so fun to hear that buzz around here, because we're starting some of the MAP training with our supervisors. Not the full-blown MAP, but Jim Wichterman comes in and trains our supervisors. They are eager to learn more about Vital Factors because they know it's so important to our management group. They all want to bring it back to their departments and use Vital Factors. The whole format is so great. We do our Vital Factor Meetings in the Southwest, and every branch gives their report on their Vital Factors. It takes two and a half hours. We don't talk a lot about Goals and Controls; they're either done or not done. And if they're not done, each person presents their corrective actions. They've absorbed the entire process.

In talking about the many changes that MAP has set into motion, Tammy talks in terms of leadership, focus, discipline, accountability, and profitability. But one strong, consistent theme runs throughout her conversation: *clear communication*. After all, how do the most effective leaders motivate and inspire their people? Through clear communication. How do they instill values, passion, and discipline? Through clear communication. How do they push alignment and accountability? Through clear communication. And how do they promote and sell their company's products and services? With a clear, compelling, well-targeted message. You get my point. Communicating is one of the six basic functions of management, and as a leader it is essential that you do it well. In real estate the old mantra is "location, location, location." In leadership, I believe the mantra should be "communication, communication, communication."

To me that is an undeniable truth. I don't care if your field is business, politics, sports, or the military, the most effective leaders and coaches are *all* first-rate communicators. Think about Jack Welch or Steven Jobs. Ronald Reagan or John Kennedy. Leaders like these speak clearly. They speak with passion and conviction. Their values are clear and solid, and what they say affirms their values. So people trust them. They have credibility. And their teams admire them, break their backs for them, and follow their lead. As a result we at MAP have a cardinal conviction: if you want to grow as a leader and manager, you have to learn how to be an effective, compelling communicator. And if you want your company to grow and succeed, you and your team have to master the art of clear communication.

The question is, How? And the answer is MAP.

In our workshops and on-site coaching we teach people the art of clear communication. Our starting point is that clear communication is always a two-way process. It is not enough to *speak* clearly; you have to make sure that you are being *heard and understood* clearly.

To facilitate the process we provide everyone with a primer on the basics of effective two-way communication. Here's the primer and its salient points:

I. Prepare how you will communicate.
    A. Clarify the goal of the communication.
    B. Plan carefully before sending it or having the meeting.
    C. Anticipate the receiver's viewpoint and feelings.
    D. Determine the best medium and time for the communication.
    E. Outline the vital points to be covered.

II. Deliver the message.
    A. Engage the receiver's attention and interest.
    B. Express your meaning with conviction.
    C. Relate the message to your larger goals.
    D. Identify the action that needs to be taken.
    E. Watch out for potential barriers to good communication.
    F. Encourage feedback from the other person.
    G. Finally, *confirm the other person's understanding. Make sure everything is clear.*

III. Receive the message.
    A. Always keep an open mind.
    B. Identify the key points in the message.
    C. Value constructive feedback and use it to grow.
    D. Focus on the feelings behind the message as well as the facts.
    E. Demonstrate respect for the sender's viewpoint.
    F. Listen actively—participate in the process.
    G. Finally, *confirm your understanding.*

IV. Afterward, evaluate the effectiveness of the communication.
    A. Was the process itself effective?
    B. What barriers impeded understanding?
    C. What is the impact on future communications?

V. Take corrective action as necessary.

This primer has a dual purpose. First, it helps leaders and managers to better understand the basic fundamentals of the communication process, and it gives them a checklist to guide that process. Second, it can also be used as an informal report card, enabling leaders and managers to evaluate how well they are doing in communicating with their people. In the MAP workshop, after we have covered these points, we bring into play a typical MAP action step: we have the participants set for themselves—write it down!—a *Personal Growth Goal* for their communication skills. For example: "I will do an excellent job of communicating all relevant information to my team in a clear and timely manner."

At first glance this entire approach might seem simplistic: how can anyone reduce effective communication to a short list of how-to checkpoints? But you would be amazed at how effective this primer has proved to be for thousands of managers and leaders. Going into MAP they were simply not aware of the basics of effective communication or what steps they could take to smooth the process. And I can tell you this: that simple, concluding act of *confirming understanding* can have a real clarifying effect at the end of a meeting. It shows respect, and it reminds everyone that communication is always a two-way process.

In this vein let me relate a charming little story. It comes originally from Dee Hock, the visionary business leader who helped turn Visa into the largest credit-card company in the world. In his early days in banking, Dee worked for a wonderful gentleman with Old World manners named Maxwell Carlson, who was president of what would become Rainier Bank, headquartered in Seattle. In order to confirm understanding at the end of a meeting, Carlson would ask his visitor, "Did this meeting serve your purpose?" Now that's brilliant. With one clear, engaging question, Carlson could elicit enough information to confirm understanding and evaluate the effectiveness of their communication. At the same time, he very politely conveyed his respect for his visitor and for the visitor's feelings. What an effective little management tool! With a humble bow to Maxwell Carlson, I invite you to make it your own.

Primers, of course, are not enough. So in our workshops we go deeper and analyze why, in so many companies and organizations, internal communications are so poor. We also provide managers with an extensive list of potential *barriers* to good communication. With that list leaders and managers can examine their communication skills and see where they need to improve. I'm setting forth that same list here. Let me emphasize that the stakes here are high: if you fail to appreciate any one of the following barriers, you can poison the atmosphere between you and a colleague, and you can poison the entire spirit inside your entire company. I see it happen far too often: one ill-advised or insensitive comment can do enormous damage—and it can take enormous work to undo the damage. So the next time you are drafting a letter, e-mail, or policy statement, *before you send it out* consider these potential barriers to effective communication:

1. A lack of respect in either party for the other
2. A poorly defined purpose for the communication
3. The failure to establish the best medium for the communication
4. The misuse of electronic communication devices (is e-mail or voice mail really appropriate for the task at hand?)
5. The *assumption* (rather than *certainty*) that the listener has received the message
6. The failure to be clear in intent or language
7. A message clouded by the perceptions of either party
8. A receiver or sender who is not open to constructive feedback
9. The ignoring of emotions or sensitivities
10. A failure to get on the listener's level of understanding
11. The use of approaches that activate the listener's defense mechanisms
12. The preoccupations of either party
13. Intimidation by either party
14. A failure to recognize diversity

As you can see there are many potential barriers to clear communication—some of them obvious, some not. The FIRO-B and Behavioral Analysis tests can be useful tools here in helping you understand other people's communication needs and styles. And here is the best news: the MAP system *fosters* clear, effective communication. In fact it *demands* it. The regular Vital Factor Meeting in itself establishes an ongoing process of dialogue and communication. Team Consulting, Goals and Controls, and MAP's emphasis on candor and writing it down also facilitate a healthy communication process.

Now, what specific impact did MAP and its push for clear communication have inside Border States Electric? Did the leadership lessons of *Twelve O'Clock High* stick with Tammy and her top management team in the Southwest? Yes. As Tammy explains, for a long time clear communication had not been a particular strength or a priority at Border States. Historically, the company had operated with a traditional corporate leadership model, and operations in the Southwest were hampered by poor communication among the branches and a lack of goal setting and accountability. And those problems were hurting operations and profitability. When she arrived in Phoenix, Tammy saw those problems from a new perspective. If the Phoenix operation and Border States as a whole were going to get to the next level of performance and growth, Tammy realized that she and her other managers had to find ways to improve communications throughout the company. They also had to improve alignment, planning, coordination, and problem solving. Communication, especially among the branches in the Southwest, would also have to be dramatically improved. With her MAP tools Tammy set out to address each of those problem areas. Here is some of the resulting impact:

LEADERSHIP

To set in motion lasting changes, Tammy knew she had to start by getting the members of her management team in the Southwest onto the same page, using the same language, the same tools, and the same leadership approach. With that goal in mind she asked Jim Wichterman to do another *Twelve O'Clock High* seminar. And he did. "Jim came out and we brought in all of our supervisors and managers in the region," Tammy says. "It was very well received. We were really rebuilding the team at that stage, and many of us did not have a lot of leadership skills. MAP was a methodology we all could use and use consistently."

With Debra Paterson, Bill de la Viña, and others, I have already shown you how the MAP leadership model facilitates both dialogue and collaboration; it worked the same way for Tammy and her team. Now when she chaired meetings Tammy became much more of a listener and facilitator, encouraging her team members to speak up and empowering them to come up with their own solutions—and then own them. Tammy also realized that a critical part of her responsibility was to ensure that the dialogue was always respectful and inclusive, to avoid those potential barriers to clear communication.

PLANNING

A few years ago Border States decided to make a major push to diversify its customer base. Up until then its main focus had been providing electrical supplies to utilities and other industries. Now Border States decided to move into the rapidly expanding construction market. This was a potentially lucrative strategic move, especially in the booming Phoenix market, but in the launch phase the company was slowed down by problems with planning, inventory, and supply. "We had inventory issues that needed to be communicated to the corporate office," Tammy explains. "Historically, the field offices would submit a request to beef up their inventory, and the corporate office modified those requests or sometimes didn't implement them at all. When the field offices complained, I said, 'Why didn't you come to me? If you want something and you're not getting it, take it to the next level.'"

The root problem, Tammy discovered, was not planning or inventory; it was poor communications: "The corporate office didn't understand that the field offices were trying to grow their business in the construction market, so what they had been getting historically wasn't enough." Once a better communication process was put into place, the problem virtually resolved itself.

ALIGNMENT

In its Southwest operations Border States Electric faced another thorny communication issue: how to harmonize relations between the corporate managers and the staff throughout the region. And Tammy also faced a more urgent problem: the lack of profitability in the company's El Paso, Texas, office. This branch was new to the Border States system, having come into the fold via the buyout of another company. The El Paso office had a strong operations manager who ran his shop in his own way. He was a good man, and to hold down costs he tended to do everything himself, delegating little to anyone else. On the MAP empowerment pendulum he was definitely on the extreme side, running the office like a relaxed country club. Tammy wanted to show him another way, but she didn't want to offend him or undermine his authority. It was a challenging situation; how should she handle it? By using MAP principles and tools of course.

TEAM CONSULTING

As I explained earlier, Team Consulting is a form of group brainstorming but with important modifications. There is a chairperson who presents a specific problem along with its basic facts and background. The chairperson defines the desired goal as it relates to that problem. The team members are *not* asked simply to throw out ideas. Instead they are asked to present specific *action steps* that could have a direct bearing on the problem. The process has a very definite structure, as shown in the Team Consulting guidelines on page 100. Once the chairperson has presented the problem, his or her job is to *listen* and take notes (write it down!). A key element here is time management. To keep everyone focused, the chairperson is usually given only two minutes in which to present the problem, its background, and the desired goal. Likewise, the group has a limited time for brainstorming, usually between five and seven minutes, depending on the size of the group. (This can be modified, as you will see in a moment.) The chairperson is encouraged to listen with an open mind and to solicit input from everyone; you don't want anyone to feel left out or devalued.

Now here's the part I really like: once the time period for suggested action steps has elapsed, the chairperson goes through his or her notes and *plays back* the suggestions—to confirm understanding. That closes the communications loop and averts potential misunderstandings. The chairperson is then responsible for selecting the action steps that seem best suited to solving the problem. He or she is also responsible for making sure that everyone around the table understands and accepts those action steps. This seems like a simple concluding step, but what is the underlying purpose? One, to forge alignment behind a common set of action steps. Two, to build a consensus and feeling of engagement and

Team Consulting Guidelines

I. The chairperson is responsible for the corrective action or action plan.

II. The chairperson and team agree to procedures, including choosing a timekeeper and the time to be allotted.

III. The steps in Team Consulting:

A. Chairperson presents the apparent problem.

B. Chairperson defines the goal.

C. Chairperson states the how-to question that will generate ideas about the best way to accomplish the goal.

D. Chairperson presents the facts and background of the problem.

E. Team members contribute clear action steps that could solve the problem.

F. Chairperson writes down all the suggestions made by team members.

G. Chairperson must be open to suggestions, listen, not be defensive, and definitely not reject ideas out of hand.

H. Chairperson solicits balanced participation to tap group's reserves.

I. Chairperson summarizes all the recommendations.

J. Chairperson is responsible for selecting the action steps to which he or she will be committed.

IV. Suggested time frames:

A. Two to three minutes: state the problem; state the facts.

B. Five to seven minutes: give possible solutions and action steps.

C. Two to three minutes: commit to a series of action steps.

D. One to two minutes: write it down!

Total time: ten to fifteen minutes. This can be expanded for broader problems.

commitment. Three, to make this a team decision, giving everyone ownership and responsibility for the outcome. Team Consulting also has another purpose: to put in place a reliable communication process that can be used to mold the team and address any future problems that may arise. As I have said before, building a reliable management process is often far more important than the short-term outcome.

To address the problems in the Border States El Paso office Tammy followed the MAP process of Vital Factor Meetings and Team Consulting. She decided to convene a big meeting in El Paso and bring in the managers and outside sales staff to air their issues and feelings. To focus the meeting and allow for proper preparation, Tammy drafted an agenda and distributed it beforehand, setting down the main topics they were going to address:

1. How to grow sales to reach the goal of $10 million for the year.
2. How to resolve problems with planning and inventory.
3. How to address the persistent lack of profitability in El Paso's operations.
4. How to handle a scheduling issue: namely, what time to open for business each morning? People in construction traditionally get rolling long before most of the other Border States clients. Would everyone agree to open at 6:30 A.M.?
5. How to address the lack of urgency at the sales counter.

This last issue was complicated. Construction people need rapid attention at the sales desks and they need their orders filled right away; otherwise they take their business elsewhere. The El Paso salespeople were not reacting fast enough. The pace was too country club; there was no sense of urgency. Tammy saw the problem clearly: "Industrial clients are good planners and they usually need their orders filled within a few days; construction people need their orders filled on the spot. We had to change our mindset as well as our operating procedures."

There was one more issue too, but Tammy did not write it down and put it on the agenda: how could her regional managers in Phoenix work harmoniously with a manager I will call "Miguel S." Miguel was used to running his own show in El Paso, and he didn't like outsiders from the head office telling him how to run his shop or when to open his doors. Sticky situation!

With so many complex issues to be addressed, Tammy knew this meeting was critical, and it had to be handled with special care and tact; otherwise it could become contentious and counterproductive. To set a warm, convivial tone, she chose to host the meeting in a private room at a popular Mexican restaurant in El Paso called Jaxon's. To give the meeting structure she decided to use a modified form of Team Consulting, one that omitted the tight time frames that are usually used; there were just too many issues to explore and resolve. If the discussions bogged down she could use classic Team Consulting to brainstorm any specific issues that were proving difficult to solve. In keeping with MAP's primer on communications, Tammy planned her approach well in advance, and she tried to anticipate people's sensitivities and reactions.

On the day of the big meeting Tammy was ready. The meeting had been well planned, and she knew exactly what outcome she needed to see: concrete action steps to redress the problems and improve sales and profitability. Moreover her desired goals had been clearly communicated to everyone in advance. The managers in El Paso would either find a way to deliver what she and the company needed—or, in line with the MAP system, Tammy would hold them accountable and take corrective action. In sum, her line of march was absolutely clear, and that greatly simplified the task at hand.

"We started the meeting in a casual way and then the food came," Tammy recalls:

> After we ate we picked up the conversation, and we met for about three hours. It was all productive: everyone had a lot of good comments. The Team Consulting principles gave us some structure, but we expanded the usual time frames because we had big issues to discuss and we wanted specific resolutions. We stated the problems and then went around the table. Each person contributed ideas about what the issue was and what we needed to do to improve. We had a very structured format because I knew in that environment one person could have easily taken control of the entire meeting and it would have gotten out of control. This way, every person had an opportunity to speak and share their ideas.

As it turned out, the Team Consulting process facilitated dialogue and made all the participants feel they were part of the process—and the solution. Going around the table, Tammy and the others drilled into why the sales staff were not moving with more urgency in helping construction people fill their orders. And finally, drilling deep, the truth came out: "We learned that the bonus program we had for them was really a disincentive. In the construction market it took our people a little longer to help the customer, and so they were letting that business go to the back burner. With their industrial customers they just had to enter the orders, so they could earn their margin and bonus much more quickly." Once the real source of the problem had been unearthed, it was relatively easy to establish an action step to correct it.

A few minutes later this same process brought to light another problem in the El Paso office: a lack of *discipline and accountability*. The lightning rod issue here was a Ping-Pong table. "We had a Ping-Pong table in the back of the warehouse," Tammy says. The staff used it for a little R&R during the workday. Well, OK, maybe they used it more than a little. "Our people didn't have time to take customers' orders or pick up orders, but there was time to play Ping-Pong," Tammy says. "So we said, 'Get rid of the table.'" The issue, of course, was larger than the table and so was the remedy: Tammy was communicating to the entire staff the values of the company—and she was enforcing discipline and holding people accountable for their actions.

EMPOWERING YOUR PEOPLE

Miguel S., the operations manager in El Paso, was a congenial guy. Before Border States took over the El Paso office he had been on staff for a couple of years, and when it did take over, Border States singled him out for promotion and made him operations manager. Soon, though, the country club problem emerged. Tammy was sympathetic. Under the previous regime El Paso was a tiny, isolated outpost, operating on a shoestring and with next to no supervision from the parent company. As a result Miguel had a tendency to do everything himself—a potential problem as the office made its push into the construction sector. "We needed to do simple things like remodel the counter and have more displays to meet the needs of the construction customers," Tammy explains. "Miguel did that himself. He painted the counter area, put up flat board, did all the displays. It took three or four months. But I understood: his thinking was, 'We have to save money; let's do it ourselves.'"

At MAP we have a fun term for people like Miguel who are intent on doing everything themselves: we say they are wearing the *Big Red "S."* They're trying to be Superman or Superwoman. We also explain that this approach is lose-lose: the person wearing the Big Red "S" is usually overworked, overstressed, and has no time for his family or healthy relaxation. Worse, his team feels disempowered, not listened to, not trusted, and generally devalued. Naming the problem in a light-hearted way can immediately defuse it, in a clear and supportive manner. Tammy knew the term, of course, but she didn't unfurl it at the table. She much preferred to see Miguel's staff bring the problem to light—and propose their own solutions.

Part of the problem, again, was poor communications. The people around Miguel had neither the tradition nor the proper vehicle to say to Miguel, "Let us help you, man! Let us be a part of the solution!" At the meeting it was still a bit difficult initially for some of the people to speak up, since Miguel was sitting right there. But with Tammy carefully guiding the discussion, everyone eventually was able to speak up, speak from his or her heart, and get to the root of the issue. Tammy immediately saw the shift in the group's internal dynamic: "Up to then they didn't have a communication vehicle, and if they did tell the person who was responsible, they didn't feel confident that they would be heard or that action would be taken." Now, with people free to speak their minds, the old walls came crumbling down. Deep changes were set into motion, and the stage was set for a new beginning, one based on dialogue, collaboration, and individual empowerment. Miguel seemed to get the message. Initially, Tammy was pleased with the results of the meeting: "It was great. And if we had not used the Team Consulting structure, we would not have achieved these results."

INSTILLING VALUES

Just stop and consider for a moment what Tammy had achieved with one well-planned meeting. She set a new tone for the entire El Paso operation. She resolved several operational issues. She skillfully and sensitively nudged Miguel into a new management posture. She set in motion fundamental changes inside that branch and how it does business. She also set into motion changes that would affect operations in Phoenix and beyond. By being forthright and candid she also illustrated and affirmed the guiding values of the company. Think of the values she affirmed, without even naming them: Discipline and a strong work ethic (get rid of the Ping-Pong table). Customer service (show more urgency at the sales counter). Empower your people (delegate more work and more responsibility to them). Treat everyone with respect (let them have their full say around the table and act on their suggestions). Help your people grow (don't fire Miguel; work with him and give him the help and guidance he needs to grow).

And just look at the leadership values that Tammy modeled: Check your ego at the door. Be humble. Ask questions. Don't pretend to have all the answers; let your people bring you *their* solutions. What a wonderful illustration of teaching and leading by example! Later, Tammy modeled another leadership virtue: *accountability.* Despite initial appearances, Miguel was not able to adapt to the management model, and he was not able to implement the agreed-upon changes. In keeping with the MAP guidance to *repair or replace,* Tammy reluctantly had to let him go. Still, that sent a crystal-clear message to the rest of her staff.

THE LASTING IMPACT

At MAP we love to point out that when you get it right and fully implement the MAP system, it becomes a self-perpetuating blueprint and manual for success. Tammy Miller is seeing that happen at Border States Electric. Today the MAP system is woven deeply into the company's daily operations, and to keep the process of change moving forward, Tammy has decided to push the MAP system through the entire company. The impact is plain for everyone to see. "The account managers in El Paso now feel more comfortable that we will have the resources to support the sales that they generate, as they work toward their goals, and I get updates on this task list of action items that come out of the meetings. And all of them have been done as scheduled." Now that's discipline. That's accountability.

The MAP process is now almost driving itself through the Southwest region. "In this organization it is happening even at a lower level," Tammy says. "We have our Vital Factor Meetings monthly with all of our managers. Now it's the supervisors who want more training to take that back to their departments. The office administrator, the shipping supervisor, they also want the training and tools to go back and have Vital Factors for their departments. They want specific goals and measurements for their departments, in order to drive behavior, performance, and accountability. They also can use Team Consulting as the way to get some ideas to solve their problems and facilitate meetings."

Jim Wichterman has watched the transformation of both Border States Electric and Tammy Miller. He is deeply impressed: "For the company the results have been spectacular," Jim says. "The Southwest region was losing money or barely breaking even when Tammy got there. Now the region is a leader in the company from the profit standpoint." Jim has also seen Tammy grow as a leader and as a person. "She's more confident to act now and she is much better at communicating clearly. She has become more approachable and more human without losing her focus on concrete business goals. And she has her group totally focused on the Vital Few."

Business is now booming for Border States Electric. The push into the construction market has been a huge success. Sales and profits are both on the rise. With its recent acquisition the company is projecting revenues of $610 million in fiscal 2007, and the staff now number almost one thousand people. More than that, the company's internal chemistry has undergone significant change. Communication is clear. If you want to see clear statements of mission and values, just glance at its Web site: www.borderstateselectric.com. A proven management system is in place, ensuring better discipline, accountability, and performance. Each department has pinpointed its Vital Factors and is focused on the Vital Few. With the new leadership model, employees are being empowered like never before, and Border States managers and leaders are being groomed for greater responsibility just by learning how to use the MAP system to full advantage. And one more thing: heavy-duty electrical equipment might still be a man's world, but in her short time as CEO of Border States Electric, Tammy Miller has already made an impressive mark:

"We all have an idea of what is important, but the Vital Factor scorecard really keeps us focused," she says. "And Goals and Controls works. I know that 50 percent of what we set forth on our goals last year would not have gotten done if it had not been documented via Goals and Controls. People are very, very competitive here and proud to accomplish their goals." All her managers in the Southwest are men, but no one doubts who's the boss: "Sometimes they'll come in and say, 'I didn't do that until last week,' and I'll say, 'It doesn't matter; you got it done before the deadline. I don't care if you did all of it last week, we met the goal. If that deadline gives you the pressure you need to accomplish the goal, perfect."

I agree, Tammy Miller: perfect indeed.

The Bottom Line

1. Study the two MAP primers on *clear communication*. Use them to assess your strengths and challenges as a communicator.
2. Formulate a Personal Growth Goal for your communication skills.
3. Use the MAP checklists when you write an important memo or plan your next big meeting. Afterward, objectively assess the results.
4. Seek input from your staff on how best to improve your communications.
5. With all important communications, confirm understanding.
6. With a bow to Maxwell Carlson, you might even think to ask, "Did this meeting serve your purpose?"

CHAPTER EIGHT

STRATEGIC ALIGNMENT AND BUY-IN

Transforming any big company is never a simple undertaking, especially one like Tammy Miller's with its forty-three branch offices. On many a day, though, Jose Pulido wishes he had it that easy.

Jose is city administrator of the City of San Fernando, and his job would make a circus juggler dizzy. Every day he has to manage his own staff, of course, and that's just the beginning. He also has to draw together the concerns of the mayor, the city council, the treasurer's office, the police, the firefighters, the public works people, the water department, emergency services, the teachers, the school board, the city planners, the tax collectors, the social services, and all the many political constituencies that make up his quiet little city of 25,000 people.

Life is, at least, never dull. If a traffic light goes out downtown, Jose's office gets the call. If one street misses its weekly garbage pickup, Jose's office gets the call. And if the city budget suddenly dips into the red, guess who catches the heat? But Jose Pulido wouldn't have it any other way. This is his city, this is the job he's been preparing for his entire career, and to manage it all and to keep everyone working together in unison and harmony, Jose relies on a very effective system and set of tools: Management Action Programs.

"MAP has provided the rudder for us," Jose says, during a quiet moment in his office at City Hall. "It allows our organization to move forward with everyone rowing in the same direction."

In running San Fernando, Jose has been a one-man catalyst for change, and what he has accomplished is a testament to what one proud and dedicated public servant can do. As CEO of MAP I may be a bit biased, but I think that what Jose has done is also a testament to the power and flexibility of the MAP system. As I have already illustrated the MAP system works well in big, established corporations like Wells Fargo & Company and it also works well in small, creative start-ups like Michael Caito's Restaurants on the Run. The challenges that Jose faces every day are substantially different, so I think it will be very illuminating to see how Jose has adapted the MAP system to his own specific needs and to the unusual, constantly changing needs of city government. And talk about crisis management! As fate would have it, Jose's first day on the job in San Fernando was 9/11.

Still, his job today is a perfect fit for Jose Pulido. Jose grew up in San Fernando, he went to the local schools, and then he went north to the University of California-Berkeley for his undergraduate work. "I received two BA's, one in Chicano studies and another in social science, and a minor in city and regional planning," Jose says. By the time he graduated from Berkeley, his life path was clear: he wanted to work in urban planning and city management. That said, he had no desire or plans to return to Southern California. Destiny, though, had other ideas:

"After graduating I came back and saw a job posting for the County of Los Angeles Community Development Commission, in community development," Jose recalls. "At about two o'clock in the afternoon, I went in, picked up an application, and filled it out. By the time I drove back home, which was an hour away, I already had a call asking me to interview. I interviewed the next day and they offered me a job shortly thereafter. I went back to Berkeley and packed up my belongings. . . . The rest is history. And for the most part it has been go, go, go ever since."

Working for Los Angeles County, Jose realized that he needed a graduate degree, so he went to UCLA and in 1991 graduated with a master's degree in urban planning. Now he was really on his way. For nearly a decade he worked for the City of Montebello, California, in various roles in community and economic development, and he learned the intricacies of city management from the ground up. The job was challenging: "We were facing a budget deficit in the mid-1990s as a result of the State of California's raid on local governments," Jose says, "and the city's downtown had become stagnant. Although Montebello had malls on the north side, there was a lack of economic development in the older sections of the city, and when an innovative development project came forward, it was not supported."

This was frustrating for Jose. He had passion, he had drive, and he had a noble purpose: he wanted to help people, he wanted make a difference in the quality of people's lives. He also believed in effective local government, and he believed in community development. But in Montebello his idealism and passion were constantly put to the test. Then one day his wife-to-be planted a surprising seed, one that would take a few years to germinate: "In 1996, Laura and I were driving a few blocks away from where I grew up here in San Fernando, and it was kind of a revelation for me," Jose recalls. "I had brought her here to meet my parents, and as we were driving through town she said to me, 'Jose, wouldn't it be great if you could do some of the things you're doing in Montebello over here in San Fernando?'"

Jose was intrigued by her suggestion, but he had his doubts. "I thought that my small city was a little too far gone," he says, "and at that time I didn't know anyone at the staff or political level." Also, his work in Montebello in economic and community development was starting to bear fruit: "We were able to develop an award-winning community development program in Montebello; that's what my wife was alluding to: wouldn't it be great if you could do something like that here?"

The next several years in Montebello were increasingly frustrating for Jose. The city's government was poorly structured. There was a lack of long-range planning in most areas. There was no strategic alignment and no accountability. The result was predictable enough: escalating operating deficits, year after year. Jose and his team continued to generate good ideas, but the city just didn't have the means—or the will—to do anything new or bold. As in so many government bureaucracies, lethargy, paralysis, and a general attitude of cover-your-rear reigned supreme. All of this sapped Jose's energy and enthusiasm: "We got tired of sending things up the flagpole," he says. And he saw no change in sight.

"Our staff predicted, seven years ago, that unless the city government did something about public safety—Montebello has its own fire and police—they were going to have some fiscal problems down the road, five, seven years. And guess what? They are having problems." By 2005, he says, the city's operating deficit was $1 million. As Jose sees it, Montebello now is "just kind of a ship floating out there, rudderless."

In the late summer of 2001, the city administrator's job in San Fernando opened up, and Jose immediately threw his hat in the ring. And he got the job. He was supposed to report for work later that week, but on the morning of September 11, 2001, Jose received a panicky call from the mayor: could he come in and start right away, in the next few minutes? Terrorists had hijacked planes and flown them into the World Trade Center in New York and into the Pentagon outside Washington, D.C. No one knew if more terrorist attacks might be on the way. Jose rushed in and helped take charge of fire, police, and emergency services. He also coordinated with regional and national law enforcement agencies. Welcome home, Jose. Now get to work! Help us manage this crisis!

Taking the reins that day was not a simple feat. Jose was only thirty-six, he was the new guy in the city, and he had to rally a much older group of city department heads into action. Talk about a monstrous leadership challenge! Within hours of the attack Jose was walking into an emergency meeting, to plan what to do and prepare for a possible second attack. Jose knew his mettle would be tested. "We had older managers in place that were pretty set in their ways and I was a new kid coming in. Literally, I was the youngest person that walked into the meeting that day. And it was like, 'OK, who *is* this guy?'"

Jose passed the test. But even before the shocks of 9/11 had subsided, he had other pressing problems to tackle. And he had big responsibilities: he wore the hat of city administrator and he also wore the hat of redevelopment director. And both hats butted against the same cold fact: San Fernando had an operating deficit of $600,000 per year. Back in Montebello Jose had learned a valuable lesson by seeing things done the wrong way: he now knew he had to tackle that deficit head-on and not just push the problem down the road. He also knew that being new in the city, he had some assets in his pocket. Although he had no political base and no political allies, he also had no political enemies, at least not yet, and he owed no one any political favors. "I'm staff; I've always been staff. And knock on wood, I'll always be staff," Jose says with a laugh. "Elected people, well, they get funny sometimes, especially right before elections."

During his first eighteen months on the job, Jose moved patiently, taking care to learn the city, assess its problems, win the trust of its leaders, and build bridges to its different ethnic and political constituencies. No substantive change, he knew, could be set into motion unless he had first built a base of trust and credibility with city leaders and the general public. "During the first year and a half, I was pretty much assessing what the needs were and where the city organization was going. To be more specific, I had to address what the city council wanted me to do, which was to look at the city and really turn things upside down."

Jose did turn things upside down—and he didn't like what he found. There were long-festering problems with planning, budgeting, and accountability, and there was nothing even remotely resembling a common mission or a common vision of the city's future. The resulting malaise was evident and profound. City services were weak and uneven. Housing was inadequate. Educational opportunities were poor. Young people were leaving in droves once they received their college degrees. And there were no signs of new investment in sight. In a nutshell, the local economy was stagnant, and the future was bleak, especially if the city continued to operate on its existing budget. Jose knew that if the city were a private company, it would soon be bankrupt and closed. He also knew that cleaning the situation up would be a huge and complicated task, about that he had absolutely no illusions:

"Budgetwise, I don't think things were being scrutinized as much as they should have," Jose says.

> People were just running the city on a cash-in, cash-out basis. I don't know that there was any long-term planning going on. That was one of the challenges that I saw when I came in: that the city was pretty much being run day to day. And for an organization with a $39 million budget, you can't afford to do that over the long haul. Pretty soon it catches up with you. It just so happened that when I came in, it was catching up. That was the $600,000 deficit.

We were losing funding in our parking lots, we were losing money in our water and trash services. We're pretty much a full-service city—we have everything except the fire department, which we contract out to the City of Los Angeles.

Worse, revenues from sales taxes, property taxes, business licenses, and water and other public services were, in Jose's word, "flatlined." And here too there was no relief in sight.

Given the depth of the city's problems, Jose knew that serious changes had to be set into motion; pursuing a timid policy of a tweak here and a tweak there would be an exercise in futility. Jose wanted bold action; the situation demanded it. He wanted to re-examine everything city government was doing—then overhaul it. Short term, there was going to be pain, Jose knew, but that was the only possible path to long-term gain. And in any case this sweeping rethink and overhaul was long overdue—and Jose had the mandate to do it. "My job was to look at things that were laid out ninety-plus years ago, when the city was first incorporated, and ask, Did they still make sense today? And if they didn't, what did we need to do to change it? It wasn't just me telling people, 'We need speed bumps over there, we need this over there. . . .' My responsibility was to come back and create the broader vision."

Fine. But how do you create that broader vision? How do you set in motion the necessary process of change? And how do you bring together the different city departments and services and convince them to work together, plan together, and revitalize the city together, according to a broad common vision? Jose was eager to get the process moving—the future of his city was clearly at stake—but where exactly should he start?

With MAP, of course.

Ed Stein, one of MAP's executive consultants and a specialist in working with city governments, called Jose one day in 2003 and introduced him to MAP. Ed explained a little bit about the MAP system of management and personal growth, and then he asked Jose if he would be interested in attending a MAP workshop. Jose jumped at the chance. "He was ready," Ed recalls. "And a few things I said about planning and accountability really struck a chord."

Jose was ready. He was ready for action, and he needed a plan. Right off, MAP provided Jose with just what he needed: inspiration, ideas, and a whole new set of tools for addressing problems and catalyzing change. "When I went through the MAP program, I learned, within the first hour, that this is what I needed in terms of structure, accountability, and the level of attention to detail," Jose says. "This is what I needed to bring people together." The MAP management system and tools worked well for private companies, and Jose was convinced that they could work equally well in city government. There would have to be a shift of mind-set. And there would have to be a wholehearted buy-in by his staff and other city leaders. But Jose's key premise was this: that cities should be run like private corporations, ones with a strong social conscience. Well-run governments, just like well-run businesses, need clear strategic goals, a well-planned budget, fiscal discipline, strong accountability, and a leadership style that by its nature promotes dialogue, consensus, alignment, and equal ownership of the responsibility and outcome. By the end of his three-day MAP workshop, Jose had made up his mind: he was going to bring MAP and its tools to San Fernando. It was a bold decision, with plenty of risks, but Jose was convinced: MAP was the medicine necessary to cure his city's ills.

Soon after the workshop, Jose began designing his plan. The city council had already defined his mission: "To turn things upside down and create a broader vision for the future of the city." Now Jose defined a series of action steps that he needed to take. One, secure the necessary buy-in from his staff and other city leaders and department heads. Two, shake up the entrenched bureaucracies and fiefdoms and set in motion a far-reaching, self-sustaining process of change. Three, establish an effective process of dialogue and consensus building, one that would produce a common vision and common goals; strategic alignment could then be forged. Four, take clear, effective steps to eliminate the city's operating deficit—by an agreed-upon date. Five, as a leader remain humble, be self-effacing, and play a facilitating role; for this grand experiment to work the city's leaders and many department heads would have to feel fully empowered and vested in the outcome. Six, be alert to staffing problems and possible Onboard Troublemakers. Some people might buy into the MAP system, and some might not; Jose had to be ready. If he were running a private company, Jose would at least have the power to hire, fire, and make unilateral changes in policy. But Jose had no such power. Therefore, point seven: everything would have to be done through negotiation, consensus, and gentle persuasion. Was he up to the challenge? Was the MAP system up to the challenge? Well, Jose thought, we're about to find out.

The first essential step was getting buy-in and convincing city leaders that they couldn't afford to be timid; they had to tackle the financial and budgeting crisis head-on. To that end Jose had MAP organize a *Twelve O'Clock High* seminar for himself and other department heads. The seminar, Jose says, proved to be an eye-opener for everyone. "We brought all the directors together, and when you launch the film you see what crisis management is and how some people deal with crises and how some people don't," Jose says. "For us it got the ball rolling by getting our department heads to realize that things were going to change for the better."

Next, Jose began focusing in on the budgeting process; it had to be totally overhauled. In practical terms that meant Jose had to figure out a way to get the different city departments to show some discipline and work for the common good, even if that meant cutting back on their individual department's budget demands. They could no longer continue to request a 5 percent increase in their budgets without any justification or without difficult questions being asked. But Jose knew this was treacherous ground: in years gone by the budget process had been dog-eat-dog, with most departments in it for themselves:

"The way things were funded in the past," Jose says:

whoever put on the flashiest PowerPoint presentation got the most funding, with police and public works being the beneficiaries of such a process. That created some animosities between department heads as to how the limited budget resources were allocated year in and year out. There were two or three of the departments that always got the lion's share of the limited funding, and everyone else was pretty much left whistling in the wind and hoping that some of the morsels would fall from the big boys so that they could operate their department's programs. What I wanted to do was to create a neutral, merit-based process that allowed department heads to come in and have an open discussion of the needs of the city, not just the needs of their specific departments.

Fine. But how to foster that open discussion? How to create that neutral, merit-based process? How to break the existing stalemate? Well, Jose opened his MAP toolbox and out they came: Vital Factor Meetings. Prioritizing. Planning. Focusing on the Vital Few. We at MAP had taught Jose that the best way to build teamwork is to get the team to focus on a common set of goals. So Jose convened what amounted to a government-wide Vital Factor Meeting. And he set before the assembled leaders and department heads an urgent, well-defined task: examine all city services and projects and then define ten *strategic goals* that they could all agree on, focus on, and then attack. In the best MAP tradition Jose also set a target completion date: bring me a list of those ten strategic goals within one year.

I applaud Jose's approach and leadership style. Notice that he did not set down *his* ten suggested goals—he transferred that responsibility to the people in charge of the city's departments and agencies. Like Debra Paterson, Bill de la Viña, and Tammy Miller, he was learning how to empower his people and give them responsibility and a vested stake in the outcome. Jose had become a facilitator, an asker of pertinent questions, a manager growing into a first-rate leader. What made him especially effective was that he was clear in his values, mission, and purpose. And he could communicate them with clarity and conviction. Just listen to this:

"I wasn't out here to try to take advantage of anybody; all I wanted was better services," Jose says. "I think some of the things deep down for me were, 'I wonder why these services went away?' When I was growing up, for example, our city park was twice as big; why all of a sudden was it carved up in the 1980s? In time, you learned why: they were operating in a deficit. But it was still analogous to cutting off an arm."

By asking city leaders and department heads to reexamine their work and come up with an agreed-upon list of ten strategic goals, Jose set powerful forces into motion. He was really asking everyone to put aside his or her individual pet projects and to participate in forging a united vision for the common good. What kind of city do we really want? Where do we want to shine? What problems need the most urgent attention? The process cut deep and it finally hit bedrock: *values*. What kind of values do we want to embrace and convey to our children? What kind of future do we want to create for the City of San Fernando? It amazed him, but through the ensuing process of dialogue and meetings, within a year the city's leaders and department heads had done it: they produced those ten strategic goals. That "broader vision" that Jose was seeking was now coming into focus, and a strong, healthy, self-sustaining process of change was also taking hold.

Once the strategic goals were defined, Jose could zero in on his financial goals: cutting costs, boosting revenues, and erasing that debilitating operating budget. This was the big test. City leaders and department heads had come together and achieved consensus on their vision and strategic goals; could they now bring their budgets and programs into similar alignment, in support of those goals? To do that each department and city agency was forced to sit down, see where it was spending its money, assess results, and then make some hard decisions. Departments and agencies had to prioritize. They had to cut waste. They had to do away with failed programs, programs of scant importance, and programs that did not support the ten strategic goals. Staffs had to negotiate and reach consensus inside their own departments. Then, when the department heads gathered for their next meeting, the process of prioritizing and consensus building began all over again—but now out in the open, with equality around the table and with each person focused on how best to cut costs and reduce that operating deficit.

Now this might not seem like a radical development. After all, it is routine in private businesses for presidents and CEOs to gather their department heads around the table and hammer out the budget for the following year. This is just bedrock business practice, the blocking and tackling of setting goals and priorities and fixing budgets accordingly. But guess what? This process was entirely new to the City of San Fernando. In previous years the department heads and managers had casually put down their target numbers, submitted their annual budgets, and then worked behind the scenes to get the sum of money they wanted. There was no open discussion, no transparency, no personal accountability for the outcome—or for going over the city budget. As this new process unfolded one police captain took Jose aside: "You know,

Jose, I've been here twenty-two years," he said, "and I've never had an opportunity to sit down with all the department heads like this, to have a dialogue and exchange ideas about funding or projects." In his mind the simple act of sitting down and working together toward common goals was a major breakthrough, almost a mini-revolution.

In the end the process worked. "Through the process of MAP—by then most of my department heads had been through MAP—we were able to define, over a one-year process, our ten strategic goals, each of them identifying a particular reason why all of us collectively show up to work. Those strategic goals were, in essence, a public proclamation: 'We are your management team, this is what we represent.' The city council approved all the goals, and from that point forward we were able to start creating supporting projects for each of those strategic goals, along with the Vital Factors to get them done. In two years the operating deficit was erased. Within two years we had turned it all around and got the budget under control. Now we have a $1.8 million budget reserve."

But that was just the beginning. Now a new spirit was taking hold in San Fernando, and some people responded well to it and some people didn't. Change will do that, as Jose discovered:

> We now had the ability to create unity and dialogue between the different department heads; they could actually collaborate on things instead of everybody protecting their own kingdom. Along the way I lost two of my most senior department heads, and I had two new department heads that came on board who were very much into MAP. Having that turnover and change has been very healthy for the organization in terms of creativity and camaraderie. As hokey as it may sound, it's true: when you have people sitting at the table during budget time, by the time we get to the city council we pretty much have hammered out our budget already, consistent with the ten strategic goals and consistent with the project that we have set before the council. The entire process becomes more collaborative and transparent.

The result, of course, is *consensus, strategic alignment,* and *accountability,* with each department now an owner in the outcome, for the good of the city and its broader unifying vision. Jose was delighted by the way the process unfolded: "I think MAP has provided the rudder for us to allow the municipal organization to move forward with everyone rowing in the same direction. And by that I mean department heads as well as second in commands within each department."

The City of San Fernando is now powered by MAP. Vital Factor Meetings, Goals and Controls, and Team Consulting are tightly woven into the fabric of city government. "Every other Tuesday we have department head meetings and we go through everything," Jose says. "We troubleshoot, we brainstorm every issue, and every department gets a chance to bring up issues that they want to put on the table. It helps. We're not at the point where we would limit Team Consulting to ten minutes because people are still new and they're learning the process. At this stage I think it's better for camaraderie to be built—and it's working. Had it not been for MAP, I'm telling you, we would still be upside down and rudderless."

Now that the city's vision is clear and its finances are on the mend, the process of change is rapidly spreading and attracting new projects—and new revenue. To help revitalize the city's downtown area, Jose's team planned and the city council approved a specific blueprint that allows mixed-use development in the older downtown areas. "We went through a two-and-a-half-year community-planning and participation process to do that," Jose says. "Ultimately, the council adopted the San Fernando Corridors Specific Plan in January of 2005, and right away we had development proposals for 200 to 300 condo units in the downtown area. Before, that would never have been possible. But having that broader vision, and having affordable housing and maintaining the character of our community among our ten strategic goals, it makes it very easy for us to come back and work with the city council." Everybody wins.

And there's more: to revitalize the city's education system and better prepare its youngsters for the challenges ahead, San Fernando is building an ambitious new junior college–style complex, with four academies able to accommodate 500 students each. "One is premed, one is prelaw, one is social justice, and the other is performing arts," Jose beams. "This will be in 2010." A big, new commercial center is set to open in 2010, and Jose and his planners are projecting a big boost in sales tax revenue. "It will help us," Jose says. "We're hanging on until then."

There has been another important shift in San Fernando: young people are no longer eager to pack up and leave. "Back in 1996, when I drove in with my wife, there weren't any signs of life," Jose says. "Now you're going to be quite surprised to see what unity and bringing people together has meant in terms of fostering creativity. The young people are staying, and we've actually had a couple of staff members come in from other cities because they wanted to become a part of what we are doing here. One person actually took a pay cut to come from the City of Sierra Madre because we are one of the first Latino communities to be working on a historic preservation plan and ordinance. In a Latino community you don't typically see neighborhoods where residents in their late twenties and early thirties are taking Craftsman and Victorian homes and restoring them. That's going on here."

Developments like these have validated one of Jose's basic premises: that cities ought to be run like private businesses, albeit businesses with a strong social consciousness. But as Jose has learned firsthand, that noble goal can be achieved only when cities have their vision clear, their financial house in order, and their management practices rock solid. MAP, Jose says, has been key: "MAP allows us that flexibility to identify problems, solve them, and to change course and direction as need be, on a weekly basis or a monthly basis."

MAP consultant Dorriah Rogers has been working closely with Jose and his top people, helping them implement the MAP system and adapt MAP tools to the special needs and opportunities of San Fernando's government. She has also charted the impact of the changes that Jose and MAP have set into motion. "Jose is truly an inspiration to city government," Dorriah says. "His vision has allowed the City of San Fernando to move away from the glacially paced environment typical of other bureaucratic organizations. In my work with the Tier 1 Vital Factor Team [made up of the department heads] we have made tremendous progress. We have been able to align the Vital Factors with the ten strategic city goals, measure each department's progress toward each goal, and report in a meaningful way each month what it means to the city council. My hat is off to Jose. He makes what I do worthwhile."

Looking back now on his experience in city planning and administration, Jose says he learned a lot at UC Berkeley and

UCLA, but it wasn't enough. Nor was his long on-the-ground experience in Montebello. "As a working professional I hadn't found anything in terms of a model that would bring things together," Jose says. "You always felt like you were shooting from the hip, going day to day. Within the first hour of MAP it was like, 'Bam! OK, this is it!' That's where the realization hit me that this is the component I had been missing in my professional and education background. This was the management tool that, if other cities knew about it and had the courage to implement it, I think they would be even more successful."

In Jose's view the new emphasis on clarity and accountability has removed some stubborn barriers between the government and the people. "We never before had this level of accountability," Jose says.

> It makes a big difference when your city council has approved the strategic goals. Now it's up to us to go out and implement those goals with supporting projects. It also creates a mechanism for the city council to track the work. Rather than having the perception of "Who knows what goes on between you and City Hall?" people can actually see what happens. City Hall becomes transparent. There's nowhere to hide. And people appreciate that. You get everybody on the same page, set your goals, and explain to people that you have to take tough medicine for a while because we're $600,000 in the red. People understand that. And as long as they can see that you're going to deliver them something positive as a result of the tough medicine, they'll support you every time.

Right on, Jose. And when you're done in San Fernando, how about taking some of your energy, passion, and MAP expertise over to Washington, D.C.?

The Bottom Line

1. Follow Jose's lead: identify areas of ongoing contention inside your organization—or your family.
2. Design a process of discussion, consensus building, and alignment.
3. Start by defining your common vision, values, and goals.
4. Don't impose *your* solutions; facilitate the process, and keep it focused.
5. Use the process to promote an ongoing climate of positive change, dialogue, consensus building, and personal growth.
6. Hold people accountable.
7. And if you're feeling fanciful, imagine a world where all politicians actually embrace fiscal responsibility and work for the common good—and hold themselves accountable for the results. Imagine that!

CHAPTER NINE

THE BIG RED "S"

Glenn Stearns is a high-energy, high-octane, triple-espresso kind of guy. He thinks fast, talks fast, moves fast, and he exudes boyish enthusiasm and very high spirits. Sitting in his expansive office in the plush headquarters of Stearns Lending, just south of Los Angeles, Glenn Stearns seems on top of the world. And he loves to spin stories about how he started out in the mortgage business, printing his own flyers, walking the raw streets of new housing developments, charming his way into every doorway and office, and always refusing to take no for an answer. You gotta love him. He's a special breed: the born entrepreneur, the self-made man, the star-spangled dynamo who worked hard, followed his dreams, built his company, and made himself a fortune in the process. He's a one-man bow to the American Dream.

And make no mistake about it: Glenn Stearns is one smart cookie. Like many born entrepreneurs, Glenn is a creator, a builder, a mover and shaker, a big-picture guy. He has no patience for details, and he hasn't got the velvet touch you need to be adept at managing people. But Glenn knows business and, boy, can he sell. And Glenn Stearns has one other outstanding asset, one quality that may well be one of the true secrets of his success: he knows his strengths and he knows his limitations. He focuses on what he's good at—and he hires first-rate people to do the rest. And clearly Glenn has an eye for talent; for proof of that all you need to do is spend a few minutes talking with Katherine Le, his second in command.

Katherine, too, is a star-spangled success story, but of a very different sort. I am going to tell her story in some detail, not only

because of her experience with MAP but also because her story is
so inspiring and so illustrative of what it takes to succeed in business and in life. Like Glenn, Katherine did everything herself, with
extremely heavy odds stacked against her. Listen to her story, really
take it in. And the next time you hit a rough patch, or think you
can't make the grade, stop and remember Katherine Le and all the
obstacles she had to overcome on her own path to the American
Dream. If Katherine can do it, by golly, so can you.

Katherine Le is a slender, elegant woman, and as soon as you
meet her you can see that she is a woman of great dignity and poise.
Like many Asian women she is very private by nature and not one
to wear her heart on her sleeve, and certainly not on first en-
counter. In talking about her experiences in America and in business she speaks slowly and chooses her words carefully, the way
many people do when not speaking in their mother tongue. Still,
right away you can sense the strength and feeling behind her words,
and when later, in a second conversation, she opens up and reveals
her personal story, you thank heaven you're getting it down on tape,
so you can get every word right and not miss a single nuance or
ounce of meaning.

"I was born and grew up in Saigon," Katherine begins. Her
father worked as a contractor for Shell Oil, and after the Communists came to power in 1975, life was extremely difficult for her
family, as it was for most of the families in South Vietnam. There
were waves of reprisals; many people died, countless others were
clapped in jail. In Katherine's family there were seven children:
Katherine, her four sisters, and two brothers. After Saigon fell,
their mother, Hong, was worried sick. What would happen to her
girls? What would happen to her sons? It didn't take long for Hong
to make up her mind: "I was fifteen when my mom decided to get
us out," Katherine recalls. "The country was already being gov-
erned by the Communists and to try and get out was illegal. When
she first arranged it, I tried to leave and I was captured. At fifteen,
that was my first try. I was in their camp for about a month, so I got
my first taste of what it was like. This is where they kept all the people who tried to get out illegally. I had that experience, and my
mom had to bribe the guard to get me out."

Hong did not stop there. She was a strong, resourceful, and
very determined woman; whatever it took to get her children out,

Hong would do, no matter what the price. "About a year later, my mom tried again," Katherine says, "but this time it was half-legal, because at that time the government had a program to let people go." This was 1979, and by then the new rulers of Vietnam were facilitating the exodus of ethnic Chinese, many of whom had been in Vietnam for generations. Katherine's family was not Chinese, but many Vietnamese families like hers seized the moment anyway. They begged, borrowed, and bribed to arrange permission for their loved ones to leave. In some ways that was the easy part. Then wave after wave of men, women, and children were loaded onto small, rickety boats and sent out to sea, with no certainty of where they would land. As a group these refugees became known as the *boat people*, and their plight became a shameful, heart-wrenching epilogue to the war in Vietnam.

Hong figured her children might never get a better chance to leave. So using guile and all her connections, she managed to get Katherine's two sisters and one of her brothers onto boats and out of Vietnam. Two weeks later, with more cajoling and bribing, Hong arranged for three more people to get onto a boat: Katherine and her aunt and her aunt's five-year-old son. Her aunt's husband had been a captain in the military under the old regime; he was now in prison, and no one knew when—or if—he would ever get out. So Katherine's aunt was eager to get out, with her son in tow. Katherine was eager too. She was scared, of course, but she knew she might never get a better chance. "I was Vietnamese," Katherine says, "and of course they knew that. But this was at least a half-legal way for me to get out."

Finally the hour came, and the three of them were put onto a small boat. They were not alone. "It was about a sixty-foot boat, but they got 240 people—including adults and children—onto the boat. They packed us like sardines, your shoulders touching another person's shoulder. You had no legroom and you pretty much sat in one position; that's how they packed everybody in."

The boat captains weren't doing this out of any humanitarian impulse; they were doing it for the cash. And the more people they packed in, the more money they made. Once they loaded up, most of the captains would keep their boats close in near land, then head either south toward Malaysia or north toward the Chinese mainland. A few headed due east toward the Philippines. On those

distant shores they would dump the boat people off, then return
to Saigon to pick up another load. The captain of Katherine's boat
had a somewhat different plan. "The captain of the ship, he pretty
much decided that he was going to take his chance and head
directly out to sea, where they have all the big ships traveling for
business and commercial fishing. He headed directly out with the
hope of running into a big ship, or maybe we'll die out there
because obviously the ship will not be able to handle the rough sea.
He made that decision."

For two days that little boat—with 240 men, women, and children crammed on deck—headed straight out to sea. "Then we ran
into a fishing boat, a big one from Taiwan," Katherine recalls. "In
Taiwan they had a policy that they don't pick up refugees at all. So
the captain of the fishing boat stopped and said, 'I can give you
food and water, but I can't pick you up.' Then among the sailors
they had a plan to separate all the children from the parents, and
the captain negotiated and forced it down on the Taiwanese captain. So they started loading and separating the children from the
parents. It was kind of a madness going on, and there was a lot of
crying."

Perceiving a terrible tragedy in the making, the Taiwanese captain finally relented. "We forced it down with the Taiwanese, and
so 240 people made it onto his boat," Katherine says. "And if it
wasn't for that we would probably have died the next day. Because
that same night there was a storm and our boat, the little boat, sank
because it couldn't withstand the storm. It was meant for us to live."

The Taiwanese fishing boat was bigger and sturdier, but the
boat people's ordeal was far from over. "The boat was mainly open
decks—so every one of us, all 240 people, were outside on an
open deck." On deck the refugees had no shelter from the wind
or sun or cold. "Between 4 A.M. when the sun rose and 5 o'clock
when the sun was down, you pretty much got burned. I was pretty
tan and burned from the sun. At night it was cold. It took us about
nine days to get from where we were back to Taiwan. They took us
to one of their little islands in Taiwan, and along the way we ran
into many stormy seas."

One night the storm was especially bad and the sea churned in
fury. "I still have a vivid memory of that night," Katherine says:

They had to strap all 240 of us down on the deck, under a big, sturdy plastic cover. So you can lay flat on the deck with this piece of plastic on top of you, because they anticipated a really rough sea and they didn't want anybody to be thrown overboard. I went under that plastic. And my aunt, at that time, because she had her son, she managed to get one of the sailors to give up part of his cabin. So she went in with him and I was out there all by myself. The sea was so rough for what felt like hours and hours, and it must be thousands and thousands of gallons of water pounding on top of you constantly. I was thinking that if I disappeared, because the water swept me away, no one would know—because it was the middle of the night.

The fishing boat, of course, did not have enough water or food to feed all of those refugees. So each day it was a challenge just to survive. "We had a teaspoon of water, and I had many days where there was no food to eat," Katherine says. "There was only food for the 10 people on the boat; they didn't have enough food for 240 people. Nine days we had very little water and very little food."

Just imagine what this took. All her life Katherine had lived in a privileged and protected enclave in Saigon, in a culture that was, before 1975 anyway, sophisticated and refined. Now she was crammed onto a boat, in violent seas, fighting for her life. Those nine days were the ultimate test of her character and courage. When the boat finally reached Taiwan, Katherine knew that no test would ever be as harsh.

"This would be a good experience for me," she says now, "and we made it. I can tell you that I'm pretty fortunate compared to other people that I talk to. Their story is probably a lot, lot worse than what I went through. But me being a city girl, not having ever left my mom and dad for a day, it was quite an experience for me."

Coming through an ordeal like that, Katherine learned how important it was to be resilient, resourceful, and totally self-reliant. Under those circumstances nothing small mattered; you had to stay focused on your top priority: staying alive. And you couldn't count on anyone else to help you with that; you had to rely on yourself. For nine months Katherine was held in Taiwan as a refugee. Then she got clearance to leave, to go to the United States where her sisters and brother were waiting. When she finally reached America,

Katherine was still a refugee, a woman without a home or a country, and she was facing an unknown future. But those were small concerns. The big thing was this: Katherine had survived, she had made it through, and now she was determined to take advantage of the golden opportunity for which her mother and father had paid so dear.

Katherine's first stop in America was Texas. "I stayed in Texas for about a month, then I came to California to meet with up with my sisters and brother." She and her siblings settled in Orange County, south of Los Angeles, where many other refugees from South Vietnam were busy forming a community and trying to restart their lives. Getting settled here was not a simple undertaking for any of them. In Katherine's case it meant learning a new language, discovering a new culture, and coming to grips with a new reality: she was on her own. She was going to have to build a whole new life for herself—and do it from scratch. Still, she had no fear now, and the freedom was delicious. And Katherine knew that if she could survive those boats, she could accomplish whatever else she set out to do.

For Katherine and her sisters and brother, one of their first priorities was getting their parents out of Vietnam. "My mom got us out as a family, and when I came here in 1980 I immediately sponsored my mom and the rest of the family, after I became a permanent resident. Six years later we were united as a family."

Another priority for Katherine was finishing her education and finding a way to earn a living. She enrolled at California State University at Fullerton, nearby in Orange County, and she already had an inkling of the path she would follow. "It is a pretty good school for business, and business is something I was always interested in," she says. "I learned a lot. Business is a process to learn, and in terms of management most of what they teach you in school probably you learn better on the practical side."

Katherine worked hard and did well at Fullerton, and she graduated with a BA degree in business management. Then right out of school she was recruited by Merrill Lynch. This was a wonderful opportunity and a fitting testament to the amazing distance she had traveled: in the space of just five or six years she had made the leap from helpless, homeless boat person, speaking no English, to budding junior executive, at Merrill Lynch no less. Her field was mortgage lending, and Katherine worked on a small, somewhat independent lending team. She soon discovered that in business too, you have to be resilient and resourceful.

"I was at Merrill Lynch for about two years," she says. "We made a lot of money for them, but because of a conflict between corporate and the leader of our group, they decided to close the group down. I was one who was retained by management, and we started a new group. After Merrill Lynch we moved on to a new shop called Franklin Mortgage. When I was at Franklin I worked initially as an underwriter, but I was being trained in all different departments. I decided that I did want to be an underwriter, so after doing that for five years I became chief underwriter. Then I had a group of underwriters that I managed." During this period Katherine got married, and before long the couple had two sons. I think you get the picture: in business and in life there was simply no stopping Katherine Le.

While she was working at Franklin Mortgage, Katherine met Glenn Stearns. "I worked with him," she says. "He was one of the priority brokers that Franklin serviced." While she was at Franklin, Glenn offered her a job but she declined; she felt that his operation wasn't ready for her yet. Franklin was soon bought out, and Katherine moved on to CUB Funding, which made her a branch manager in Irvine, California. Persistent fellow that he is—and a good judge of talent too—Glenn kept trying to recruit Katherine, but she kept on declining. Finally, after two years of running the branch for CUB she was ready to move on, and Glenn was eager to have her. She joined Glenn's operation in 1995, when it was named First Pacific Financial.

"Up until that point First Pacific was just doing retail lending," Katherine says. "I was in charge of the operations for the company, with the intention of starting up the wholesale division. So I pulled a lot of people that I know in the industry who came and joined us for the wholesale operation." Glenn's was a very shrewd move; Katherine delivered just what he wanted: growth and profitability. Over the next nine years their lending portfolios continued to explode, fueled by the good economy and by the hot housing market in Southern California.

By late 2004, though, Katherine could see that their rapid growth in both business and staff was taking a heavy toll on her and other top managers at the company, which changed its name to

Stearns Lending that same year. They had more work than they knew how to handle. And some of the salespeople they had promoted to manager were simply not up to the job. So Katherine sat down with Glenn and Bob Telles, the CFO (chief financial officer), and shared her concerns. "One of the things I was struggling with in our company is management," Katherine recalls. "We have many managers that became a manager for the wrong reason." In the lending business, what everyone wants from his or her salespeople is "production, production, production," and when someone really produces the next step is a promotion to manager. The problem, Katherine explains, is that good salespeople do not always make good managers. "We had C players, people who didn't know how to manage," Katherine says. "I said that we should bring somebody else in, a consultant group, to talk to us about management."

Enter MAP.

CFO Bob Telles had been through a MAP workshop when he was at another company, and Bob now recommended the MAP system to Glenn and Katherine. It could be just what the company needed, he said. Glenn and Katherine agreed to take a close look. Bob then called Randy Halle, a former president of MAP and now the head of MAP's office in Sherman Oaks, California. Randy is a unique figure at MAP. He started back in the days of Eric Gillberg, and no one else has his experience or his longevity—or his network of devoted friends and clients. As soon as he got the call from Bob Telles, Randy turned to Dorriah Rogers, one of MAP's most able senior consultants, and she agreed to present the MAP system to Glenn's top executives at Stearns Lending's forthcoming management summit in Las Vegas. By all accounts Dorriah put on a dazzling show.

"She did a wonderful job and that's how MAP was introduced here," Katherine says now. "Afterwards, Glenn and I sat down and said this is something we need in our company." The primary problem was not hard to define: Stearns Lending had grown at a furious pace, and its management system had simply not kept pace. A glance at the numbers tells the story. "When I came on in 1995, the company was funding $5 million in loans a month," Katherine says. "Then it was $60 million a month, and now we are funding about $200 million in loans a month." The simple truth was that Stearns Lending couldn't groom competent managers fast enough to handle the mounting workload. And when the managers fumbled, guess who kept picking up their slack? Yes, you're right: Katherine Le.

Katherine never complained out loud, but we at MAP could see exactly what was going on: Katherine was wearing *the Big Red "S."* She tried to be Superwoman and do everything herself. You can understand why. From the moment she had set foot on that boat Katherine had learned to be tough, resilient, and resourceful. If you want something done, do it yourself. To succeed, work harder and smarter than everyone else. And if you get tired and overworked, and if you're not spending enough time with your husband and your kids, well, guess what? That's just too darn bad. Life is hard. And working in a modern financial office was a Sunday picnic next to what she'd been through.

Katherine would never express herself in exactly those terms, of course, but we understood. In her years of climbing the corporate ladder, her do-it-yourself work ethic and management model had served her perfectly well. She had delivered the goods; she had always provided the answers. She was emblematic of what Jack Welch once said, as I mentioned earlier: on the way up, your job is to provide answers. But when you reach the top, your job is to ask questions and get your people to bring you solutions. To be successful as a leader you have to learn how to delegate and empower your people. You have to teach your people to bring you answers—and not dump their own problems onto you. Katherine needed to see that light. And at the MAP workshop she finally did:

"It was enlightening," Katherine says. "I found that the workshop helped because as a manager you know the concept, but you are so busy just trying to go with the flow and grow the production that you tend to lose focus." Through the workshop process and the 360-degree feedback she received from her peers and her staff, Katherine saw many areas where she needed to grow as a manager and a leader. Just as important, she also learned exactly what she had to do to change. Here are some of the specific challenges she faced and how she overcame them.

LACK OF FOCUS

"For years I was just covering the waterfront. In our offices we were kind of overwhelmed, and we were just trying to check off our lists." The solution? Prioritizing. Focusing on the Vital Few. And the Pareto principle, realizing that 20 percent of what you do often produces 80 percent of the results. "Now I'm much more focused," Katherine says. "A lot of the exercises we went through were very helpful." Her main lesson was this: "Go after the Vital Few, stay focused on the Vital Few. You have to stay focused on the things that make the biggest difference."

Alignment and Accountability

"In our business, if you're lucky, you have people with a good work ethic and a sense of responsibility and teamwork," she says. "But you also have others who don't see that duty clearly. As a manager you have to get everybody to work together and hold them accountable for what they are there for." At the workshop Katherine realized she wasn't doing that. The solution? Goals and Controls. "If you spell out your goal and everybody together accepts that goal, and you have a plan of action, then when you talk to them personally it's not about them. It's about the team. It's about helping each other meet the goal. That's one way to hold people accountable for what they say they're going to do."

Empowering Your People

Katherine is a very humble person. As she is the first to emphasize, "I couldn't do what I have done here at Stearns for the last ten years without my great people. We all work really hard. And I owe so much to them." Learning how to delegate and how to empower her people has proved to be one of the most valuable lessons of her entire life. She also believes strongly in working with each of her fellow managers to help them grow and mature. "You have to work with each employee and get the best out of them in a positive way," Katherine says. "When somebody comes to me and says, 'This is the issue, what do you think?' sometimes I give them the answer, and that's obviously not the right way of doing it. At that point, already the ball has been shifted back to you. So that person is now going to wait for you, so you have more work instead of empowering them to come up with the solution. Also, when you give them the answer there's a dependence, and that doesn't help you or them."

Through MAP Katherine saw this tendency of hers much more clearly and she saw the solution: she had to drop the Big Red "S." She had to drop her ingrained tendency to do everything herself. "The coaching that hit me is that my job is *not* to give them the answer. My job is to coach them to come up with the answer on their own. MAP helped me as far as seeing that I need to do that more."

Dorriah Rogers worked closely with Katherine in helping her grow as a leader and manager, and Dorriah was delighted at how quickly Katherine grasped the changes she needed to make. "From my perspective Katherine had all the earmarks of a successful woman executive," Dorriah explains:

> She had adapted to wearing the Big Red "S" at work, at home, and in everything else she did. Her innate intelligence enabled her to figure out how to juggle all of this, while the mother in her wanted to do the right thing for everyone. Enter what we call the *monkey concept*. Katherine was allowing those around her, including Glenn, to dump their monkeys squarely upon her shoulders. In response she would graciously accept—and excel—in whatever they asked her to do. . . .
>
> Unfortunately, Katherine was working harder, not smarter. And she was stressed out and exhausted, another hallmark of successful women executives. When I began my work with her, the first place I started was to enable her to say no. It took a while to help her understand that her productivity would increase by delegating the monkeys and empowering those around her to do more. The Katherine I see now stands more upright; the weight of the monkeys has been lifted from her shoulders.

KATHERINE'S LEADERSHIP MODEL

When you drop the Big Red "S," and when you stop supplying everyone with the answers, your leadership model naturally shifts to the leader as coach and facilitator. You ask more questions, and you have more time to look at the big picture and plan for the future. All this proved true for Katherine. "I do try to hire A-level players, and once I have faith in their ability, I let them run with it," she says. "I do believe in empowering. I tell them all the time that I don't care how they are going to do it, it doesn't necessarily have to be a certain way. I can share with them my way of approaching it, but I also tell them that it is up to them. If they have a better idea and way of doing things, more power to them. They can do it as long as we get to the same result. It doesn't matter to me."

Katherine says that same lesson is now being driven home to the other managers at Stearns Lending. "MAP is still new with our company. Until now, my first tier of management has attended the MAP workshop. And now my second tier is going through it. With the first tier, as a collective team, it has helped us realize that, 'You know what? We need to stop being a doer and get enough resources in here.' We have to go through the process of identifying our A, B, and C players, and get additional resources so we can remove ourselves from always being the doer."

PLANNING

Historically, planning has not been a strong suit of management at Stearns Lending, Katherine says.

> Planning is something that I think, as a company, we definitely lack. Obviously, every day we do plan out our projects, but it's not long-term planning and as leaders we need to do that. From the MAP workshop that's another thing we got. Now we are focused on developing our three- and five-year plans, and we talk about what we need to get to our goals. You have to get your team off the field and make them coaches so you can really sit down and plan the next phases of the company's development and not be burdened day to day with getting the job done.

Planning is one of the topics that MAP addresses head-on in its workshops. And MAP helps companies make effective planning a solid cornerstone of their management system. One of our tools is the *Planning Checklist*, shown on pages 135–136, which we use to structure the process. This is an important document. It is a blueprint for how to use the MAP management system, and it brings together many of the MAP components we have discussed so far.

MAP's Planning Checklist: Developing Goals and Strategies for Future Action

I. Create a strategically aligned organization.
   A. Develop strategic thinking—the big-picture vision.
   B. Create a long-range (three- to five-year) business plan, setting down your company's vital strategic objectives.
   C. Create a one-year operating plan, setting down your company's vital goals and strategies.
II. Go through the planning process.
   A. Identify the planning team.
   B. Select a facilitator.
   C. Conduct a preplanning meeting.
   D. Conduct the planning retreat.
   E. Review the first draft.
   F. Finalize the plan document.
III. Create the plan.
   A. Examine the past.
      1. Growth pattern, trends.
      2. Major events, milestones.
      3. Successes and failures.
      4. Industry and competition (historical impact).
   B. Study the present (*situation analysis*).
      1. Strengths and weaknesses (internal).
      2. Opportunities and threats (external).
      3. Social, political, economic, regulatory, environmental, and technological issues.
      4. Image and reputation.
      5. Vision, mission, and values.
      6. Customer satisfaction (internal and external).
      7. Critical success factors.
   C. Design the future (*goals and needs*).
      1. Vision, mission, and values statements.
      2. Forecasts and projections.
      3. Key objectives and initiatives.
      4. Vital performance goals.
      5. Resources needed (capital, equipment, personnel, technology, systems).
   D. Develop strategies and action plans.
      1. Corporate plan.
      2. Departmental plans.

MAP's Planning Checklist: Developing Goals and Strategies
for Future Action, continued

      3. Functional group plans.
      4. Individual employee plans.
   E. Assign action steps with due dates.
      1. Key 30-day and quarterly goals.
      2. Vital Factor or goal spreadsheets.
      3. Milestone charting.
      4. Task lists.
IV. Implement the plan.
   A. Communicate the plan throughout the organization.
 V. Measure and regularly report progress in achieving the plan.
   A. Conduct regular Vital Factor Team Meetings, with Goals and Controls.
   B. Broadcast results.
   C. Celebrate successes.
   D. Review and modify plans as vital issues require.

In her coaching work with Stearns Lending, Dorriah has used the Planning Checklist as a means to guide and structure the process of change. The impact, she says, has been enormous.

> My first reaction upon working with Stearns was "Wow." Glenn was moving at 100 miles per hour, Katherine was gamely trying to implement every change he proposed, and Bob Telles was steadfastly trying to implement systems to manage all of it. . . .
>
> Although they thought they were moving in alignment, the reality was they were not. I find this in many organizations. Management feels that if they are being successful with their top-line numbers (in the case of Stearns this means the volume of loans), then the company itself is being successful. In my coaching, however, I always emphasize that growth and good numbers are not the sole measurements of success. In the case of Stearns they were headed for problems due to continued internal growth—and rising expenses—and a changing and potentially volatile mortgage marketplace. As with Katherine the challenge for the entire organization was to work smarter, not harder, and thus increase efficiency and profit. So the first place we started was with the Stearns infra-

structure. First, we completely revamped their organizational chart. Then we developed a three- to five-year Strategic Plan, a twelve-month Operations Plan, changed out a number of C players, created a training plan for B players, and promoted and rewarded the A players. Simultaneously, we began implementing the Vital Factor Teams throughout the entire organization, from California to Maryland. Glenn, as is his style, wanted everything to happen at lightning speed. So we made it happen. As a result, Stearns significantly reduced internal branch expenditures and is well on its way to successful and profitable growth. I am thrilled with the results. Glenn, Katherine, and Bob are now in absolute alignment, and I believe that their combined foresight and leadership will carry Stearns to even greater success.

TRAINING

Planning is especially important in the mortgage lending business, and proper planning includes putting into place an effective training process. "It's either feast or famine in our business," Katherine says. "When the interest rate is low and business is booming, there is never enough manpower, so you get whatever people you can. Many times we were forced into a Band-Aid situation." Through MAP Katherine saw that better planning brings better staffing and better training—and fewer Band-Aids. Now she shares a core MAP belief: if you want to grow your business, start by growing your people. Before MAP, Stearns managers had it backward. They were growing the company first, and then scrambling to make do.

COMMUNICATING YOUR VALUES

No one at MAP had to teach Katherine Le the importance of having strong values. And no one had to teach her the importance of transmitting those values to the people around you. Everything Katherine needed to know about values she had learned from her mother, Hong, both from her mother's words and from her deeds. America has changed Katherine's life and brought her success and material comforts. Nothing, though, has changed her values:

"Always in America we have to remind ourselves of how good we have it," she says. "Freedom comes with a cost. Ultimately, we have such a good life here, but most of us take it for granted.

Sometimes here our children—if we don't watch what they do—they are just so self-centered and not realizing what they have. I do want to make sure that my children appreciate what they have and are aware of what is going on around us and around the world, of how other people are so much less fortunate than we are. This helps us appreciate and have compassion for other people."

Bless you, Katherine. And for all of us at MAP, thank you for holding our torch so proud and high.

The Bottom Line

1. Take a page from Glenn and Katherine: become aware of your strengths and liabilities. Act accordingly. Make changes accordingly.

2. If you tend to wear the Big Red "S," stop. Drop it entirely.

3. If you spot that tendency in the people you work with—or live with—help them understand the impact and help them change. They'll win—and so will you.

4. Never take for granted your freedom and opportunities. And don't let your children take them for granted either.

5. And if some day you're feeling frustrated, or sorry for yourself, or near the end of your rope, stop for a moment and think of Katherine Le. Then thank your lucky stars, and get on with the job.

CHAPTER TEN

HOW TO BUILD A WINNING TEAM

I love Katherine Le's story. What an amazing and inspiring woman she is! And her experience at Stearns Lending leads us into a crucial component of the MAP management process: recruiting, hiring, and building a winning team.

Almost every book or expert on leadership and management will tell you that the one thing you should write down, memorize, and emblazon on your wall is this: "People Are Our Greatest Asset." Yes. And we have already seen the truth of that. When Stearns Lending started going great guns, what was its biggest problem? Not having enough top-quality people on board to handle the increasing workload. When Border States Electric made its strategic push into the construction industry, what was one of Tammy Miller's most serious problems? Some of her people couldn't make the adjustment. And I'm sure you remember Bill de la Viña's staffing problem: when he tried to implement a bonus program for his people at Sigue, some of his kingpins stood in the way. As Bill found out the hard way, they were Onboard Troublemakers, working against his vision and his goals.

So simply proclaiming that "People Are Our Greatest Asset" really doesn't take you very far. The real question is, What kind of actions do you take in support of that proclamation? In my experience every manager and business leader loves to pay lip service to people being the company's most important asset. But the sad truth is that leaders' actions rarely back up their words. If you really want to make hiring and keeping the best people your No. 1 priority, here are some basic questions you have to address: How do you go about finding the best people? How do you determine if someone is really right for the job? How do you spot potential problems before you bring someone on board? Once you do bring someone on board, how do you manage his or her integration into your team? Finally, how do you groom your people for long-term success, job satisfaction, and ongoing personal growth? The truth is that many companies never seriously examine these fundamental questions. And many of them have no system for structuring their hiring process, grooming their people, and retaining their top performers. They just wing it—as Stearns Lending used to do.

MAP has a better way. And I'm going to lay it out for you right here.

To start, let me say this, and it comes straight from the heart: your most important job as a manager or a leader is managing and developing your people. If you want to succeed in business or any other form of group endeavor, you have to learn how to hire the best people, how to define their jobs and responsibilities, how to train them, how to set them on the road to success, and how to keep them focused, challenged, rewarded, and always growing and becoming better at what they do. As I said in Chapter One the most successful companies understand, deep in their marrow, that their people are their greatest asset—and they act that way. It's simple: if you want to grow your business, start by growing your people.

To drive this point home let me put it in football terms. You might be a brilliant coach, and you might have absolutely ingenious systems for both offense and defense, and you might have a clear and inspiring goal: to win the Super Bowl. But guess what? If you don't have a team filled with top-quality players who can band together, learn your systems, and execute your game plans, you're not going to the Super Bowl. No way, no how. In business it's the same: you can have the best ideas, the best game plans, and even the biggest budgets, but whether you succeed or fail will still depend on one thing and one thing only: the quality of your people.

With that bald truth in mind I'm now going to show you how Management Action Programs helps you hire the best people and build a winning team. I'm going to give you some tools to get the job done, and for an illustration I'm going to walk you through the phases that we at MAP use to recruit, hire, and train our most important people. Then I'm going to do something more: I'm going to bring in Don O'Neill from Stewart Title Company to tell you how he uses MAP tools to manage his staffing process and to help his people grow and prosper. I urge you to pay close attention here: how you hire and develop your people is the biggest test you face as a manager and leader—and it is one of MAP's richest areas of expertise. As you will recall, Eric Gillberg created MAP on the foundation of his own gifts and expertise as a trainer in the U.S. Navy and in business. Eric knew how to identify men and women who had the Right Stuff, and he knew how to train them to excel at their jobs and fulfill their highest potential. Winning players make winning teams. If they win, you win; it's that simple. And that tenet remains central to MAP's mission and work today. Now, let me show you how to get the job done.

Basic Principles

Every company is always looking for good people. There isn't a client I have today that isn't looking for good people. A book published a few years ago, titled *Topgrading*, took the view that you have to hire the A players and you have to go through an elaborate selection process to do it. Well, OK. Given my experience, though, I see one major problem with that approach: the A players are usually working for someone else. That means the only way you're going to hire them is by hunting them down, and that generally means outside recruitment. It also means paying the person substantially more money than he or she is making in his or her present job. Every once in a while an A player will walk in your door, or you will find that elusive diamond in the rough while reading résumés, but those are exceptions. The statistic I've heard bandied about—and I don't know how accurate it really is—is that seven out of ten new hires turn out to be the wrong choice. Think of that: seven out of ten wind up wrong for the job! That is an alarming number, and one that costs companies heavily in terms of money, energy, and staff time. But you can do far better than that—provided you have an effective system for managing your hiring process and building your team.

To build a winning team you have to do six fundamental things:

- First, hold your Vital Factor Team Meetings every month. That ensures accountability and keeps your people focused on the right things, with specific ways to measure their performance. These meetings are also your early warning system: they help you spot emerging personnel problems—who's doing the job and who isn't.
- Second, you need a sound, well thought out business plan. This is the rudder of your ship, the tool that keeps you on course. The plan makes clear to your team members exactly what they have to do to succeed. In addition, it helps you see down the road and plan well in advance for expansion and new hiring—*before* it's an urgent necessity. (Learn from the experience of Katherine Le and Stearns Lending.)
- Third, before you hire anyone, write a clear, detailed job description. This is critical, as I'll explain in a moment.
- Fourth, put in place a multilayered interviewing process, to bring together as much information and analysis as you can about your list of candidates. Again, I'll provide details in a moment.
- Fifth, once you do decide to bring someone new on board, give him or her a ninety-day training plan, with specific goals to meet. The first ninety days is the honeymoon period. If a person can't meet the ninety-day goals, then you have to evaluate whether or not you have made the right choice. Give the person specific, measurable, results-oriented goals; those provide the clearest yardsticks of performance.
- Six, create a detailed Personal Development Plan for each of your top people. This is each person's blueprint for ongoing success, job satisfaction, and personal growth. This is also a strategy for retention: when you invest in your top people like this they are more likely to be happy and stay. There's no mystery here: if you want to build a Super Bowl team, you have to attract and hire the best people, train them—and keep them.

MAP's HIRING PROCESS

OK, those are the six fundamental things you need to do. Now I'm going to go deeper. To illustrate how to apply these six steps, I'm going to walk you through the process that we use to hire senior consultants at MAP. These are the men and women who give MAP workshops and coach our clients. They have to be first-rate performers, with long experience in real-world business leadership; our clients expect that and our reputation depends on it. So we are extremely careful about whom we hire—and how we hire. Again, we are *modeling* best practices. Once our senior consultants have come through this process, they understand firsthand the process their clients should adopt for recruiting and staffing. Here are the building blocks of effective hiring, the ones we use at MAP:

BE PROACTIVE: PLAN AHEAD

At MAP we always try to plan ahead for jobs that we anticipate opening down the road. As I showed in discussing Stearns Lending, too many companies *reactively* recruit, meaning they wait until they urgently need to fill a particular position. The result is often terrible. When managers are under that kind of pressure to hire and hire fast, they often get desperate. And if they can't find Mr. or Ms. Right, they settle for Mr. or Ms. Make-Do. Needless to say, that is *not* the best practice. So we never hire people under duress. I urge you to likewise plan ahead; it will cut down on your chances of making a mistake.

PREPARE A DETAILED JOB DESCRIPTION

Preparing a detailed job description is critical: the job description anchors your entire recruitment and hiring process. An ideal job description includes the overall purpose of the job, its specific duties and responsibilities, the background experience required, and the specific competencies required. Don't just say you are looking for broad management competency; list the soft skills and technical skills you are looking for. Also, be clear about the management skills a person needs to be successful in the job: personal organization, time management, negotiation skills, listening skills, initiative, creativity, whatever. For instance, when we at MAP are looking for a senior consultant, we say in the job description that applicants need to have many years of hands-on experience in business. They also need to have first-class skills in leadership and communication; they will be modeling those in this position. Be sure to state how the person is going to spend his or her time. Also, identify the authority that comes with the job: the kinds of decisions the person will make—and the kinds he or she won't be responsible for. Also be clear about the Vital Factors that will be used to evaluate the person's performance. Finally, be sure to include the reporting structure: the position to which this position reports and vice versa. These are all important components of a job description that can become a clear blueprint and action plan for your employee's future success. They will also set out the criteria you should use in the process of interviewing candidates.

Search Multiple Sources

To find the best people in today's world, you have to use multiple sources. Gone are the days when you could rely solely on ads in newspapers and business journals. To find a top consultant MAP pursues many avenues. First, we go to our employees and our customers for referrals; if we can find someone already in the MAP family and familiar with the MAP system, so much the better. Second, we use business journals and professional recruiters. Third, more and more we are using recruitment sites on the Internet to look for the best people. And fourth, to facilitate the networking and recruiting process for ourselves and our clients and customers, we have created a MAP alumni network. It is now available online at www.mapconsulting.com.

Examine Résumés and References

As every job applicant should know, a poorly done résumé can kill an application on the spot. But with today's preformatted résumé forms, readily available online or on DVDs, a smart-looking résumé doesn't say all that much about the candidate either. It is the content that counts, the richness of the experience. Again, though, lots of candidates look great on paper, so in our initial screenings we don't put too much stock in résumés. The same is true these days for references. In today's world, references are not always a reliable guide: many companies are too afraid of lawsuits to deliver an honest appraisal. We're also finding that more and more companies have established policies *against* giving out references. So résumés and references can be useful as first indicators, but I would never view them as reliable tools.

Conduct the Interview

Once you get a group of promising candidates in the door, what do you do next? Before I interview someone, I take that candidate to a waiting room, give him or her the job description, and tell him or her to read it carefully. Then I say that the interview will start in about ten minutes. When the interview starts, one of the first questions I then ask is, "What is it in your background and experience that tells you you're qualified for this job, based on your reading of the job description?" That immediately gives me an idea of whether or not the candidate has read the job description carefully and really comprehends what the job entails. I also invite the candidate to ask me questions about the job; that tells me whether or not people have done their homework before coming to see me. I often learn more from candidates' questions than from the questions I ask them. During that first interview I do form opinions, of course, but then I always seek other people's views. At MAP we're firm believers in multiple interviewing.

Get Different Points of View

Don't look at candidates just once, look at them several times and have different people join the process. In my view the more good brains you apply to any decision making the better, and that is especially true in hiring. My colleagues often spot qualities and potential in job candidates that I have totally missed. It is especially important to include in the interviewing and decision-making process the people who will be working directly with the new hire. They know best what the job demands and how the new hire will fit into the work. In staffing as in other areas it always pays to empower your people.

Administer the Behavioral Style Analysis

If a person gets through the first series of interviews, we then have him or her take the Behavioral Style Analysis. We have found this test to be a very effective way for us to narrow the field and determine if a given candidate seems likely to fit into our organization, its mission, and of course the job at hand. We urge our MAP clients to do the same: narrow the field down to about three good candidates and then have them take the Behavioral Style Analysis. For more information you can link onto our Web site (www.mapconsulting.com) and we will guide you to the asssessment.

The Behavioral Style Analysis is a fascinating tool. Developed in its original form in the 1920s by William M. Marston, a pioneering psychologist, the test evaluates people's behavioral patterns on four dimensions:

- Dominance (D): how they respond to problems and challenges
- Influence (I): how they attempt to influence other people
- Steadiness (S): how they respond to the pace of an environment
- Compliance (C): how they respond to rules and procedures

These four dimensions are often referred to by the acronym DISC. A DISC assessment can be a very useful guide in hiring and managing your people. Job applicants can take it via the Internet, and then employers receive an illuminating personality and behavioral profile of the applicant, showing his or her expected patterns of behavior in periods of calm—and in periods of pressure. I have been using the assessment for years. In short order it shows me whether someone is, for instance, a high D, meaning she is likely to try to forcefully dominate a situation, or a high I, meaning he is likely to try to achieve his aims via more subtle means of persuasion. From the resulting profile I can also get an idea whether the candidate is a good fit for the specific position I want to fill. For instance, for a sales position I might want a tiger who is a high D or I, but if I'm filling a position in accounting, I look for a high C or a high S, two behavioral styles that tend to be compliant and detail oriented. In other words, I'm happy to have cowboys and free thinkers in my boardroom—only insecure leaders want to be surrounded by yes-people—but I sure don't want cowboys and free thinkers doing our books or tax forms!

Now let me give you a little taste of how an actual DISC Behavioral Style Analysis profile reads and the personality qualities it might highlight: "Mr. So and So is extremely results-oriented, with a sense of urgency to complete projects quickly. He is often frustrated when working with others who do not share the same sense of urgency. He likes to be forceful and direct when dealing with others. His desire for results is readily apparent to the people with whom he works. . . . He has high ego strengths and may be viewed by some as egotistical. He prefers an environment with variety and change."

The full portrait is much more extensive than that, but as an employer I am already seeing both strengths and potential liabilities. This is clearly a reliable, take-charge guy who will deliver results. And that's all to the good. But I see red flags too. Will he have the patience to work effectively with people who aren't quite as quick or as forceful as he is? Will he prove to be a good team player—or more of a loner? I also see that this person prefers "an environment of variety and change." That might be a good characteristic if I'm looking for a workshop leader and MAP coach but not if I'm looking for someone whose job is to sit at a desk all day and make telephone sales calls. On good days he'd be uncomfortable, and on bad days he'd probably be irritable or totally bored out of his mind.

Now, do I take these profiles as gospel? No. The profile is a good *indicator* of how people behave, but I would never rule out a promising candidate based only on the results of this test. Still, the Behavioral Style Analysis is a good interviewing and management tool. When I call someone in for an interview, I will often let the person read the test's general characteristics pages, and then I'll say, "Is that you?" Most of the time he or she will say, "Oh, yeah, that's me." (The Behavioral Style Analysis has a predictive probability of over 90 percent. It's a highly validated instrument.) Then I will tailor some of my questions around the strengths and liabilities indicated by the profile. For example, if someone's profile says something like, "This individual has a tendency to take on too many duties and too much that he or she can't handle," I'll ask the person a question around that. I'll also ask if on a past job he or she has indeed had a tendency to take on too much. Then I'll say, "What did you learn from that? And how do you deal with those situations now?"

One page of the test report lists areas for improvement. I'll also turn to that page and say, "Now look down this list of areas of improvement—they might not all be right—but pick one that you know is right and tell me what you have done to improve in that area." I've had candidates who say, "Well, none of these apply," and that sends up a red flag right away. Do they themselves know their strengths and liabilities? Are they in denial? What's going on? One more thing: if we do decide to take someone on, these profiles can play a further role. For instance, if we are concerned that someone might prove to be too much of a loner, when we provide training and a ninety-day training plan (described later in this chapter), we can emphasize the importance of working well with one's Vital Factor Team and we can make "improved teamwork" a stated—and written—personal growth goal for the new hire.

CONDUCT A GROUP EVALUATION

After I do an interview I fill out a worksheet for myself. It has two columns: one is labeled "Positive Attributes" and the other is labeled "Concerns/Issues for Further Exploration." This worksheet moves the process of evaluation forward. If we have multiple people interviewing a candidate, the evaluators can then sit down with their worksheets and have a more thorough discussion and evaluation. In some cases we use a formal evaluation sheet that asks each evaluator to assess a candidate according to a specific set of attributes and then we compare our evaluations. Don O'Neill of Stewart Title does that with his hiring team, as you will see in a moment. With MAP's evaluation team, if we are all in agreement— whether it's a thumbs up or a thumbs down—we keep the process moving forward in an orderly, well-anchored way.

GO DEEPER

As you know by now, we at MAP insist on planning ahead and promoting alignment and buy-in. This is especially true for staffing. Our workshop leaders and coaches play a vital role in caring for our clients, promoting our brand, bringing in new business, and maintaining our reputation. In sum, all of us at MAP have a stake in making sure that we hire the best workshop leaders and consultants that we can find. So when it comes to interviewing candidates, it's not just that I want my colleagues to give me their views on a given candidate; I want to make sure they are aligned with a final decision and fully buy into it. To achieve these multilayered goals, in our company or yours, *managers have to carefully structure the final stages of their selection process.*

Now, how do you do that? As you proceed with multiple interviews, have different people interview the candidate with regard to different strengths and competencies. In our case, if we're looking for a senior MAP consultant and coach, we say to one of our interviewers, "We want you to look at so-and-so's ability to coach," and we'll say to another interviewer, "Look at this person's ability to stand up and deliver workshops. Tell us how effectively she presents the material." If, in contrast, we're looking for an executive consultant, someone who calls on companies and seeks out new business, we'll say to an interviewer, "Look at this person's ability and confidence level when he talks to CEOs and presents MAP to them. How refined is his style? How effective is his presentation? How well does he present our brand?"

Using multiple interviewing goals helps us develop a well-rounded look at each candidate. If a candidate makes it through Round One—the preliminary interviews—and Round Two—the more specialized interviews—then we put the candidate into Round Three, the *work sample*. In essence we simulate a real-life MAP situation. We give the candidate a task that applies to the job that she is going to be doing, and we ask her to prove her ability to do it. For instance, I'll give the candidate a business case study that I have made up about a fictitious client. I'll include a dummy Vital Factor Spreadsheet, and I will clearly define the task to be done: "Your goal is to come in and facilitate the discussion of the management team of this organization. You have to identify the three most important issues that are in front of that organization, then help management decide what steps to take to resolve those issues. You'll have thirty minutes to do the facilitation."

We then make the simulation as real as possible. In preparation we create for the fictitious company a management team, using our own people from MAP. Each of us takes on a simulated role: one is president, one is VP of sales, one is VP of operations, and sometimes we'll throw in a fourth person as CFO. Then we role-play a team meeting and put the candidate into the situation as MAP consultant and coach. Then the real fun begins. We throw out all kinds of wacky ideas and curve balls, and sometimes we even bicker and argue. This isn't pointless theatrics: real-life Vital Factor Meetings can be extremely difficult to manage; there are always a few oversized egos in the room and there are always some very big issues on the table. So MAP coaches need to be able to manage those meetings; they need to be strong leaders and effective facilitators. As you may recall, Steve Campbell of Campbell Concrete referred to our man Lew Herbst as the Enforcer. Well, he didn't earn that title by being walked over at Vital Factor Meetings or by letting Steve's foremen ignore their Goals and Controls. So this simulation phase of the hiring process is very important. We all need to see how the candidate works under pressure. Does she get flustered? Does she run for cover? Does she have the leadership skills necessary to manage a business crisis? It is right here that we put our candidates to the test.

We also evaluate their leadership style. Once in a while we'll have a candidate come in and do a fabulous PowerPoint presentation, explaining the strategy he or she is recommending, outlining where that strategy will take the numbers on the Vital Factor Spreadsheet, and regurgitating those numbers into a whole bunch of graphs and charts. But we already know what our numbers are! So all the talk and pretty graphs are somewhat beside the point. What I really evaluate is this: does the candidate do all the talking? Or does he or she ask tough questions and get us, the management team, to respond with real solutions? And what is the candidate's leadership style? Does he or she showboat? Or truly lead? In essence I assess how well the candidate has assimilated the MAP leadership model and made it his or her own. This is a very difficult test; many very promising candidates flunk out right here.

Take Candidates into a Real Business Situation

Those candidates that do pass that test get a reward of sorts: they get to go with me to a MAP client to observe a real Vital Factor Team Meeting. I ask the candidate to watch carefully, maybe take notes, observe the management team, and observe me as well. In particular I tell him or her to watch how I work with the client. These meetings can run a half-day or an entire day, and they really put the candidate to the test. Afterward, I ask him or her a series of questions: What did you observe that I did? What did you learn from it? What would you have done differently? This is always very revealing. I pay close attention to how much detail the candidate gives me in reply and how carefully he or she has observed and understood the MAP process. I also love to see how candidates' minds work and where their own process of inquiry takes them. Afterward, I add the new material to my ongoing written evaluation of each candidate's performance.

Seek Outside Opinions

If a candidate proves his or her mettle in observing a Vital Factor Meeting, I now seek help from people I trust outside MAP. I often turn for help to a longtime MAP client—a Michael Caito or a Bill de la Viña—and ask that client to meet with the candidate and talk about the client's business and its challenges. Afterward, I ask the client the big question, the bottom-line question: "Would you hire this person to do your MAP consulting for you?" The client's answer will not only be informative but will take me right to MAP's own bottom line: does this candidate generate the necessary trust and confidence from established MAP clients? Would they pay for his or her services? Does the candidate uphold our standards at MAP? Will the candidate bring in new business and help us grow and prosper? Will he or she help our client companies grow and prosper? I've actually had cases where the clients give the candidate a thumbs down, saying "No, I don't think I'd hire this person." You can't get any clearer than that.

Apply the Final Tests

If a trusted MAP client gives a candidate a clear thumbs up, we on the MAP hiring team usually make up our minds right there, and by now we have good grounds to do so. We have put the candidate through an extensive process of interviewing, testing, and evaluation, both from inside our house and outside. Sometimes, though, just to be sure, I put the candidate through a final test: I have him or her come in and do a coaching session with me, with the candidate acting as my personal coach. He or she has seen me in action, and I say, "So tell me: What can I do better? Where do I need to grow?" I ask the candidate for specifics, sometimes even action steps that I can take to grow as a manager and leader. The point is, I want to see how the candidate coaches, how he or she works one on one with people.

At the end of a hiring process we sometimes bring in our last evaluation tool: the *Randy Halle test,* because it was Randy, MAP's former president and most senior hand, who devised it. Here, the intrepid candidate sits down with a group of MAP executive consultants—all of them experienced salespeople—who fire questions at the candidate. About different aspects of the MAP process. About business basics. About how to handle an *SOB*—the son of the boss (one of the worst nightmares any consultant can face!). And about any other business challenge they can think of. And I can tell you, the grilling can be rough!

Now, what's the point of the Randy Halle test? To see how the candidate reacts under fire. To see just how unflappable he or she can be. This is not a gratuitous exercise; our coaches are frequently going to be in the line of fire, and they have to be able to handle the situation. After all, our clients place their faith, trust, and the fate of their companies in our hands; we have to be up to the job! Let me say too that this kind of rigorous battle-testing is embedded in our company DNA. As you will recall from Chapter One, our founder, Eric Gillberg, trained Navy pilots for combat, and part of their training involved throwing them in the Dumpster, to see how they managed the crisis—and to prepare them for the next one. The Randy Halle test is our equivalent of the Dumpster.

ONGOING TRAINING AND SUPPORT

When a candidate makes it through MAP's gauntlet and is finally invited to join our team, our work is not over; it has only just begun. This is where a lot of companies fail. They bring a new hire in, and they basically say, "Here's your desk; here's your phone. Good luck! See you later." That's not us. Once we've gone through all this effort to find a well-qualified candidate, we feel we have a responsibility to make sure that our new colleague will be successful. That's part of our job. Again, it helps to think in football terms. You land a first-rate player in the college draft or in a trade with another team, and is your job done? Of course not. You still have to integrate him into your team, teach him your playbook, and infuse him with your team's special spirit, and then you have to guide him to success and help him get even better at what he does. And all this takes an entire team of coaches and advisers. At MAP we work with new hires in the exact same way.

The Ninety-Day Plan

For each new hire you need to create a detailed ninety-day training plan. In our case, when a new senior consultant comes on board we present him or her with a set of valuable tools—an orientation notebook and a "who-you-can-call" notebook—and we also create a special mentoring team for the new hire. The team is made up of three or four people. One is the team leader, who will serve as the new hire's field trainer. The second person is the new hire's branch manager, the person he or she directly reports to, and the third person is an executive consultant, a sales specialist who will do everything possible to support the new person and help him or her be successful in the new job.

To get the process properly started, we have a first mentoring meeting where we explain what the role of the mentoring team is: namely, to ensure the success of our new hire. Roles and goals are clearly spelled out. For example, the executive consultant's role is to help the new hire get new clients and develop a network of people to call. It is also to give the new hire many different forms of support: telling him who to work with inside MAP, how to approach prospective clients, what political minefields to watch for, and the like. The branch manager is responsible for ensuring that the ninety-day training plan is being followed. The team leader is responsible for the field training as well as for offering feedback and coaching on the new hire's performance. During the first ninety days we have a mentoring team meeting once a month with the new hire. The team reviews the person's progress and gives feedback on his or her performance. The new hire can of course ask for any other form of help and guidance that he or she feels is needed. The primary goal is to create a group of people who can guide and support the new hire, bring him or her into the MAP family, and do everything possible to help the new hire succeed. This is our method of teaching, coaching, supporting, and building a winning team.

VALIDATION

This mentoring process demonstrates to the new hire that we want him or her to be successful. That means a lot to new people coming on board, and it sets a positive and supportive tone for the entire organization. The ninety-day training plan is really an empowerment tool, a blueprint for success. It is also a way to teach new hires the essence and particulars of the MAP system. For instance the goals we set down are always measurable and come with deadlines. For example: "the new hire will complete 80 percent of the training steps in the first thirty days." If you are bringing in a new salesperson, a typical goal could be: "At the end of ninety days the new hire will have closed X amount of business and generated X amount of new sales dollars." The key is to set specific, measurable goals. That sets the tone and lets the new hire know that you're going to measure performance and how you will measure it. It also gives you a way of evaluating and critiquing his or her performance.

ACCOUNTABILITY

If you are going to build a winning team, you have to make sure there is accountability up and down your organization. And accountability never flows in just one direction. When new hires fail to meet their ninety-day goals, it is not just their fault; it is also the fault of everyone on the mentoring team. And if new hires then can't raise the level of their performance and wash out of the company completely, again that is not entirely their fault either. The hiring team has to hold itself accountable too. When that happens at MAP, we go back through our hiring process, pinpoint what we did wrong, and then correct the process for the next time. If you are making computer chips or coffee mugs, you can approach a product success rate of 100 percent. But not in hiring. Let's face it: in hiring you are going to make mistakes. In the selection process you can peel the onion back only so far. There simply is no foolproof system for hiring. So if you make a mistake, be candid and let the person go. Don't keep the failed hire on; that solves nothing and usually makes matters much worse. If you don't have the courage or integrity to face up to your mistake and you keep the failed employee on, you are doing your company a great disservice. You are also doing that person a great disservice. He or she will never fully succeed in your organization, and you are only damaging his or her chances of moving on and getting a better job at a more opportune age. In sum, in staffing, as in other areas, always be candid and always hold your people—and yourself—fully accountable. In the long run it always pays.

Letting People Go

Inevitably, some hires just don't work out. Inevitably, too, as your company matures not everyone grows as well as you had hoped. And then you come to the moment of decision: Do I try further training? Do I move the employee to a different job inside the company? Or do I let the employee go? This is one of the hardest decisions a manager or leader has to make. At MAP we often say, "Repair or replace," but that is never an easy decision.

Dennis Troggio, president of Achen-Gardner Engineering, one of the most respected highway general contractors in the Phoenix area, works incredibly hard to retain his best people. He regularly sends them to various personal growth seminars and retreats, including MAP workshops, and he encourages them to find interests and passions outside of work, so they can grow as individuals. Still, there have been times when Dennis and his top managers have found that one of their people was just not doing the job. And then comes the toughest part, a moment that every manager or leader will sooner or later face, usually with dread:

"About eight or nine years ago we started putting large-diameter pipe in the ground in serious quantity," Dennis recalls.

> We had a guy that we made our general pipe superintendent. He did a tremendous job for awhile, but then he reached his level of incompetence. Rather than sitting down and telling him, "Look, right now your communication and management skills have to take precedence over your technical skills," we tried to make changes to

mask it. And that was a big mistake. We were managing around him. It got so bad that we had a choice: we either fire him or we end up losing three or four other people. When we got to that point we had no other choice. He was fired and the change was instantaneous: people who had left us before were calling us up and asking to come back—they had left because of him. You just shake your head and say, "My gosh, why didn't I do that a long time ago!"

Looking back now, Dennis sees in that episode an important lesson for his company and for other managers and leaders as well. "Every time we have parted company with someone like that we have gotten better. If you don't confront, you allow one bad apple to threaten the whole barrel. And that's not doing anybody any good. You're not helping the employee, yourself, or your organization. Nonetheless, it's still difficult. One of the hardest things is to let people go."

ONGOING COACHING

After ten brilliant years in the NFL, do superstars like Jerry Rice or Brett Favre no longer need coaching? Of course not. The best athletes always want more coaching; they are always striving to be better, to be the best they can be. If you're going to be an effective manager or leader, you have to learn how to coach effectively and then do so on an ongoing basis. That's the only way you're going to build a winning team. One of the things I encourage my clients to do is to prepare an annual development plan for each of their managers, a plan that is concrete, is written down, and has specific, measurable goals of course. That provides the foundation for ongoing coaching.

As I have already shown, good managers are good teachers: they don't give their people answers; they get their people to think for themselves and form their own answers, as Katherine Le learned to do. In my experience too many managers are just not good teachers. Instead of empowering their people they act like the Answer Man. Here's a tip: when people come to you with a problem, turn it around and say, "What do you recommend we do?" If they don't have an answer, send them back to do their homework. Say to them, "When you have a couple of solutions, come back and tell me which one you're going to use."

In this vein I like to tell a story about John Wooden, the legendary basketball coach at UCLA. At Wooden's postgame interview after his last basketball game as head coach, one reporter raised his hand and said, "So, what did it feel like to coach your last game?" Wooden's response was simple and telling: "Tonight I taught my last basketball game." The key word, of course, was *taught*. Good leaders are good teachers. And to build a winning team you have to constantly teach your people how to improve, how to work better together, and how to win. Wooden understood that. His teams compiled exceptional records not because he had devised some breakthrough basketball strategy but because he was a patient coach, teacher, and mentor, always grooming his people, always leading them to a higher level of performance. Wooden understood the demands of enlightened leadership, and I've learned more about how to build a winning team from him than I have from reading a shelf full of books by so-called business gurus and experts.

Drilling Deep

What are your duties as coach and mentor? For one thing you should meet regularly with your top people, work with them, and see how they are doing with their Personal Development Plans. You should encourage them to read books, encourage them to expand their minds. You should always challenge them with insightful questions too, encouraging them to drill deeper into what they're doing. Don't ask them fluff questions. The fluff questions are questions that can be answered with not much more than yes or no. "Did you do everything you could on that?" That's a fluff question. The tough question is, "Why didn't you succeed in your goal?" And you keep asking why until the person gives you the answer. Don't assume the first answer is the real or the right answer.

Let me give you an example. The other day I was in a Vital Factor Team Meeting, and one individual had not achieved any of his goals. I looked at him and said, "Why didn't you achieve any of your goals?" And he said, "Well, I had a lot of things going this last month." I said, "No, that's not the answer. Why didn't you achieve your goals?" "Well, I had to meet with so-and-so and do this . . ." I said, "No, you still haven't answered the question." "Well, truthfully, I ran out of time." "Why did you run out of time?" What followed was a long, pregnant pause, and I knew we were getting down to the truth. "Well, truthfully, I didn't do a good job of prioritizing this month." "Why not?" "I didn't pay attention to it." "OK, what are you going to do differently this next month?"

As this example illustrates, what you have to do is drill down. You have to get people to think. So I said, "What can the team do to help you on prioritizing?" From there we launched a Team Consulting session. If you use Team Consulting and other MAP tools, like Goals and Controls, it's a simple process to challenge your people to think and go deeper. Just focus them on their fundamentals. That will help them focus and grow, and it will help you build a winning team.

DEVELOPMENT AND RETENTION

As I said before, managers and leaders love to talk about people being their most important asset, but many of them don't put real dollars into developing their people. MAP clients do. They send their people to our three-day workshops, our one-day *Twelve O'Clock High* leadership seminars, and the various refresher courses that we offer throughout the year. Other companies send their people to various workshops and training programs as well. That is money well spent. To my mind, though, the best development is on-the-job development. It's coaching your people through good situations and bad. If someone on your team makes a mistake, ask him or her, "What did you learn from that?" In a Vital Factor Team Meeting I like to ask people, "What did you learn from that? Why did you achieve your goal?" What I really want them to do is play back the process they used and see that there was value in it—and then learn from what they did right. And always keep this in mind: good coaching is not just focusing on mistakes; it's building on the positives.

Effective coaching also has a side benefit: it's a good way to ensure that you keep your best people. Part of retaining people is developing them. People want to work for companies that give them new tools to put in their toolbox, tools they can use in their present job—or their next one. As I have emphasized before, people want to feel appreciated; the two biggest motivators are recognition and pride. So if you invest in someone's development and personal growth, that is a demonstration of your faith in that person; you are recognizing his or her worth and potential. You are building his or her pride. Smart people don't leave companies that show them that kind of respect. You'll see how true that is in Chapter Fourteen, when Joe Daquino tells you his personal story.

TAKING THE "PERSONAL" OUT OF PERSONNEL

How have MAP clients integrated MAP's precepts about staffing and team building into their own companies? Don O'Neill is a great example. Don started out as a lawyer, and then he moved into business. Today he is a top executive with Stewart Title Company, one of the nation's oldest and most respected real estate information and title insurance companies, with 9,300 offices and agencies in the United States and fifteen international markets. When Don talks about his experience with MAP, two words come frequently to his lips: *discipline* and *maturity*. He and many of his closest colleagues at Stewart Title have embraced the MAP system, and Don says they find it particularly valuable when it comes to hiring the best people, keeping them on track, and building their team into a disciplined, mature, winning unit. In fact Don has creatively melded our precepts on staffing with one of his favorite MAP tools, Team Consulting. Like us, the managers at Stewart Title interview and evaluate as a group, according to a fixed set of criteria that they believe will lead to success in that particular job.

"One thing we try to do is understand the difference between finding 'a job for a person' versus finding 'the right person for the job,'" Don explains. "We try to say, 'OK, what's the job we're trying to fill? And here are the five or six major criteria for the position.' Then we look across the entire roster of candidates to find the right person for the job." Often, though, they come upon a trap: "We find ourselves saying, 'I know a guy . . .' That's how the sentence always starts, 'I know a guy who might be able to do that. . . .' As soon as those words come out of your mouth, you're trying to find a job for the person, not the right person for the job."

The solution? Team Consulting. And zeroing in on the Vital Factors that define that particular position. "Using Team Consulting, we identify the job's criteria. Say we're trying to fill the position of operations manager. That is a really critical job with very specific skills necessary to be successful. We go to our organizational chart, look at the key positions, where the reporting lines are, then we identify the three or four primary characteristics of this operations manager." They then take their list of candidates and begin their evaluation process. "We go around the room and grade everybody on the list."

The process is orderly and structured. As Don explains: "I say, 'Here are the selection criteria. Candidate Smith is the first candidate to be evaluated against these criteria'—which are specific to the position and designed to match skills to those necessary for job success: things such as proven ability to successfully manage a similar business or operation; ability to direct, control, and hold people accountable; ability to manage outside vendors; experience developing budgets, forecasts, and pro formas; success managing a P&L; ability to manage people at multiple sites, and so forth. Then we rate candidate Smith on a scale of 1 to 5 in each category."

By using the Team Consulting framework and time constraints the hiring group stays tightly focused on the candidate and the hiring criteria. "Remember some of the requirements of Team Consulting," Don says. "This isn't a debate or a discussion. It isn't one person advocating why the candidate is a great guy. We concentrate on the task at hand—that is to identify the best-qualified candidate for the position, based on the job-specific criteria. We all work from the same agreed-to selection criteria, and we all use the same 1 to 5 scale to rank each candidate against the criteria."

I tell you, folks, what Don is describing is the MAP process at its best: there is a clear goal, a tightly focused decision-making process, and clear, measurable criteria for making the final selection. "There's little or no debate at this point," Don says. "The process takes away most of the subjectivity because the candidates are graded based on their experience, skills, and abilities compared to the selection criteria. Usually the best candidate clearly stands out. Often there is a significant difference in score between the score of the top candidate and the score of the next best."

If there is no clear winner, what then? Don and his hiring team take an even more rigorous look at their job criteria and drill down deeper. "We might then modify the Team Consulting format but with discipline; we're not going to debate irrelevant things. We keep everything in a systematic framework and identify the skills and attributes necessary to successfully master the position. We go around the table again, getting new scores from the members of the group and trying to solve this problem: who's the best-qualified candidate?"

Over the years, Don and his team have mastered the staffing process. "In the best situations we just naturally drop into Team Consulting: you've got thirty seconds to give me your opinion, we're going to go around the table, and at the end of it we'll be done with it. To have that discipline, that common tool—everyone in the room knows what we're going to do—makes the process of hiring so much easier. This has become an absolutely invaluable tool in the way we do business."

This is music to my ears. Don O'Neill's experience highlights the value of one of our core mantras at MAP: "When we deal in generalities, we shall never succeed. When we deal in specifics, we shall rarely have a failure. When performance is measured, performance improves. And when performance is measured and reported, the rate of improvement accelerates."

One last point that Don O'Neill makes: the Vital Factor process, because it evaluates performance using objective, measurable criteria, takes the messiness out of potentially difficult personnel issues. Every month each person sets his or her goals and then at the Vital Factor Meeting the report card comes in. The person has either met his goals or he hasn't. "There is nowhere to hide," Don explains. "We're sitting around the table together, and each person has to take responsibility for their own performance. It takes the bs out of it. Vital Factors and their measurement highlight performance and leave little to be hidden or explained away."

This process, Don says, instills discipline and maturity in your team, and that can only make them stronger. Winners don't give excuses. They accept responsibility. If they make a mistake they own up to it, learn the lesson, and move on. Just ask Jerry Rice. Or Brett Favre. Or John Wooden. "My goal is to reach that level of skill and discipline with my managers," Don explains. "I want to push it down a layer or two in the organization, so it seeps in and becomes an institutional practice, not just a practice that makes the boss happy, but it becomes the discipline of the overall organization. We've had great success there, and sometimes we've had less than great success. But we're always learning, always striving to do better."

That, my friends, is the stuff from which champions are made.

The Bottom Line

1. Your most important job as a leader or manager is to develop your people. Be a coach; understand the principles of coaching and what good coaching entails.
2. Be candid. Confront. Ask tough questions. Have written development plans for your top people, with specific directions and accountability. Make these plans an important part of your coaching process.
3. When you recruit and hire new people, start with a well-defined job description and have a well-structured hiring process in place. It doesn't have to be as elaborate as the MAP process for bringing in consultants, but do your homework on a candidate and don't just accept the first look. Do multiple interviews, conducted by multiple people.
4. Once you've hired someone, set him or her up for success. Have a ninety-day training plan. Back the person up with a support team. Give him or her top-level coaching and mentoring.
5. Talk and walk this fundamental truth: People are your most important asset. If you want to build a winning team, you have to hire—and retain—the best players. Just ask Bill Walsh. Or John Wooden.

CHAPTER ELEVEN

UNEARTHING THE BURIED JEWELS

It is now time to go deeper. Much deeper.

In previous chapters I have shown how many different organizations have adopted the MAP system and used it to transform their operations, motivate their people, and improve their performance. I have also shown you how to use several different MAP concepts and tools—Vital Factor Meetings, the Vital Few, Goals and Controls, Team Consulting, and the Big Red "S"—and I have described the deep and lasting impact that these concepts and tools can have when you use them in managing your organization. I have shown you what it takes to build a winning team and how MAP can improve the way your team executes the six functions of management: leading, communicating, planning, organizing, staffing, and controlling.

I have also demonstrated the power and impact of the MAP leadership model: it facilitates clear communication, empowers your people, and promotes strategic alignment and buy-in. And you have seen how Debra Paterson, Bill de la Viña, Michael Caito, Doug Ducey, Steve Campbell, Jose Pulido, Tammy Miller, and Katherine Le have adopted the MAP leadership model and used it with success, be it in banking, food delivery, construction, mortgage lending, ice cream franchising, or even running a city government.

That's a good start, but there are far greater riches ahead. What I want to examine now is what the MAP process can do for you over the longer term, once you have embraced the MAP system and embedded it inside your organization. As I often emphasize, implementing MAP is not a one-time event; it's a process, one that continually helps you better understand your business and improve your results. In the coming chapters you will hear from a number of other business leaders and managers who have used the MAP system over an extended period of time, and many of them will tell you how the MAP process helped them achieve their highest business goals and ambitions. Some will also explain how they brought the MAP philosophy and tools home to their families, and how MAP helped them improve their relationships, their parenting, their life planning, and the work they do in their communities. That's a lot of ground to cover. But if you enjoyed the first part of this book, all I can say is, "My friends, you ain't seen nothin' yet!"

To show you what MAP can do over the long term, let me start by telling you about a man named Robert Wexler, the creator of Wexler Video, one of the largest broadcast video production and postproduction equipment rental houses in the Los Angeles area. When people in Hollywood are making a movie or a TV show, Wexler Video is one of the first places they call for high-end cameras, sound systems, and editing suites. It's a big business, and Bob Wexler built it from scratch. MAP played a key role in the long-term development of Wexler Video, but it was an unusual role, and I think it offers valuable lessons for other business leaders. It also offers valuable lessons for entrepreneurs in Bob Wexler's mold: the kind of men and women who are dynamic and clever and who love the start-up phase of building a company but who become restless with the day-to-day chores and obligations of management. If that describes you, then really listen up! Bob found some wonderful solutions, and you can too.

Bob Wexler grew up in Philadelphia, and from an early age he liked working with his hands. So did his dad. "My father was a junior high industrial arts teacher, and he ran his own printing shop," Bob says. "He always said, 'If you want to get anywhere, learn a trade.'" Bob took that to heart. In high school he studied electronics, and afterward he went to a two-year vocational school, majoring in electronics and communication technology. Electronic gear that might look like the Cyrillic alphabet to most of us, Bob found to be as simple as the ABCs. "I had this passion for electronics and taking things apart," he explains. "If you gave me something, the first thing I would do is take it apart and see how it works. That's really the foundation for my background in being an engineer: knowing how to repair, take apart, and put things back together, understanding how things work."

After graduating from technical school Bob opened a shop in Miami Beach to repair television sets. A few years later he wound up in Southern California working for a TV production company that made documentary films. "I maintained all their equipment," Bob says. "They had several cameras and editing consoles. I knew very little about the equipment, but presented with something I can pick it up pretty quickly if it's technical." Pick it up he did. Before long Bob was chief engineer of another company, one that specialized in renting film and video equipment, just as Wexler Video does today. Soon he became restless again.

"I had the entrepreneurial itch," Bob says. "Working for someone else didn't satisfy me. Also, I was always looking for ways to supplement my income and supplement what I do, and I wanted to capitalize on the fact that I was working for this big equipment rental company. So I took all the money I had and went to the bank." With a little finagling he convinced the bank to give him a modest line of credit. Then he used that credit to make a down payment on a television camera worth between $30,000 and $40,000. Then he went a step further: "I purchased a tape machine, a microphone, a light kit, and so there I am. I'm in business."

At this juncture many headstrong entrepreneurs might have plunged ahead and started making a film or documentary of their own. Not Bob Wexler. "The problem is, I'm not a cameraman. I'm not creative. I don't have a creative bone in my body," he says. "So I became known as this engineer who worked at a rental equipment company but who had his own equipment. People would call me directly, on weekends and after hours, and they would hire me, with my camera and equipment, and they would operate it. I would just ensure that the equipment worked properly. And that was the start of Wexler Video."

Before long Bob's business was "booming," meaning he had two cameras to rent out instead of just one. And he had something more: showmanship and flair.

I moved the operation from my garage and leased a 1,000-square-foot storefront; then I hired some really cute secretaries. They really helped to bring in the business. Customers always enjoyed coming by the office to check things out. Everyone would help around the shop, and my secretaries also helped out with errands and equipment deliveries. So I developed a reputation for having the best equipment in town with the finest help. Another thing I did was I collected empty camera and shipping cases. The more cases I had lined up against the wall, the more equipment it looked like I had, even though I only had two cameras. So people would come and say, "Wow, look at this place!" The next thing I know, I had five, six, ten cameras going out on jobs. I purchased more microphones and accessories and next thing I knew I was running a company.

I love that story. It's a classic entrepreneurial start-up story. A man finds his passion. Then with a lot of energy and a lot of street smarts he turns it into a thriving business. And I think there is a vital lesson here for other entrepreneurs: first, know yourself. Know your strengths. Know your limitations. And then act accordingly, just as Bob did. He knew he was an able technician and not a film-maker, so he built on his strengths and *served* creative people. They win, he wins, and his business booms. As Bob Wexler soon learned, though, energy and street smarts can get you up and running, but to build a company that will succeed over the longer term, you need more: You need structure. You need organization. You need planning. You need a system of management. And here Bob's life lesson of "know thyself" soon took on much greater depth and meaning.

As Wexler Video grew and grew, becoming one of the top broadcast video equipment rental houses in Los Angeles, Bob realized he was getting frustrated. He simply didn't like the day-to-day chores and obligations of running a company. In fact he hated them. And the more his company grew, the further away he was from what he loved most: technology, electronics, and fixing equipment—and the daily juice of building a company and solving problems. As a result Bob's company had no management system and no steadying hand; the result often looked like chaos. "I had no employee manual, no systems in place," Bob says. "If somebody wanted a vacation they'd say, 'Bob I need a vacation,' and I'd say

'OK.' Then they'd say, 'Can I get paid for my vacation?' 'Well,' I'd say, 'maybe, maybe not. It depends on how I feel.' Basically it was me every day shooting from the hip, putting out fires one at a time. . . . I drank a bottle of Pepto-Bismol a day."

What to do?

As a first step, Bob got married. To a well-organized woman with a systems background. "People use different parts of their brain," Bob explains. "I'm tactile; I'm very hands-on. But ask me what movie I saw yesterday and I can't tell you. You have to know what your limitations are. I knew one of my limitations was organization; I wasn't very organized. My wife, Cindy, who is extremely organized, who can master huge construction projects, and who worked supervising union employees in the insurance division of a local hospital, came in to help me, and she said, 'Look, we need to put together an employee manual for this company.'"

The next logical step was MAP. And the timing was serendipitous. While the Wexlers were putting together their employee manual, Bob received a call from one of our consultants. Would Bob be interested in attending a management workshop? Bob was about to hang up on him, but the consultant told Bob that MAP was doing some consulting work for a competing equipment rental company—one much bigger than his. That immediately perked Bob's interest. "I always want to know what my competitors are doing," Bob says. "Obviously, it's worked for them because they're ten times larger than I am, and when I say ten times, I'm talking about Richter-scale bigger. I was nothing compared to them."

A Buried Jewel

Now this story would be extremely simple if I could report that Bob went to a MAP workshop, embraced the system, used it to transform his business, and everyone lived happily ever after. But it did not happen quite that way. Bob did go through a MAP workshop, but he came away feeling that MAP was not for him. "It was tough for me to go through that program because I'm a hands-on guy and I'm in this room with some very accomplished, academically strong people," he says. "There was the CEO of a baked goods company, someone else who was an organic farmer, someone else who was from a prominent bakery, you know—a complex mix of people. I'm not good in this type of environment. This is not my environment, to sit in a room where there's some guy up there and you have to write something down and present it. I felt like it was a great program, I learned a lot, but it wasn't for me."

I understand that. MAP requires focus and discipline, and as Bob is the first to admit, focus and discipline are not his strengths. Also, he was hoping that MAP would be a quick-fix solution but it isn't; it's a long-term process. And Bob, being as restless as he is, just didn't have the patience to stay with it. Still, he knew full well what it takes to succeed in business. And he knew that the challenges he faced in running his company were only going to get bigger. So even though Bob felt that MAP was not for him personally, he felt it was exactly what his company needed. So as a next step he brought in Dane Henriksen, one of our most experienced coaches and mentors. Dane installed the MAP system—Vital Factor Meetings, Goals and Controls, Team Consulting, the works—and before long the MAP process began to take hold inside Wexler Video. Bob Wexler was thrilled.

"I started sending my managers to the workshop," Bob says, "and then every month we had our Vital Factor Meetings and we were seeing how well we were hitting our goals." Right away, too, Bob saw that MAP would help him fulfill one of his top personal goals: pulling back from the day-to-day management of the company. "The more I got my managers involved in the program over the years, the more I could back away. For me to be involved at a discipline level like that, it was stressing me out more than helping. But I knew it was absolutely necessary. I knew that the company could not grow with the model that I had laid out for it. It had to have structure."

MAP provided the structure, and that enabled Bob to begin focusing on his next priority: finding and grooming someone to fill his shoes and manage the daily grind. But who? The answer came in a most unexpected form. "The first really big TV show that Wexler Video did was *Candid Camera*," Bob recalls:

> The remake of *Candid Camera*, not the original. Doing that show took every ounce of equipment we had, and pretty much I was working on it full-time. There was always that worry: what happens if the show gets cancelled? What happens when they pay me slow,

which they did—very slow? You have to make payroll. Well, that show did get cancelled, and all the producers and cameramen and engineers went to five other shows. So the next thing I know, I'm providing equipment for five other shows. It wasn't much longer after that that Chris Thompson came to work for us as a rental agent. I don't think I had more than fifteen employees at the time.

At first, Bob did not see Chris Thompson as the kind of guy he might one day elevate to the position of president and CEO. He was brash and a little rough around the edges. "When he came to work for me, Chris was a total shoot-from-the-hip kind of guy, but he got a lot of work done," Bob says. "He had a degree and experience, and he knew the industry really well. He got people to perform. Before I hired him, his previous employer told me: 'You can hire Chris. Your customers will love him; your employees won't.' I thought, 'OK, I have to get my people to perform. We're looking at the lion tamer.'"

Chris worked at Wexler for many months as a rental agent and he did well. He may have looked and dressed at times like a laid-back Southern California surfer, but Chris knew how to get results. And he had plenty of confidence and fire in his belly. Six months or so after starting at Wexler, Chris went in to see the boss. The lion tamer was ready for more. "Chris basically said to me, 'Bob, I feel like I can run the rental department.' He said, 'I can do it!' And I said, 'You know what? You *can* do it. You're hired. Do it! Take over the department.'"

This was a key moment in the evolution of Wexler Video. Bob was eager to pull back from the day-to-day grind; he wanted to pour his energies into new areas of exploration. And Wexler Video needed a lion tamer, a leader who could take the reins, maintain discipline, and take the company into a new phase of maturity and sustained growth and profitability. Was Chris Thompson the right guy? Was he the buried jewel who could take charge of the company and take it to the next level? In his gut Bob felt the answer was yes. But Bob also took out an insurance policy: Chris had to go through MAP. He had to work closely with MAP's Dane Henriksen. And he had to grow as a manager and a leader.

Chris himself was ready for change and personal growth in principle, but he was not at all sure that he was ready for MAP. "In the beginning I resisted MAP," Chris says now. "I'm not a joiner; I'm anything but a joiner. I saw MAP as snake oil at first. Years ago I was running a company for someone else and they brought an outside consultant in and, well . . . My experience has been they come in, they know very little about your business, they have one size that fits all, and they make evaluations that they don't have to live with or see the fruition of. That was what I perceived MAP to be. And I thought, 'Gee, this is all I need.'"

Still, Chris realized that this was his moment: he had to put up or shut up. So he put aside his reservations and went to a three-day MAP workshop; Dane was the facilitator. Right away it produced an awakening. "I had my eyes opened," Chris says. "MAP gave me a way to do business. I know that sounds kind of simple, but you have all these pressures in business: financial pressures, employee pressures, competitive pressures. Most people, whether they come from a business background or not, don't have a way of organizing all these things and solving them. MAP gives you that skill."

During the workshop Chris and Dane forged a strong personal bond, one based on mutual trust and a blunt, warts-and-all candor. Looking back now Chris says that the MAP workshop and working with Dane proved to be a critical turning point in his life. "What the MAP toolkit does for you is it allows you to know that you can do it. That's the truth. Everything else is great—the Pareto principle and all the wonderful stuff that MAP talks about—it's all good. But the truth is you go through the MAP process and you realize, 'You know what? I can do this! I can accomplish this. It's doable.' They even give you tools to work with other people and present the problem to them and let them solve the problem for you."

Sound familiar? Like Katherine Le and others, Chris felt he had to do it all himself. He was wearing the Big Red "S." He rarely delegated, rarely empowered his people. Dane and MAP showed him a different way of thinking, a different way of leading. The critical first step for Chris was learning humility and accepting his own limitations: "MAP allows you to be graceful in coming up with the realization that 'oh yeah, I'm not so smart but I can do it.' It's humbling. Working with Dane is extremely humbling," Chris says. "What you realize going through all this is that you're not that smart. You can use the power of others to help. I had to make a deal with myself that not only could I be wrong but that I'm often wrong and that I had to listen more to the advice of others and allow more input from others. Now I'm more of a traffic cop for ideas, rather than the person who says yes and no, and it's my way or the highway."

What I hear there is Chris accepting the value of the MAP leadership model: facilitating, delegating, empowering your people, and having them bring you solutions instead of their problems. And after his MAP workshop that was the new leadership model that Chris brought back to Wexler Video. In this case Chris did not have to launch the MAP management system; thanks to Dane it was already in place and functioning very well. But now Chris took the MAP tools and philosophy and pushed them much deeper into the organization. And his goals as leader were clear and specific: structure, focus, discipline, accountability, clear communication, alignment, and buy-in. In sum, the MAP blueprint for success.

As he moved deep into the MAP process, with Dane as his guide, Chris also made big changes in his personal life. He cut his ponytail, bought more business suits, and transformed his personal relationships too. "MAP has extreme ramifications throughout—if you really believe in it and are honestly looking at your business and yourself. You'll make personal and business decisions that are painful but will get you to a better place," he says. "MAP helped me make decisions in my personal life that I would never have been able to make otherwise."

As Chris was discovering, MAP helps you manage both the business of work and the business of life. "Many people think they have everything in hand, but the truth is most of the time you're just whistling in the dark. MAP gave me simple skills that are repeatable, that I can use in my personal life and my business life, and that I can use forever. Business schools talk about all this high fallutin', wonderful stuff—about how to run a business, about how you can measure this and that—but MAP actually teaches you how to organize, manage, and succeed."

Now we are seeing what happens when the MAP process works its way deep into an organization and into the people who run it: it changes their behavior and it changes the psychodynamics of the leadership team. As Chris grew as a leader and became more confident in his abilities, he became more humble and more willing to reach out for help. His leadership ways became more supple and understanding. This smoothed relations with his staff and with his boss, Bob Wexler. As Chris now saw clearly, he and Bob had very different strengths and limitations, but they could still work comfortably and effectively together.

Bob Wexler had to do some growing too. Early on, even as he and Cindy were stepping out of the day-to-day management of his company, Bob would openly balk at some of Chris's decisions. But he soon realized this was counterproductive: it only undermined Chris's authority. If Bob was going to empower Chris, he really had to cut the cord and go all the way. And Bob did come to that realization: "I stopped working with MAP directly and Chris started," Bob says. "I made Chris the president, he started working with Dane and MAP, and he started changing the way he played the game. Still, there are a lot of things that I don't approve of and I don't necessarily like, but I've learned in a company, if you try and step in and undermine everything somebody does, they become ineffective."

Bob also learned other valuable lessons. "I learned—and I don't know if I learned it from MAP or not—that you rise to your level of competence, and then you let someone else take over. You always hire people who are better than you in a given area. I see so many companies where the companies revolve around one individual, and as Dane always used to say, 'What happens if that person gets hit by the pie truck? Where does that leave you?'" With regard to planning too, Bob has come to understand the wisdom of the MAP approach. "The philosophy I have is this: any plan is a good plan as long as you have a plan. The only bad plan is no plan at all. If you have a plan or a map to follow, you'll know when you're off course. If you don't have a plan you are destined to get lost or fail. It's just shooting from the hip."

With Chris and the Wexlers now working in sync and with the MAP system humming along inside the company, growing the business should have been a lot easier. Fat chance. Now, though, the problems came from *outside* the company. The first was the dot.com craze of several years ago, when every entrepreneur and venture capitalist in the country was scrambling for ways to make fast money via the Internet and the boom in e-commerce. At that time, scores of suitors knocked on Wexler's door, peddling ideas, looking for support, and offering up a piece of the action. With their usual entrepreneurial spirit the Wexlers were eager to find a way to jump on board. But not Chris Thompson. By now he was a stickler for hard facts. Measurable results. Tough-minded business plans. And no-nonsense projections.

"During the dot.com craze the owners were all over me to open up some kind of dot.com enterprise related to Wexler," Chris recalls.

> They wanted to get in somehow; they saw it as a huge advantage. My staff and I looked at opportunities, and every time we'd run it through the different matrixes we had developed with MAP, and you know what? It never penciled out. A lot of our competitors got involved in dot.com businesses and several of them went under. MAP creates a very rational program for you to evaluate your business and other business opportunities, and again, no matter how much schooling you have, how much education, MAP is different. It gives you practical tools and it gives you discipline."

The result? When the dot.com bubble burst, Wexler Video came through with nary a scratch.

Then came 9/11. How did Wexler Video fare? "Every month we do our Vital Factors, our Goals and Controls, and everyone laughs because they sound so darn simple," Chris says.

> My controller came from an accounting background and also from Sony Studios. When she came in we were doing all the MAP stuff, and she thought it was hysterical. "What's all this stuff about?" she'd say. "It's just mumbo-jumbo!" Well, it's the kind of mumbo-jumbo that when 9/11 happened, we were able to—in one week—evaluate what was going to happen to our business, make the business corrections, lay off fourteen people, and change our purchasing decisions, so that we still made a profit that year. Using our MAP tools we acted quickly and we were able to really succeed where everybody else was just hammered.

Another Buried Jewel

As Chris said, the process of MAP—its discipline and the tight focus it puts on Vital Factors and the key drivers of a business—helped Wexler Video avoid the business catastrophes that many other companies experienced after the dot.com bust and the terrorist attack of 9/11. And there were other dividends as well. As Chris and his management team pushed the Vital Factor process deeper and deeper into the operational life of their company, they got down to the real root of their business. And boy, were they surprised!

"When MAP came in here, we had no mission statement and no internal understanding of what we do for a living," Chris says. "To someone coming from the outside, we look like an equipment rental company." Huh? Isn't that what Wexler does? Rents video equipment? High-end cameras, sound systems, editing consoles? Yes, Chris says, at one level that is exactly what Wexler does. But what really drives the bottom line? Going through the MAP process Chris and his team discovered this:

"MAP let us understand that we're not a rental company at all," Chris says.

> What we are is a finance company. We borrow money from someone else, we turn the money into equipment, we rent the equipment out, we pay off the equipment, and we keep the difference. That simple understanding of what our business is, that's the difference between our being successful and not being successful. We can talk about customer service, we can talk about new technologies, we can talk about all that wonderful stuff, but the truth is we're a finance company. Borrow money as low as we can borrow it, turn it into something we can rent, rent it, pay the money back, and keep the difference. That's really what we do. That's what really determines our level of profit and potential growth.

This was a huge revelation and it took Chris awhile to fully accept it. "Dane and I came to the realization . . . it was really more his idea and me going, 'Gee, you're right.'" Some other people inside the company didn't buy it all. But the more carefully Chris examined his business—and the way its profit was generated—the more convinced he became. Cut away all the top layers, and Wexler was not a rental company; it was a finance company. That's what drove the bottom line. By using MAP principles and tools to peel back the onion, Chris finally saw it clearly: "Find whatever becomes your bottom line, what impacts it the most, what you're borrowing money at, what you're buying your equipment at, how quickly you're getting your return on your investment, and good-bye. When you've peeled all that back and clarified it, you're at the wheel of what generates your profit."

This revelation of course catalyzed important changes inside Wexler. To be precise, Chris and his financial team began focusing more tightly on a different set of Vital Factors: lending rates, equipment costs, how quickly new equipment was being paid off. Priorities shifted too: if Wexler's service team did not generate bottom-line profit, how could the service staff be streamlined? If Wexler wasn't really a technology company, did it make financial sense to always be shelling out big bucks for the latest model of a high-definition camera? And if your priority as a finance company was to pay off your equipment as quickly as possible, shouldn't you adjust your pricing structure to help you achieve that goal?

Through the MAP process those shifting priorities were quickly fed into Wexler's planning process. As Chris had learned through MAP, your business plan should not be some static document that sits on a shelf gathering dust; it should be a dynamic and flexible plan of action. (MAP stands for Management Action Programs, remember?) When conditions change, as they did in the dot.com bust, or crises arrive, as they did on 9/11, you can rework your business plan to meet the challenge, just as Chris and his team did. And with that plan you always stay on course.

"The MAP process creates alignment," Chris says.

> If you go through the process and you get key people involved in MAP, there's alignment because now you know what's vital. You work through the business plan, you start working your plans for the course of the year. I'm constantly talking to competitors, vendors, manufacturers, and I say, "What's your business plan?" and they all look at me like, "Business plan?" They have nothing. Even big businesses. The business plan that you write when you're using the MAP process is an operational business plan that basically gets you through your year. If you do things right, you're very successful. It's a blueprint for success.

Now here's the big question: once the top managers realized Wexler Video was really a finance company, where, in concrete, measurable terms, did that lead them? Did that peeling back process lead them to greater success and profitability? The answer is yes. That revelation led Wexler into a period of unprecedented performance and growth. "We all speak the same language now," Chris says. "We understand what's vital, what's not vital. We were able to take the company from where it was just kind of getting along, going along, to being an industry leader. For the past several years, we have been among the top 100 fastest-growing companies in Los Angeles. Growth is up from 15 to 25 percent per year. In 2004, our growth was up 33 percent."

Those are delicious numbers, but for Chris and Bob Wexler some other results of the MAP process are sweeter still. Now free of the day-to-day stress and chores of running his company, Bob has entered an exciting new field: craniopathy, the study of the human skull, the brain, and the nervous system. He keeps an elaborate skull collection in his office, in a glass case, so that he can pursue his research whenever he feels the urge. Always the fix-it engineer and the savvy entrepreneur, Bob has two design patents on his research, one for a golf visor that by applying gentle pressure to key parts of the skull improves focus and concentration, and he claims it actually helps improve your swing. The other patent has medical applications. Bob also has more time to be with his kids, and he and Cindy are enjoying a more balanced and fulfilling quality of life.

Chris Thompson, too, has created more balance in his life. "Through the MAP process I stopped having to work the kind of hours I used to work, because you start making changes that create processes and practices that allow you to get through your day successfully," Chris explains. He's also more comfortable dealing with his staff:

> You make it less personal and more about "here are the numbers, look at the problem." Taking the personal part out and making it more about the numbers makes it so it's a better day. The thing that is so funny—you say it and it sounds so damn simple, but it's true—every business is about the numbers, but you have to have a roadmap, a blueprint, a recipe—all the metaphors they use—and MAP gives them all to you. It's a process, an educational process, a teaching process. I've spent a lot of time in a lot of different parts of the world looking at systems that work, don't work; governments that work, don't work; film operations that never work. MAP gets the job done. It gives people a platform, a philosophy, a belief system.

Though implementing MAP has been very hard, Chris says there has been an unexpected payoff: now that the MAP system has become ingrained in Wexler's daily operations, Chris has become freer to innovate and be creative. "We are incredibly innovative in the technology that we apply to solve problems for our customers," he says. "We get to introduce a wide variety of new products into the industry and pride ourselves on being able to do that. You can't do that if you're putting out fires everywhere. So there's this trade-off with the discipline and rigorousness that MAP requires, which in turn gives you the ability to do the fun stuff in your business."

As Chris learned how to apply MAP inside Wexler Video, Dane nudged him to take a further step. One day, in a one-on-one coaching session, Dane said to him, "I'm sure you realize that you are also the president and CEO of the Chris Thompson Corporation, right?"

Chris nodded in agreement.

"And you have shareholders there too, right?"

Again Chris nodded.

"Well," Dane said, "what is *that* president supposed to do?"

Chris laughed. "Plan. Forecast. Budget. Set goals. Measure performance. Have a Plan B. Monitor cash flow. Have a mission, vision and values. Right?"

Dane smiled with joy: his student had absorbed all the lessons. "Right! Now install the MAP system in your personal life. Craft a Life Plan and apply to it all the MAP principles and tools."

Chris did exactly that—and it changed his life. In life, as in business, his watchwords became Responsibility. Honor. Candor. And as MAP taught him, it is not enough to speak the words; you have to manage your life in accordance with those values. In business and in life that's a proven path to deep and lasting success.

I salute you, Chris Thompson. Your story shows how MAP can help people become the best they can be. And I salute you, Bob Wexler. You saw a buried jewel inside your company, and then you worked with him, polished him, and helped him grow into a winning manager, leader, and person. You both win. Your company wins. And your entire team wins. May your story be an inspiration to us all.

The Bottom Line

1. In building your team, keep an eye out for the *buried jewel*. The best players might not come wrapped in the packages you expect.

2. Use the Vital Factor process to drill down deep into your company and find those other buried jewels, the hidden Vital Factors that can clarify and transform your business, just the way they did for Chris and Bob.

3. And always keep in mind that profound change never comes from a quick fix; it comes from a long-term process of growth and maturity. As Robert Mondavi will tell you, the finest grapes and the finest wines come from older vines, the ones with roots that are strong and deep and rich in character.

CHAPTER TWELVE

MANAGING CREATIVITY

Now we come to one of the most interesting aspects of our work at MAP: working with people and companies who are succeeding in highly creative fields.

Building a business is always a creative endeavor, but building a business based solely on creative output is especially demanding. In fields like film production, television, software design, architecture, and advertising, what drives a business is its ability to generate new ideas: ideas that excite, ideas that sell, ideas that transform the way people work and the way people live. Think of how a seemingly simple idea like Scotch tape or the Post-it changed every office in America and beyond. And think about how much the animation studio Pixar has done for children in America and around the world by brilliantly marrying computer animation technology with highly inventive characters and storytelling. And when it comes to turning creativity into business success, I can sum up every entrepreneur's dreams in a single word: iPod.

The question is, how do they do it? How does a company like Pixar or Apple generate winning creative ideas? How do company managers recruit—and manage—highly creative people? What is their secret? And what tools can they use to facilitate the process? For answers to those questions I now turn to a brilliant young man named Ted Price. Ted is the cofounder and president of Insomniac Games, a highly creative company in a frenzied, high-stakes, idea-driven industry: computer gaming. This is an industry where companies rise or fall on the strength of their creative ideas—and their ability to turn those ideas into winning products. But creativity is not enough. A game company like Ted's has to turn out its products on time, on budget, and with zero mistakes. And as Ted can tell you, your team can have the most ingenious ideas on the planet, but if you can't turn them into attractive, cost-effective products, then your company is going to get beaten in the marketplace, and sooner or later it will head into ruin. The bottom line here is simple: managing creative people can be one of the toughest challenges in the world of business, and Ted Price and his team are now mastering that challenge. And I'm eager to tell you how.

First, let me tell me you about Ted the man. At first glance, when you meet him in the offices of Insomniac Games in Los Angeles, Ted does not come across as a business pioneer. He's tall and lanky, with an unruly shock of black hair that plays freely across his forehead. Though he's in his late thirties, Ted Price retains a distinctly boyish spirit and enthusiasm—especially about his lifelong passion for computer games. If he told you that he had grown up in Southern California and had been swept up into computer gaming during a surfing year in Malibu, you wouldn't doubt it for an instant. As with Tammy Miller, though, first impressions can be deceiving. And as soon as he settles back into a comfortable chair in his office, a very different Ted Price comes to the fore.

"I was born in Richmond, Virginia, in 1968, right around the time that the first video games were making their way onto mainframe computers," Ted begins. "In 1972, when the Magnavox Odyssey came out, I had a little girlfriend whose father bought her one of these first machines. You could only play PONG on it, but I loved it. That was my first real exposure to video games. I was five or six. It was one of my earliest memories. I can still remember getting really excited to see this little plastic console in front of her TV and these two paddles with balls moving back and forth. Each time I was really looking forward to that."

A few years later Atari brought out its 2600 system, and Ted remembers that vividly as well. "That was a huge success in terms of the video game industry," he says.

It really opened the door for home video game consoles. It sold a total of three million consoles over its lifetime, but spawned some great games, like Combat—simple concepts but a lot of fun. My parents were cool enough to actually buy a 2600 for my sister and me, and they allowed us to play it for many hours—as long as we did our homework. The Atari 2600 was what solidified my interest in video games at an extremely early age. From there I went on to play games on the Apple II. When I was ten I told my dad that if he bought me an Apple II, I would program a game on it and make a million dollars.

As you can see, Ted's passion for video games came with an accompanying understanding that gaming wasn't just child's play; it was a business—a very *big* business, with potential windfalls in the tens of millions of dollars. And there was something else—the games were an exciting mental challenge:

> I loved reading, but games were a much more involved experience where I could solve puzzles and be constantly challenged. Some of my favorite games were text-based adventures on the computer. I would spend hours drawing maps to figure out how to get through these games and basically navigate through these games. They challenge your imagination. You had to come up with the images behind the words, and I think that, in particular, helped me many years down the road in running Insomniac Games. You have to be able to visualize the design concept and explain it to other people.

As he talks, Ted Price proves that he's extraordinarily bright, extraordinarily articulate, and very ambitious and focused. His parents always emphasized hard work, education, and discipline, and Ted grew up putting a premium on challenge, imagination, problem solving, and personal achievement—all the attributes he would later need as a creative entrepreneur. First, though, Ted went to Princeton. There, when not studying, he played lacrosse, soccer, and squash, and he found that many of his classmates shared his passion for video games. "I played video games throughout my Princeton years," Ted says. By then the Super Nintendo system was all the rage. "I spent hours playing Zelda and Mario Brothers and Super Metroid, one of the best games of all time, with my roommates. It wasn't that we were social outcasts or not doing what college kids do. That just happened to be another one of our pastimes."

During his senior year at Princeton, Ted began planning his future. Games were his passion, but Ted, like his father and other men in his family, was also drawn to business and other forms of leadership. So while many of his classmates were headed for big jobs on Wall Street, Ted was determined to go his own way, and one day an unexpected door opened in front of him:

> My uncle worked in San Diego. He had just started a medical company named Call Doctor, Inc. It was a house-call service that had vans equipped at the level of a hospital emergency room. A van could bring a doctor and technician out to the homes of people, mostly elderly folks, and give them the same level of care they could get in a hospital. It was a groundbreaking idea. And he said to me, "Why don't you come out? Until you decide what you want to do, you can help me on the vans."

Ted agreed. He went to San Diego and helped staff the vans for awhile, doing emergency calls with physicians and paramedics and learning the mechanics of the business. "Then my uncle suggested I track the market research for all the house calls we were going on. He wanted to do this because we were trying to get better reimbursement from the government for all the Medicare patients we treated, and to do that we had to have data showing how we were actually saving the government money. I started by learning a database language, and then I basically created the databases for storing, collating, and reporting on most of the data we were collecting during the house calls." Now Ted was taking his passion and his talent for computers and applying them to business management.

"Then one day the controller of the company quit," Ted says. "So my uncle came in, put an accounting book on my desk, and said, 'You have a week to read this book and learn it because you're our new controller.' That was one of the most helpful experiences I ever could have had because it forced me to learn finance from the ground up. I didn't know what a debit was, a credit was, and within a week I got lucky and figured it out."

The book his uncle had given him was a basic college economics textbook. "I had taken economics in college and that was my worst grade ever," Ted says, "but I liked the application of economics, of accounting. I was controller for a couple years, then we brought in a new CEO who wanted a CFO who actually had a real accounting background. I ended up working for the CFO and realized it still wasn't my passion. The medical field was great, and I learned a lot about start-up companies and finance, but I wanted to do something for myself. I was working 80, 90, 100 hours a week, and I realized I was going to burn out if I didn't strike out on my own."

Now the stage was set. Ted had his passion and his dreams, and now he had hands-on training in business, finance, and management systems. He was eager to make his mark in the world, and he knew exactly what path he wanted to follow: "At that point I realized I wanted to start a video game company," Ted says. "My uncle was really supportive, and he suggested I consult for his company while I figured out the next step. I did. I maintained their databases and helped with their programs while I started Insomniac Games. The year was 1993. I rented an office and began writing a concept for our first game."

Ted first had to assess where the computer game industry was going. The hot company, he decided, was an outfit called 3DO. "The company was started by Tripp Hawkins, one of the founders of Electronic Arts (EA), and he had this vision where the game industry would move away from cartridges and instead build games on CD-ROMs. His was the first commercially successful CD-ROM system. I signed up as a licensed developer for 3DO. Doing this meant that I had a license to develop titles for that platform. But I still had to get funding, build a game, and somehow distribute it."

Ted's start-up costs were not gigantic: "You didn't need to do anything other than buy a development station. I had saved enough money from doing consulting to lease a development station for about $8,000. Then I bought a couple of computers for running an office, and I suddenly realized that even though I had this concept, and I could maybe do some of the art, my programming skills were terrible. My hope was that I could build a demo with some help and then shop it around to a publisher who could help us finish the game."

The idea was enthralling, but Ted soon realized he needed help. "I had no idea how to make a game," Ted admits:

> I had played them for a long time, I knew something about game theory, and I thought I could figure it out as I went. I was pretty

wrong on that. I was very, very lucky to run into a guy named
Al Hastings. He is our current CTO [Chief Technical Officer] and
a partner in the company. At the time, in 1993, he was a senior
at Princeton. We had never met, but one day my mom was at a
Christmas party, and she bragged to her friends that I had started
a video game company. One friend said, "Your son should talk to
my son's roommate at Princeton. He brags about this guy being
the smartest guy he's ever met." My mom gave me his number
and I called him up.

Ah, the hand of destiny: from his mother's chance meeting at
a Christmas party an amazing creative partnership was born. Ted
still remembers that first call to Al Hastings: "Al is a guy who doesn't
say much, and our conversation was about three sentences long.
But in those three sentences he agreed to come out and meet me
in California. He flew out, we met, hit it off, and he agreed to not
go for all those stable jobs he could have gotten out of college.
Instead he agreed to take a risk and join me at Insomniac. It was
pretty cool. Neither of us knew what the hell we were doing." Maybe
not, but Ted intuitively understood that it was important for him,
as a leader, to surround himself with people who shared his passion
and values, as Al Hastings did.

After graduation Al flew out to San Diego and settled in. "He
was living on my couch in my rented apartment," Ted recalls.

He and I put together the demo for our first game, called Disruptor, in a month. He did all the programming, and I did all the art
and sound. We videotaped the game play and started shopping it
around. We drove up and down the West Coast, cold-calling publishers. We must have visited eight or ten publishers, showed them
the videotape, and asked them to work with us. In every single
instance they blew us off, either because they had a game like what
we were doing or because we didn't have enough experience or
they didn't like what they saw. No one was going to spend millions
of dollars on us.

Then they got their break. "We were very lucky to run into a
guy named Mark Cerny at Universal Interactive Studios. He was an
industry veteran who had come in to help launch Universal's interactive division," Ted says.

He looked at the demo and said, "You guys are the most talented amateurs I've ever seen." He was mostly talking about Al's engine, because it was pretty impressive for a month's worth of work. At that point we were completely out of money. I'd gone through everything. I'd saved $30,000 at the beginning and we'd spent every cent. So at that point it was do or die. Then came one of the most exhilarating moments of my life. I was driving back to San Diego from LA, and I found a message on my answering machine from Mark saying, "Let's do it!" I couldn't believe it. He had decided to take a chance on us.

Mark Cerny did more than "take a chance." He advanced development money to Insomniac Games and gave Ted and Al a three-game deal. But they still had to build a creative team. "At that point it was just Al and me, and we knew we needed a lot of help," Ted recalls.

When I asked Al if he knew any good programmers, he said the best he'd ever met was his brother. So we called Al's brother, Brian Hastings, who is now our chief creative officer. He'd been working at a pacemaker company, doing programming and technical documentation for them. Brian came on board in August of 1994 and the three of us continued to work on Disruptor. We didn't really know what we were doing. And when you have no experience, it's really easy to be inefficient in what you do. Six months rolled around, and we really weren't that far along. Our first playable was actually due at our publishers, up at Universal.

The next step in their evolution came as a brutal shock. "We drove up to Universal with a videotape of what we thought was our first playable, and we just got slammed," Ted recalls. "Mark said, 'You have to be kidding. This is not playable; this is not even a game. What are you doing wasting our money?'"

Those words hit Ted and Al like freezing cold water. In an instant they learned that it was one thing to be brilliant and creative; it was quite another to turn their talents into the necessary fundamentals of business success. They needed to make changes. They needed coaching. They needed to learn discipline, accountability, and focus; in essence they needed a management system like MAP and the Vital Factors. They were in the infant steps of their journey, but their instincts were right on the money. "We decided to move up to Los Angeles," Ted says. "It would help us attract more talent because we couldn't find people who would join us in San Diego—and it would put us closer to Mark Cerny. For me Mark really was a mentor. He knew what it took to make a great game, and he gave us a lot of solid advice."

While their first game was in production, the 3DO platform went belly up; as I said, this is a high-risk business. But Ted and his team nimbly shifted gears and converted their game to work on Sony's hot new PlayStation platform. "Al rewrote the engine for the PlayStation, and we eventually released the game," Ted says. "It got a lot of good reviews. It was one of the few first-person shooters on PlayStation. It won several awards for the best first-person shooter. We were excited because it was the first game we'd ever done." As Ted explains, a *first-person shooter* is a game played from the main character's perspective: "You don't see the character that you're controlling; all you see is a gun."

Now Ted and his team got another painful business lesson: despite the good reviews for their game, Universal didn't support it with effective marketing. "There were two magazine ads and a PR tour where we had some editors come in and look at the game. That was it," Ted says. "No TV ads, nothing. One of the articles written about Disruptor called it, 'The best game that no one ever heard of.' So, despite all the critical acclaim we got, we sold enough to break even and that was it. We didn't make a profit."

Now Insomniac Games was at a critical crossroads. "We had about five people in the company and needed to decide what to do next," Ted says. "Disruptor was a dark, serious game. It was not bloody, but it was violent, and the mood in the office was not terribly positive either. So we said, 'What can we do that's different?' Again, Mark Cerny made a very good suggestion: 'One of the places PlayStation is lacking is the kids' market. There is a vacuum right now that is only being filled by Nintendo on its competing system. Why don't you guys consider making a game aimed at a younger or broader market instead of targeting the hard-core enthusiasts?'"

Let me put on my MAP hat here and explain exactly what Mark Cerny was telling Ted's team. He was saying, "Guys, look at this marketplace opportunity—and grab it." Be flexible, be proactive. Focus your creative output on a niche with enormous commercial potential. If you want to survive as a company, identify your broadest possible customer base, then build a product to serve that base. You might call that Business 101, but guess what? It holds true whether you are in the cookie business, the construction business, the electric cable business, the money transfer business, or the video game business. To their credit, Ted and his team took Mark's advice and refocused their energies.

"One day," Ted says:

> We were discussing ideas and one of our artists, Craig Stitt, said, "I've always wanted to do a game about a dragon." At that point Spyro was born, and we began conceptualizing the character. It took us a long time, with some outside help, to figure out what this character really looked like. We ended up going from a cocky, mean dragon to a very cute dragon. Al had also been working on a new engine for the PlayStation which could display panoramic views. It allowed us to display these huge vistas, and it really helped us create an immersive world of castles and wide-open fields. It all worked well together.

Spyro ended up being a huge success. "We released it in 1998 and it ended up selling over five or six million copies," Ted says. "We followed it up with a sequel in 1999, Spyro II: Ripto's Rage, and we followed that with Spyro: Year of the Dragon." Then Ted and his team decided to abandon the Spyro series—for smart business reasons. "The reason was twofold," Ted explains. "We found ourselves in a three-party deal. Universal was supposed to be our publisher but they sublicensed the rights to Spyro to Sony. That was good and bad for us. Good because Sony really made Spyro a worldwide name; they put a ton of marketing money into it. It was bad because it cut our royalties in half. Any profit we made on the game was being shared equally with Universal. Even though we were making a good profit, we should have been making a whole lot more as creators of the project."

Now Ted and Al were learning valuable lessons about creative output, including the lesson that the best friend any creator can have is a lawyer with real expertise in copyright law, intellectual property, and protecting the creator's rights in a rambunctious global marketplace. Then came another key lesson: the Insomniac team spent six months developing a new game, a dark adventure game featuring a Mayan-inspired heroine who used a staff to perform works of magic. But the game never really gelled, and when Insomniac's publishing partners at Sony suggested that Ted and his team move in a different direction, they agreed to drop it. Six months of time, energy, and creative output went for naught. But Ted and his team had learned that if a creative idea doesn't pan out, you have to be willing to bite the bullet and make a rapid change in course. Your long-term business survival may depend on it.

Their next creation was a game called Ratchet & Clank, and it was released in 2002. "It did very well," Ted says. "It won a lot of awards, and it has sold several million copies. Spyro in total has sold 11.5 million copies. The Ratchet series, which now has four games in it, has sold about nine million copies at this point. So, we went on to develop Ratchet and then three more sequels to Ratchet."

With the success of Ratchet & Clank, Insomniac Games entered a new phase of growth and development. And Ted Price laid down two primary goals for the years ahead: stay economically viable in a rapidly changing industry—and stay innovative and creative. "In this industry, where there aren't very many independent developers left, it makes staying alive and independent even more important to me personally," Ted explains. "I would like to prove that an independent developer can survive and thrive in the era where games are costing upwards of $20 million to develop. I want to prove that we can maintain a small-company culture, where everybody's voice is heard, everybody has creative ownership of the product, and making games is fun—versus succumbing to this much larger game culture where very large companies are churning out these games en masse with, I think, a little less attention to innovation and creativity."

To meet those goals Ted did have an inspiring model to follow: Pixar. In early 2006, Pixar animation studios, creators of pioneering computer animation technology and such enchanting blockbusters as *Toy Story, Monsters, Inc.,* and *Finding Nemo,* crowned its meteoric rise with a historic merger with Disney. "Pixar is one of those companies that really has held its own against the much larger movie companies," Ted says, "and they've maintained this incredible creativity and pride of ownership. I feel that here at Insomniac. All of our guys feel it. A lot of them came from much bigger companies, and they came here because we do it differently."

Still, Ted realized that he now had to make some fundamental changes both at work and at home. He was now running a successful, rapidly expanding company, and like Bob Wexler back at Wexler Video, Ted's responsibilities—and his life—were spinning into a danger zone. For one thing he was working sixteen-hour days. That was a particular strain because he and his wife were starting a family. Also, the nature of Ted's work had dramatically changed. "In the beginning I was spending 90 percent of my time on creation and 10 percent on management," he says. "Then it evolved to 95 percent on management and only 5 percent on asset creation, by which I mean generating designs or stories. Most of what I do is managing. When we got to the third Ratchet—Ratchet & Clank: Up Your Arsenal III—I realized that the company had grown to the point where, if we didn't implement a more coherent structure within the company, we would collapse. That was in the spring of 2004."

At that point Ted knew in his bones that Insomniac Games had reached a crisis point. "It's not that I thought we were going to go under. I just thought we had reached the limits of our ability to expand and continue to make great games," Ted says. "We were between 80 and 100 people and we had departments set up, but we didn't have a good reporting structure. We didn't have good communication within the company. And we didn't have any accountability set up within the company. We were still developing games as though we were a garage developer: everything was last-minute, tons of things were falling through the cracks. We were operating by the seat of our pants."

There was another festering problem too: burnout of his people—and burnout of Ted himself. "We are one of the fastest development companies in our field," Ted says. "We turn very big games around very quickly. But there's a huge toll taken on our folks. People work insane hours, they get burned out easily, and we were finding that people were dropping by the wayside and losing their enthusiasm for what we do. Our department heads and I realized we had to do something to fix it, because long term we would definitely collapse." Ted knew that he too might collapse. He had to find a better balance in his life, and he had to find a way to spend more time with his wife and kids.

There was an underlying truth here, and no one had to spell it out for Ted Price: this was a serious test of his leadership. And like the best leaders Ted did not respond with a know-it-all arrogance. He responded with humility. "I realized that my job as CEO was to establish a long-term plan for the company," Ted says now.

> I had these nebulous ideas for creating our own intellectual property *not* owned by publishers and for building more teams, but I had no idea how to get there. Unless I could enunciate that to the rest of the company, it would never actually happen. I had little idea how to develop a strategic plan. I needed something that would kick me in the ass and make me think more cogently about how to really develop a plan. It was clear that we all needed some advice on how to structure the company better. So that's where MAP came in.

Back in 2002, Carrie Oliff, Ted's director of human resources, had met Lana Elliott, one of MAP's top executive consultants, when Carrie was working at Disney Feature Animation. Two years later, when Ted was looking for help and guidance, Carrie called Lana and set up a meeting with Ted. Lana explained the MAP system to him, and Ted was impressed. "We researched three different management training companies and ended up deciding on MAP based on the testimonials we saw and their client list," Ted says. "What clinched it for us was talking to Lana. She explained the MAP process really well, and I was impressed by how much follow-up and follow-through they had with their clients. I was worried about taking the company down this road and then suddenly veering off. So it was nice to know that the people at MAP would keep us honest and force us to stick to what we said we would do."

In previous chapters you have seen how MAP helped transform Michael Caito's restaurant delivery business, Bill de la Viña's money transfer business, Glenn Stearns's mortgage company, Steve Campbell's concrete firm, Tammy Miller's electric cable company, and

Jose Pulido's city administration. Those are pretty classic corporate outfits. But what about a wild, creative, adrenaline-driven company like Ted Price's? There is nothing corporate about Insomniac Games. Its headquarters in LA looks and feels like a video circus. Huge posters of game heroes and villains dot the walls, the wails of computer-generated sound effects echo through the halls, and every nook and cranny seems to be filled with young game fanatics and technical whizzes. It is a safe bet that anyone coming in wearing a suit and tie would be viewed by Ted's team as an alien from outer space. So how was MAP going to fit into a culture like that? And what about Ted's freewheeling staff? How would they respond to the MAP system, with its rigorous structure, its discipline, and its Goals and Controls? At the outset Ted had his misgivings. But he was still willing to give MAP a try.

COMMITMENT AND BUY-IN

Ted knew, instinctively, that if the MAP system was going to work, he had to personally commit to MAP and lead the way. He also knew that if he and his team were going to transform the culture inside Insomniac Games, it would not happen overnight. They had to commit to an ongoing, long-term process of self-examination, restructuring, and on-the-job training. Ted was ready. To take his business to the next level, he knew he needed fresh ideas and a management system with a proven track record in management and leadership. After talking with Lana, Ted started the process in September of 2004 by personally attending a three-day MAP workshop.

At MAP we carefully planned Ted's workshop experience. For starters Lana Elliott put Ted into a workshop led by Dorriah Rogers, one of our most able coaches and consultants. Lana figured that Dorriah and Ted would be a very good match. They were close in age, they were both extraordinarily bright and articulate, and Dorriah had a technology background. Ted knew gaming; Dorriah knew business. Together, Lana felt, Ted and Dorriah could move mountains. In an added twist, Ted and Dorriah had been born on the same day, though a few years apart, and both had three young daughters of approximately the same ages. In Lana's eyes there was something else too: "Dorriah thinks outside the box.

I knew the MAP system would have to be specially tailored to fit Ted's needs, and I thought Dorriah was just the person to do that."

Still, on day one of the workshop Ted did have misgivings about how well MAP would mesh with the unique culture at Insomniac Games. "One of the things I thought immediately was, 'Oh my god, I better not bring any of the terminology back to Insomniac or my guys will flip,' " Ted says, "because the terminology is appropriate but very corporate. And the last thing Insomniac is is corporate."

As Lana had envisioned, though, Ted and Dorriah formed an immediate bond. And they quickly established a common vision of how they could adapt the MAP system to Ted's specific needs, in terms of both business and creative output. "We worked with Dorriah to figure out how we could establish goals that were unique to a creative company," Ted says. "We're still figuring that out. It was not a turnkey approach for us at all; we had to modify it significantly to work for Insomniac."

For her part Dorriah was very impressed by Ted's intelligence and natural gifts as a leader. And she was not alone in that judgment. On the third day of the workshop the group did a leadership exercise and Dorriah asked everyone to point to one person in the room whom he or she felt was a true leader. Everyone pointed to Ted. "I'd never had that happen before," Dorriah says. "At that point I knew I wanted to work with this guy. In subsequent workshops now, I always cite Ted as an example of a truly inspiring leader."

MISSION AND VALUES

Before MAP came along, Ted and his team had already established their mission and values statement. Still, being creative, they gave it their own special twist. "Well before we went to MAP we established five pillars for the company, and they do guide what we do here," Ted says. Here they are:

1. Independence.
2. Collaboration. (Everybody in this company has the opportunity to contribute to the titles, creativity, and success of our business.)

3. Quality over quantity. (Creativity goes without saying.)
4. Innovation. (If we can't create a fresh experience for the consumer every time, then our games won't sell.)
5. Efficiency.

Efficiency was where Insomniac needed the most improvement, Ted says: "The companies that survive this next generation are going to be the ones that are most efficient because the profits are shrinking and the budgets are expanding. Something has to give. Hopefully what will happen is that more and more people will be playing games and perhaps the retail price of games will rise. We're trying to hedge our bets by becoming more efficient."

STRATEGIC PLANNING

One of Dorriah's first action steps was to help Ted and his team develop a strategic business plan for the company. Where were they going? Where did they want Insomniac to be in five years? We at MAP have a specific method for developing business plans, starting with a process we call *Planning the Plan.* You will find a primer on that in the back of this book (see the section titled "The MAP Management System's Monday Morning Action Plan"). As I said before, we believe that every company should take the time to draft a mission statement, a values statement, and a business plan, one that lays down where you want to go and how you intend to get there. Dorriah helped Ted and his team develop exactly that sort of plan, to be the rudder of their ship.

"Now that was an experience," Dorriah recalls with a laugh. "I had been used to strategic planning sessions with fairly straightforward corporate structures and personnel. Ted's group was a whole different ball game. I came into a room full of very young, very intelligent guys, all of whom had a very healthy skepticism of what I could do for them. I decided from the get-go to turn my normal process on its head and see what I could learn from them instead."

That approach proved to be the right one. Dorriah was able to use their input and quickly put together a solid three- to five-year Strategic Plan and a twelve-month Operations Plan. For Ted the MAP planning process proved to be enlightening. "When the department heads and I came back from MAP, we didn't say a whole lot about what MAP did for us," he explains.

> What we did instead was go immediately into a two- to three-day strategic planning session where we laid out the goals for the company over the next three years. That included laying out all the projects and describing the project structure we would implement. Then I presented that to the entire company. That's where I said, "This is what MAP showed us, and this is why we're putting the new structure into place." What I wanted to do was show that by doing more projects everyone here can make more money. Our projects generate a lot of bonus money for people, so as we grow it's important to release more and more projects. The only way we can do that is by being more efficient. That has the added benefit of allowing you to be more creative. So it all worked together.

VITAL FACTORS

Dorriah's next step was to help Ted's team implement monthly goals meetings, designed to support the Vital Factors and the long-term objectives set down in the business plan. Here Dorriah and Ted confronted the big question: Can a system as structured as Vital Factors, with its emphasis on monthly meetings and measurable goals, really work inside a creative outfit like Insomniac Games? Would Ted's creative people buy into the MAP system—or reject it? At this stage Ted still had misgivings. And he was concerned about the possibility of "death by meeting." He knew that too many meetings could kill the very spirit that made Insomniac Games the exciting, creative, fun, productive place that it was.

Here, though, Ted got his first surprise. Once Dorriah set the Vital Factor process into motion, Ted found little resistance from his department heads. In fact the Vital Factor process proved to be a healthy tonic, spurring discussion about what really worked well in Insomniac's production process and what did not. "Even though MAP isn't a big proponent of having a lot of meetings, it opened us up to the idea of having more," Ted says.

> One of the things MAP helped us with was learning how to structure meetings so they could be more efficient. MAP helped us real-

ize what the basic ground rules were—have an agenda, a time-keeper, someone in charge of the meetings; never run over time; distribute minutes afterward—commonsense stuff that we never used. Not that we followed these ground rules all the time, but paying attention to the rules helped us reach consensus more quickly and keep track of the decisions we had made. The rules sound like basic things, but for us they were new territory. It was the yin to our yang.

SETTING GOALS

One of Dorriah's most complicated challenges was to work with Ted and his team to devise monthly goals that made sense within the framework of the company's creative output. After all, how can you measure creative output? How do you put numbers on ideas? Again, going into the process Ted had his misgivings on this point. "I realized that the way MAP enforces accountability through setting goals wouldn't necessarily work for us because our goals, as a creative company, are not measured in dollars or hours billed or any of that stuff. Our goals are much more nebulous; they're warm and fuzzy. For a game to work, not only does it have to not crash but it has to feel good, it has to play well. And that's a very subjective thing."

Dorriah tackled this difficult issue head on. While she agreed that it was very difficult to quantify creativity or measure "fun," she pointed out that Insomniac was not setting straightforward production goals for the construction of its games. She urged the department heads to begin providing regular and measurable targets for their groups. Also, accepting that the MAP terminology would not fit a creation-driven team like Insomniac, she and Ted modified the terms to better fit the style and spirit of the company.

ACCOUNTABILITY

Through the Vital Factor process Dorriah and Ted saw that they had to make fundamental changes in the way Insomniac Games managed its creative people and projects. There had to be true accountability and more buy-in from the staff. That would result,

Dorriah believed, in greater efficiency and better cost management. Her action step here was "restructure the creative teams." Ted saw the impact right away. "One of the things we did after we went to MAP was to change the way we structure project leadership," Ted says. "We now have a project manager and a creative director on each project. We never had that before. I was kind of serving as both." The result? "While our people have always taken ownership of the creative output, there is now more discipline, accountability, and more checks and balances. Our project managers are responsible for setting the schedules—and enforcing them. What they say goes."

TIME MANAGEMENT

As the MAP system took hold inside Insomniac Games, Dorriah and Ted tackled another key issue: time management. At MAP we often say that either you manage time or time will manage you. At Insomniac Games no one works a nine-to-five job—then or now. And people rarely work a 40-hour week, especially when the company is working against a deadline to bring a game to market. Then it is all hands on deck, doing whatever needs to be done. Still, implementing the MAP system made an immediate difference. "It used to be an average of 80 hours a week," Ted says.

> When we got toward deadlines, crunch time, maybe over 100 hours a week. Now I am usually working 70 hours or so, 65 hours most of the time. Admittedly I'm a workaholic—I love my job. But I've seen that with many of the other workaholics here too. This year, because we've instituted better structure and put our project management system into place, our guys are working far fewer hours than they used to. We certainly still have our crunches, but I know for a fact that a lot fewer people are spending their weekends and nights at the office. And yet we're still maintaining the quality of our games.

QUALITY OF LIFE AND STAFF RETENTION

MAP made a big difference in people's quality of life and employee retention too. "Avoiding burnout, that's key," Ted explains:

And one of the hot buttons in this industry is quality of life. There have been some major issues with a couple of the larger publishers where they have had lawsuits over inappropriate overtime. Quality of life was important for us before it was addressed in the industry because a lot of us are now having kids and realizing we need to spend some time with our families. Even before going to MAP, I was very vocal about the need for everyone here to have more balance in their lives. So figuring out how to achieve that balance provided yet another reason to go to MAP. I wanted ideas on how to achieve a more structured approach to creating games so we could all spend more time with our families. I have to say it is generally paying off.

Staff retention in the video game industry is notoriously low, but Insomniac has historically had a high retention rate. MAP's insistence on setting clear goals and instituting more accountability has helped keep that rate high. "We have not been without casualties," Ted says.

At this point, out of 155 people, I think we have lost 7 people. And the majority of those people who left, when asked why they left, said, "I really liked it when we were smaller." At the same time, I know for a fact that a few of those people do not like structure. They told me they prefer to be left on their own, finish up their stuff, and show it when it's done. That used to be our approach when we were smaller, but we can't do that anymore. There are too many people involved with a project; there has to be constant communication. This new structure doesn't work for everybody, but that's OK. We knew that to make an omelet, you've got to break eggs.

THE BIG SURPRISE

Ted's people are not traditional career builders. They don't focus on medical plans, 401(k)s, or heaven forbid, pensions. The bonuses they receive when a game sells well are welcome, sure. But what really drives them is passion. What they love is the hunt, the quest for something new, something totally engaging, a game that pushes out the frontiers of their world and culture. What they detest above all is tedium. Routine. A game they can master with little or no effort. In their world the biggest enemy—and the biggest demotivator—is boredom.

It is here that implementing the MAP system produced the biggest surprise. It did not generate resistance or boredom. Nor did the MAP tools dull the team's creative energy; they just channeled it in a clearer, more focused direction. "These very simple tools, they liberate you," Ted says.

> Creative people need—maybe more so than other people—simple tools so they can get the mundane stuff out of the way and do what they love. Your people aren't going to be driven by bonuses or medical plans or anything that's corporate by way of incentive; they're here for the juice. They're here to express themselves. So you have to figure out a structure that helps them do that and keeps everything they don't want to do out of the way. MAP, by streamlining the system and giving you some order and simple tools, helps you do that. MAP didn't present us with things we couldn't understand. They just helped us realize what we already knew: common sense and an organized approach would help liberate us. When you have goals you tend to be more efficient. You know what's going on, and therefore more of your time is freed up to be creative.

HELPING YOUR PEOPLE GROW

One of Ted's biggest ongoing challenges is helping his team members grow, mature, and take on the responsibilities of management. Here again, the MAP system produced a surprise. "I thought people were going to be completely resistant to having goals set, to instituting more accountability, but the fact is we have a lot of very professional but creative folks here. We don't have any prima donnas, we don't have folks who are more about being 'the artiste.' We have folks who understand that to get things done you have to be efficient. To be the best artist you can be, you have to be efficient. They appreciated the additional structure we created because they recognized that this was liberating."

To help his people grow, Ted now regularly sends them to MAP's management and leadership seminars. After each workshop

Dorriah and Ted discuss how his people performed and how Ted can best continue the grooming process. Still, grooming a staff like Ted's poses challenges:

> We still have an ongoing problem when new people come in. We're still struggling with how to educate them. They haven't been here through the whole transformation from garage developer to where we are now. We have a long way to go in terms of becoming the company that I would like us to be because we're still not close to efficient. I would love for our games to be a turnkey process. I'd like to have a very clear preproduction cycle, where there are steps that are taken to make the game, then an efficient production cycle, and a good, clear postproduction cycle. I think we're still a few years away from that.

Writing It Down

In grooming his people and working hard to develop that turnkey process, Ted has come to see the value of writing it down:

> MAP has forced us to keep better records of things: we have minutes for most of our meetings, and those include postmortem meetings, and they're all available on our SharePoint site. We can go back and see what really bit us in the ass on our last project and fix the problems the next time through. We have had a habit through the last ten years of making the same mistakes over and over again. I think we're at the point where we won't be doing that as frequently. We had been only as good as our memory, my memory. We tried to bring the lessons forward each time to get a little bit better, but it wasn't systematic. We were still a garage company really. Now we are definitely putting many more systems in place, and we never had systems before 2004. These systems will stay with us as we transition from platform to platform.

Empowering Your People

As Ted has learned, when it comes to managing creative people, you can't dictate; you have to empower.

Almost without exception people here are creative. Whether they're a designer, an engine programmer, or a character artist, people are constantly contributing ideas to the projects, and that's an environment that we have fostered from the very beginning. We constantly ask for people's feedback. We can't make the games that we make without having many, many people contribute because there's much more going on than one person can possibly come up with. Most of the people here are interested in collaborating. So you have to work hard at getting buy-in from team members. Plus everyone has to feel creatively engaged, they have to feel like the whole company is there working for them as well as they're working for the company. The way we do that is we don't micromanage. We give everybody in the company a lot of freedom to create and to suggest—versus being told what to do. And that's at every level of the company. So from the bottom up you've got a lot of people feeling like they can create. They're not being constrained.

THE ULTIMATE PAYOFF

Ted Price has come to understand a fundamental truth. Creative people want and need one thing above all others: that freedom to create. They want an environment where they will be empowered to create and, when they succeed, one that will give them the pride and recognition they crave. As any serious actor will tell you, while actors might enjoy the money they earn, what really draws them back again and again is the applause of the public and the appreciation of their peers. Their chosen medium is different, but at heart Ted's young creators are really no different. They want to be free to create and free to pursue their dreams. At the close of a long conversation, Ted Price brings it all together in a single, illuminating insight, one that casts light into every cell of himself and his creative team at Insomniac Games: "That's what's fun about games. Games allow you to make your craziest dreams come to life, no matter what type of game you're making, because there's no script. You're pulling it out of your head every single time."

Thanks, Ted. May your experience and wisdom inspire other young creators as they pursue their own passions, dreams, and destinies, making our own dreams so much richer in the process.

The Bottom Line

1. Don't be fooled: you *can* manage the creative process.
2. To do it, start with the basics: vision, mission, values; a strong, written business plan; accountability; and alignment and buy-in.
3. Learn from Ted: always be agile, be flexible. And never be afraid to drop a project and change course.
4. Understand what you do well, and stay focused on that.
5. Set time management priorities—and stick to them.
6. Keep balance in your life. You may be prepared to work eighty hours a week to produce a winning product, but you don't want to lose your spouse and your children along the way.

CHAPTER THIRTEEN

DRAMATIC RESULTS

The pictures are enchanting.

In one a young boy holds up a brightly colored mask he created, and he's beaming with pride. In another a young girl looks up from her painting, and in her smile you can see her excitement and her sense of accomplishment. And in a third another girl is sitting in front of her Math in a Basket project, and she's thrusting both arms skyward in a glorious expression of pride and victory. When you see these pictures, one feeling comes through loud and strong: these kids are happy, they're succeeding, they feel proud, and they feel empowered. But that, my friends, is just the beginning of the story.

Not long before these pictures were taken, these kids—like thousands of others in the Long Beach, California, school system—were failing in school. And they were failing in life. Many come from immigrant families brand-new to America. Many come from broken homes. Many come from parents who themselves have no basic skills in reading, math, or the English language. Schools across America call kids like these *disadvantaged* or *at risk*, and that is to put the case mildly. The plain truth is that most of these kids are condemned to fail; no one has helped them build a foundation for success. For years that was true in Long Beach too, until Christi Wilkins came along and vowed to help.

Christi understands the many challenges that immigrant kids face when they first come to our shores; she was once an immigrant kid herself. But Christi made it through, and to help other disadvantaged kids do the same she created a pioneering nonprofit organization called Dramatic Results. Her group goes into schools and puts on twelve- to twenty-four-week special programs for these at-risk kids. More specifically, her group of specially trained teachers uses art, music, and creative play to get kids excited about learning and to help them absorb basic skills in math, reading, and English. (To learn more, see the organization's Web site at www.dramaticresults.org.)

One innovative program that Christi's teachers developed is called Math in a Basket. Here, the teachers have the kids weave their own colorful baskets, using the weaving process to teach an array of basic math skills. Math in a Basket gets results. In 2005, kids who had been through the program scored higher on standardized math tests than the norm throughout California—some 20 points higher! Other creative programs from Dramatic Results help at-risk kids realize that learning can be fun, instead of an exercise in frustration and failure. At the same time, the program helps kids build self-esteem, improve their language skills, and generally feel more comfortable at school and in life. One further measurement of progress is very telling: over the course of one academic year a full 75 percent of Christi's kids improve their grades in reading and math.

With local schools and community leaders, Christi and her program have long since proved their worth, credibility, and cost effectiveness. Since its launch in 1992, Dramatic Results has helped some 10,000 at-risk kids in Long Beach and (in a sister program) in Oakland, California. And what is the cost to the family of the at-risk child? Not a single dime. Christi's entire program is funded by outside grants and by the schools themselves. From the schools' perspective, helping to subsidize Christi makes perfect business sense: it is cheaper for them than staffing and running their own programs for special needs kids. As a result the Long Beach school system and the local business community are now helping Christi and her team expand their mission across the school district and beyond. They win, Dramatic Results wins, and above all, the kids win.

Those are the basics. But I do want to delve deeper into Christi's story, and I want to do so for a number of reasons. As I said at the outset of this book the MAP management system can help transform big corporations like Wells Fargo and also small start-up companies like Michael Caito's Restaurants on the Run. MAP can also transform concrete companies like Steve Campbell's, city administrations like Jose Pulido's, and even highly creative companies like Ted Price's. But Christi Wilkins's story moves us into a whole new realm, the realm of nonprofit organizations. Many nonprofit groups do fine work and are very well managed. Many others, though, suffer from poor administration, a total lack of discipline and accountability, poor focus, and what in the private sector would be called a poor return on investment. That is not a blueprint for success. As Christi herself will tell you, nobility of purpose is a wonderful starting point, but if you fail to manage your organization effectively, it will never fulfill its mission.

MAP can help. And Christi's story will show you how.

First of all, why is Dramatic Results getting enthusiastic support from both the school district and the business community in Long Beach? I believe you could sum it up in a single word: *credibility.* Christi and her team have established their credibility in the Long Beach area and also in the wider educational community. And that credibility flows from two interlocking sources. First, their pioneering work is showing proven—and measurable—results. And second, Christi runs her nonprofit organization as though it were a for-profit company, meaning she runs it with the same rock-solid business fundamentals. She and her team have a strong mission statement, a clear values statement, and a far-sighted but flexible business plan. Her staff are disciplined, aligned, passionate, and committed. They know exactly what their Vital Factors are, and they stay focused, month in, month out, on the Vital Few. They also measure their results on a regular basis, manage to their values, and emphasize clear communication among themselves and also with their partner schools, who are in effect, their *clients.* In sum, Christi Wilkins and her team are on a noble mission, and we are proud to say that today their mission is powered by MAP.

But there is something more. As you will see, Christi's pioneering work with at-risk kids dovetails perfectly with how we at MAP pursue our own mission and purpose. She and her team prepare children for success; we at MAP prepare people and organizations for success. Our goals converge, and it has been our privilege to learn from each other. Now, let me give the floor to Christi, for no one tells her story more eloquently than she does.

CHRISTI'S AWAKENING

"I was born here in the United States," Christi begins, "but before I turned two, my mother and I moved to Iran. So for my formative years I was raised as a Farsi-speaking Muslim child. When my mother decided it was time to return to the United States, it was quite an adventure. First, because we were smuggled out of Iran, via the U.S. military. And second, upon returning to the United States we settled into a very tiny rural community in central California, a region that I like to affectionately call Smith & Wesson Country."

Coming "home," Christi faced turmoil on every front. She was American, but she spoke no English, and many of her teachers were thoroughly confused. And they themselves had no skills for teaching Christi a brand-new language. How to reach her? How to integrate her into the close-knit community inside the school? And how in the world could they teach her reading and math when she spoke no English? In New York or Chicago or San Francisco the school systems have well-established programs for integrating new-comers, but there was no such thing in her corner of rural Cali-fornia. Christi was equally lost when it came to how to behave at school. In Iran the relationship between teacher and child was entirely different, and schoolwork was entirely different too, right down to the way kids take tests. On top of that, there was another barrier between Christi and her new schoolmates: she knew noth-ing at all about American culture. The food was new, the music was new, TV was new, and the sports were new. To make matters more complicated still, Christi and her mom returned in 1967, and the entire nation was in turmoil over the war in Vietnam. Christi watched the drama on the nightly news, but she understood next to nothing of what she saw. She was a young girl who felt terribly alone and totally estranged from the world around her—not exactly a formula for happiness or future success.

"I came back to this country not speaking the language, not knowing anything about the culture, and it was quite a shock for me," Christi says.

> I was blond-haired and blue-eyed and people expected me to be fluent in English. They responded with a lot of shock when I would

open my mouth and out would come Farsi or some garbled English. At that point they still gave IQ tests, and needless to say I did not know enough English to even complete a test. They told my mother that they had determined I was marginally retarded and suggested special education for me. That in itself is a complicated process in a rural community, because the resources are so sparse and far between. I would have been seven. My mother was offended and said "No, my child is *not* retarded! It's a language and cultural issue."

Just imagine it: here was a bright young girl being deemed retarded because the school failed to appreciate her special circumstances. How many other immigrant kids face that same cruel judgment every single day? Christi, though, was lucky. When faced with that same situation, many immigrant parents simply abide by the school's decision; they have no understanding of what it means to have their child labeled *retarded,* and they don't know how to respond. So their kids are often stigmatized from day one, setting them up for long-term failure in school and in life. Fortunately for Christi her mother stood her ground: "She spent the next six months working hard to teach me English. She is American and fluent in English so it wasn't a problem," Christi says. "For the next six months, between watching the war live on TV and watching lots of other TV and having my mother work with me, I learned English. And by some miracle, six months or so later, when they retested me, I was no longer retarded. In fact they decided they needed to put me ahead a grade."

For Christi this experience was the first in a series of profound shocks. "It started a love/hate relationship with education," she says.

It was compounded by two other factors. One was that within the first week of attending school I managed to be suspended for cheating. My mother had to come in and explain what I was doing when the teacher handed out the test and I took the test in my hand and promptly walked over to the desk of a girl who I had early on identified as the smartest kid in the class. Whereas in U.S. culture that's considered cheating, that's a very careful learning pattern that I had learned in Iran in school. There everything is done collaboratively in groups, on small rectangular chalkboards. You don't have separate desks and pencils like we do in the U.S. So

I was labeled as a cheater despite the fact that what I did was based on a strong cultural difference.

From there things got even worse, with a second traumatizing experience. "When we arrived from Iran, my mother was eight months pregnant," Christi continues.

Unfortunately, after she gave birth to my brother, at three months old he was murdered by my grandfather, and unfortunately, I was the only witness to it. That was in an era in which there was a lot of drug running happening in the area, and my grandfather was deeply involved. So was the local sheriff. So there was nothing done about the murder. Also, neither the school district nor the county had the resources to deal with those kind of social service issues. Help didn't exist. So when I did start school, I was angry, confused, and not liking a lot of what I was learning about the U.S. culture. That really helped shape my early view of education in America, and that set a very strong tone. When I was fifteen, I chose to drop out.

Art was her ultimate salvation. For seven years she wandered around the United States and beyond, eventually earning her high school diploma through a graduate equivalency program, then gathering college units here and there toward a bachelor of arts degree. Christi might have continued to drift if she hadn't met two mentors who took her in hand.

Throughout all this, what was so pronounced for me was art and the fact that I had two people take real interest in me, two adults. One was an artist and the other was a librarian. Both these people chose to see real promise in me and put a lot of energy and heart and soul into helping me. Those are two people I've never forgotten, and what I learned from both of them was the absolute joy and power that comes from art and books, and they really turned me on to reading and art. Those two lifelines have always stayed with me, and it's really my love for both of those things that prompted me, at the age of thirty-two, to start Dramatic Results.

By then Christi brought wide horizons to her calling. In London she had worked in marketing for the Royal Institute of British

Architects. In Denmark she had worked on a dairy farm, and in Germany she had gone to school. She had also traveled widely in South and Central America and in the Middle East. The impact was profound. "It gave me very different views and perspectives," she says. "Upon returning from Denmark in 1988, I went to work for a nonprofit theater company in Orange County. Before then, I had never heard of such a thing as a nonprofit. There I found that I had some saleable skills in writing and grant writing and that I had a good business head."

But Christi became frustrated there. She wanted to make a real difference in people's lives, and in her view the theater company was not fulfilling its potential. "I had very strong ideas and was willing to stand behind them. And I could tolerate risk. My poor mother and boyfriend at that point were putting up with my kvetching, and finally my mother said, 'Here's $2,500; I'm tired of hearing you complain. Go do something, and I don't want to hear about it anymore!'"

With that $2,500 as her seed money Christi launched a pilot program in an elementary school and secured nonprofit status for Dramatic Results. She was on her way. "In the course of the successive fourteen years, we've gone from serving 15 children in one school to serving an average of 1,200 students a year with a staff of 22," she says. And from day one she knew the importance of accountability and having results that could be measured and demonstrated to skeptical eyes in the worlds of education, business, and local politics. "We started doing very heavy-duty program evaluation from day one, where we were looking at the academic impact of art on kids," she says. "I really wanted to establish the measurable linkage between kids' involvement in arts and their academic progress." In order to measure results, she and her team examined report cards and standardized test scores, and they did extensive surveys with both teachers and students before and after the Dramatic Results programs. And for fourteen years Christi's sense of purpose has never wavered: "The mission comes from my heart, which is that I want no child to ever have to experience what I did in the public school system. My mission is for every child to experience success in school through hands-on arts experiences."

Why does her approach work? "It works because we do everything on a tiny ratio of one adult to every five children, which is a stark contrast to the one to thirty ratio in a standard public class-room," she explains. Moreover, their approach with each child is long term:

> Rather than come in for a fitness spurt, a one- or two-hour work-shop, we have the same grown-ups work with the same children consistently each week for anywhere from three months to three years. Same child, same grown-up. There's a tremendous amount of bonding and personalized attention that happens between the grown-up and the child over an extended period of time. And we do art, we laugh, we say nice things to each other, we practice com-pliments, we learn social skills, we learn trust, and what it's like to be a fuller human being and to express ourselves. I have yet to meet any child or adult who doesn't like the opportunity to create and express themselves.

Their focus is tight:

> Our target group is fourth to sixth graders, approximately ten to twelve years old. The reason we targeted that age in particular was that empirical research showed that a child's decision to drop out of school was fostered, or the seed was planted, in third and fourth grade. By then the child starts to feel that they can't win, that school is not a good place for them. Usually by the time they've hit middle school they've pretty much decided—those who are going to drop out—that that's the path they're going to take. So from fourth through sixth grade is a really critical time.

Each child who goes into Dramatic Results is selected by a school counselor as "a child at risk of dropping out without more immediate and intensive intervention."

With those kids designated as at risk, Christi and her team face challenges right from the first minute:

> The first time we step onto a campus, when no one knows us, the kids who are selected come into the space we're in, and almost to the last child they'll look at the group and say, "Oh, this is a group for bad kids," or, "Oh, this is a group for dummies." Very strong negative labels are attached. We spend the first two weeks just trying to reassure them that they're not stupid or bad and in

fact it's a privilege to be with us and they get to do art when the other kids don't. What we find is that at the end of whatever amount of time we have with them, twelve weeks, three years, we typically have other kids asking to be added to the list and to be included in the group. It goes from being stigmatized to "I want to do it too!"

Like any organization, Dramatic Results needs alignment and buy-in, from staff and from partner schools. At the outset, Christi says, for many schools employing Dramatic Results is a leap of faith.

They give us time on their campuses to take these kids out of class when, especially with the No Child Left Behind program, schools are under horrendous pressure to bring up test scores and show that the kids are meeting all necessary requirements to go on to the next grade level. So they're taking a big leap to have us come in and take their poorest performing kids out when, in theory, they're the ones who need more core instruction than anyone else. Secondly, they give us space to do it and access to the family, which is wonderful, especially for the counselors. Thirdly, and really critical, is they provide us with financial support.

One clear measure of Christi's success is the evolution of that financial support. "Back in 1992, after having the first program launched, the schools were so pleased they gave us a $2,500 contract," she says. "That contract has now grown into an annual support of over $100,000 a year from the school district. In the case of Long Beach Unified, we are the single and only program they support like that."

From a business perspective you might call this *outsourcing*. The Long Beach and Oakland school systems are in effect outsourcing their at-risk kids to Dramatic Results. Christi understands that perspective: "People sometimes have difficulty knowing how to categorize us. Sometimes they want to call us art therapists, sometimes educators, social workers. That's why we like the term *arts education*, because we like staying in a gray area. None of my staff are licensed therapists, because that's not the angle from which we come. We come at it from the perspective of educators and artists."

Now, where does MAP fit into Christi's mission and management?

"My introduction to MAP was serendipitous. I was at a neighborhood event and I met Randy Halle, who at that point was CEO of MAP. I got to talking with him, and Randy expressed an interest in what we were doing. He then arranged for me to come in and experience one of their all-day seminars." This was a *Twelve O'Clock High* leadership seminar, and the facilitator was Dorriah Rogers. "She was terrific," Christi says, "and I really appreciated her style. She was able to make the lessons real and personal for each one of us, in ways that we could put toward our own work. It gave me a personal wake-up call for my management style. We like to say that 'when the student is ready, the teacher appears,' and it was like that for me with MAP."

Right from her first exposure to MAP, Christi realized that she needed to bring real structure to her organization and run it like a for-profit company—the same realization that Jose Pulido came to regarding running the City of San Fernando. At MAP Christi also came face to face with her tendency to wear the Big Red "S." All this was an important awakening. "Up to then, I express it as being a crustacean: I had the hard coat on the outside but it was all mushy on the inside," Christi says.

> I was the only administrative person, and I knew that if we were going to grow, I could not remain the sole administrator. I had to develop a team around me. I had a lot to learn about what kind of people are needed to make a good team and how to quantify the results, both so that I could justify the expense of our professional development and justify to our funders and our board the costs for having the overhead of administrators and management people. MAP has been wonderfully helpful in making that clear and quantifiable and helping us demonstrate the effectiveness and the need for core management to sustain the program.

For her next step in the MAP process, Christi came to Newport Beach for a three-day MAP workshop, and I, Lee Froschheiser, had the privilege of leading Christi's group. She and I were both thrilled to realize that her personal leadership style was already well in line with the model we teach at MAP. "What I found was a real eye-opener for me," Christi says now. "There is a very clear difference between nonprofits and for-profits in the way the decisions are made. What I found is that my style—which is much more common in the nonprofit world than in the for-profit world—is consensus building and team building."

At the workshop Christi also realized that by wearing the Big Red "S" she was losing on two fronts. First, she was disempowering her people. And second, she was so drawn into the minutiae of day-to-day management that she was neglecting one of the essential responsibilities of leadership: keeping her guiding vision clearly in focus. "I came away seeing how vital it is to keep enough distance between yourself and the people around you so that you as a leader can continue to see the big picture," she explains. "If you let yourself get too sucked into the day-to-day crises, all the things that are immediately in front of you, then not only will you not reach your goal but you're going to get sucked in and get it eaten up by the very problem you're trying to cure. What came across very clearly for me was that I needed to step back and truly look at myself differently. In my midnight hours I would try to capture the vision and process things in my head, and all day I was putting out fires." From that point forward she knew she had to build an effective management team, even though it would mean extra cost and overhead.

To her utter surprise, Christi's board immediately approved her decision. "I have to tell you it didn't take much to convince my board," she says. "They were looking at me saying, 'Hello, we've been waiting for this to happen, but you had to be ready to let go of some of the control in order to grow.'"

Once she did step back Christi could clearly see a problem that she says affects many people in the nonprofit world: burnout. "It's very common to come into the nonprofit world not from the perspective of making a lot of money but from having a passion for the particular issue. As a result, people are often working horrendously long hours with a lot of fatigue and a lot of financial and emotional uncertainties. That can wear people down. I think for my board, having us get involved with MAP, has reassured them that they're not as much at risk of losing me to burnout, and that I can in fact hold true to our vision for a much longer time."

Now, how has the MAP system transformed Dramatic Results? Working with Dorriah Rogers, Christi put together a strong management team, consisting of a staff director, an operations manager, and a lead teacher. To do that Christi used the DISC Behavioral Style Analysis to help her make good hires and to ensure that her team members had complementary skills and temperaments. Using MAP principles, Christi and her team also built a base of clear communication within their staff and for reaching out to their partner schools and the larger community. "It's been really nice because MAP and the MAP toolbox have helped us form a language to articulate what it is that we do, both internally and in our role in the community. It has also provided the rest of my management team, none of whom come from a business background, with a whole new vocabulary and structure by which they can relate to and compare themselves to for-profit organizations. They could never do that before."

The Warm, Fuzzy Blob Problem

Through MAP, Christi was able to solve a problem that many nonprofit organizations face, what she calls the "warm, fuzzy blob" problem. As she explains, many nonprofits produce results that are "warm and fuzzy" and not concrete or easily measurable. Unlike for-profit companies the nonprofits can't really judge their performance and results using bottom-line dollars and cents. How do you put a dollar figure, after all, on saving an at-risk child? More to the point, when you are dealing with outcomes that are warm and fuzzy how do you prove to your funders that your programs are cost effective and that their money is being well spent? Here, Christi says, the MAP system has been an enormous help:

> Dorriah helped us quantify what used to be a more social service, warm, fuzzy blob. She helped us see that no, what we do has sharp edges that can be measured. That's significant for us. One of the things Dorriah honed us down to is our need to measure the effectiveness of our programs on our classroom teachers, the ones we were interacting with, and find out from them, anecdotally, how did they like what we were doing, what was effective, and what needed to be changed. That's a very critical internal monitoring tool. We were able to assemble a series of questions that everybody agreed on, and we asked the classroom teachers to answer each

question on a scale of 1 to 10. How would you rate us on prompt-
ness, responsiveness to your children's needs, and the delivery of
curriculum? There were fifteen questions that we asked of twenty-
nine teachers in November, and we asked the same questions again
in April. It was really amazing for us to see the difference.

In my view, there is an important lesson here for all nonprofits: "What gets measured gets done." As you recall, that's one of
our favorite mantras at MAP, and it is just as important for nonprofits as it is for for-profit companies. Moreover, appropriate
measurements help you and your team define your Vital Factors,
and they give you a yardstick by which you can evaluate your
improvement. Christi saw the impact of that firsthand when those
twenty-nine teachers gave Dramatic Results its report card. "In
November 2004, on a scale of 1 to 10, our aggregate was 9.0,"
Christi says. "We were thrilled to get that, but we picked out the
comments and said, 'OK here's our next goal: let's try to get a 9.4.'
I was concerned that in April the score might go down because
the teachers and students would become more familiar with us.
My management came back and said, 'No, we're going to set a
goal of 9.4.' I said, 'OK, OK.' "

What happened next amazed Christi:

We took the anecdotal surveys and the information that came from
the teachers and applied it immediately to our program. We started
making the exact changes they suggested. When it came time in
April 2005 to do the survey again we were thrilled because the
aggregate was 9.4. We hit our goal. That did two powerful things
for us. One, it really did help us realize we were doing something
good and effective, and it gave us a number to apply to it. It also
gave our staff a sense of, "Hey, I picked a number out of the air and
we achieved that number. Next year I want 9.5." It was really fun to
see the management team get revved up about that and start to set
future goals for themselves like that.

That process, in sum, put an end to the warm, fuzzy blob problem, and it gave Christi and her team real, measurable results that
they could show their partner schools and their funders. One simple MAP tool transformed a critical aspect of their entire operation.

INTERNALIZING MAP

As we have seen in earlier chapters, when a company defines its Vital Factors and its Vital Few, the key measurables come in such realms as cost per delivery (Restaurants on the Run), profit per project (Campbell Concrete), and new sales per month (Stearns Lending). But how does a nonprofit like Christi's define its Vital Factors and its Vital Few? In a larger sense too, does the process of the monthly Vital Factor Meeting make sense for a nonprofit organization? Christi Wilkins says the answer is a resounding yes, with some modifications.

"With Dorriah here, we have the Vital Factor Meeting on a monthly basis," Christi says. "With her, they're very structured. But we also have on a weekly basis our internal management meeting where we don't follow that set protocol and we don't use those tools exactly." But the MAP principles are now deeply ingrained anyway. "We find that we keep coming back to, 'OK, have we accomplished what we said we'd do the last time? What's the follow-up?' The holding of accountability for each other is significantly higher now. The process has been really helpful. It's a living entity that gets readjusted as we go. We constantly say, why are we here? What do we need to do to make sure we're the best thing since sliced bread out there—and that we're doing the very best we can?"

Through the MAP process Christi herself has grown as a leader. Gone are the days when she ran Dramatic Results like a one-woman show. She has built her team, given the team members a system of management and a common vocabulary, and now she understands—and practices—the MAP precept of empower your people. The result has been a complete transformation of both the management process and the internal chemistry of her organization.

"Each one of us has such a distinctive role, whether it's operations, human resources, program delivery, or fundraising," Christi says.

Each of us also comes in with a unique perspective, so it's very easy within our group of four to have the discussions and come at issues from different angles. And it has changed my role and the way we work. For example, for so long I was accustomed to deciding which programs we were going to do, and depending on how much money I raised for that program, I determined how much of that particular program we did. Now management team members have started coming in, saying, "No, that's not balanced; we need more of this, more of that." And they are able to ask questions, such as, "Is this realistic?" "Is this not?" I make far fewer unilateral decisions than I ever have before. And there's more trust in the process after having gone through it with my staff.

Dorriah Rogers has worked closely with Christi and her team, and she considers it a rare privilege. "I was truly touched by Christi and her management team. My approach with them was very different than with my usual business clients," Dorriah explains. "They are kind, gentle people who are deeply passionate and inspired by their work. I felt my job was to nurture them, not bully them. My approach needed to be a mixture of compassion and business acumen, a way to touch their core with how the MAP system could impact the mission of their organization.

"I decided to do this in several ways," Dorriah continues:

> First, I decided to do some work pro bono, as a way to contribute to their cause and show them my commitment. Second, I decided to guide them through the process in a way that would create a for-profit mind-set in a nonprofit setting, without sacrificing the warm, fuzzy blob. And finally, I worked hard to put them in touch with my higher-profile corporate clients in an effort to help them find additional funding. As a result I am honored to be a part of something that is so worthwhile doing. Christi is an amazing being. With her intelligence and determination she could easily be making a six-figure salary in a corporate setting. But she has chosen the higher calling, and for that she is my hero.

Well said, Dorriah. And we totally agree. All of us at MAP salute you, Christi. You have taken the MAP system, made it your own, and used it to further your noble mission. For us, it is a source of deep and lasting satisfaction to think that in some small way we are helping you save those kids and helping them build a foundation for success. Your work inspires us all, and we would love to see it become a model for school programs all across America.

The Bottom Line

1. As a leader, keep your eye on your long-term vision and mission. Don't let yourself get bogged down in day-to-day trivia. Delegate that.
2. Even with a warm, fuzzy mission, you can find ways to measure your Vital Factors and improve your performance. Do it.
3. Measuring your progress helps build pride and recognition among your team members.
4. Whether your organization is a for-profit business, a nonprofit group, or even a city government, the Vital Factors process works. Indeed, in all three arenas it can create *dramatic results*.

CHAPTER FOURTEEN

THE LIFE PLAN

Again, it is time to go deeper. Much deeper.

Through the stories of Ted Price and Christi Wilkins, you have seen how the MAP system and its Vital Factor tools can be adapted to suit the needs of highly creative companies and of non-profit organizations. And through the stories of Bob Wexler and Chris Thompson you have seen how the MAP process helps people grow and mature as leaders and managers. You have also seen how profound and far-reaching the changes can be when leaders and their people have learned and absorbed the MAP system and have woven it into the daily operations of their company or organization.

In the next three chapters I want to go many steps further. I want to show you how you can use the MAP system and tools to manage your personal life and to fulfill your highest goals and ambitions. Do you want to build a happy, fulfilling marriage or relationship? Achieve financial independence? Raise happy, successful children? Maintain tiptop health and fitness? Whatever goals you set for yourself, the MAP process and its Vital Factor tools can help you achieve them. You have already seen how the MAP system can transform companies and organizations; now you are going to see how MAP can transform your life. As you will see, the process is the same as with your business: define your mission, your vision, and your values, and then set down—in writing!—the specific goals that you want to achieve. Next, formulate an action plan with clear, concrete, and measurable action steps—with target completion dates—that will guide you on your way. And here is the best news:

there is one powerful, easy-to-use MAP tool that can really anchor and guide the transformation process for you. And this same tool can lead you into an exciting period of personal growth and development. I am speaking of the Life Plan.

For many years I and many other MAP coaches have been helping people sit down and write for themselves a comprehensive Life Plan. And I can tell you this: the process works. Doing a Life Plan can be one of the most illuminating—and most empowering— steps that you will ever take. The process itself is fun, it's easy, and the impact can be enormous. Over and over I have had people tell me, "Lee, doing a Life Plan transformed everything. For the first time, I now have a roadmap of where I want to go—and how to get there. It's one of the best things I've ever done for myself. Thank you, thank you!"

Still, as always, I don't want you to just take my word for it. I want you to see for yourself what the Life Plan process can do, and I want you to hear about it right from the horse's mouth. With that in mind I asked several of our coaches at MAP this basic question: Who would be best to describe the Life Plan process? Who could best explain how to do a Life Plan and how to use it effectively to transform your life? All the answers I received pointed to one man: Joe Daquino. Joe is leading a happy, fulfilling, and balanced life, and he has used his Life Plan as both foundation and guide. In fact he calls his Life Plan "the book of my life." Joe has elevated the Life Plan process to a living art form, and I want you to hear about it directly from him. Besides, Joe can tell his personal story far more eloquently than I can.

"I was born and raised in Cleveland," Joe begins.

Ours was a single parent family, and I have two brothers younger than me. We were raised by my mom, and it was not a very eventful upbringing. I wasn't the first person in my family to go to college because my uncle went to Oberlin and had a PhD in music and was a concert pianist. After him I was the first of my generation to go to college. I went to Case Western Reserve University in Cleveland. I thought I was going to be a doctor until I realized I didn't really care for sick people all that much. So then I did a major in English and psychology—without even knowing what I was going to do with that.

After graduation, on a lark, Joe packed his bags and moved to Southern California. And right away he heard about an opportunity at an outfit called TL Enterprises, which published journals and ran specialized programs for people with RVs, recreational vehicles. "A friend of a friend who worked for a publishing company said, 'You have a degree in English, maybe you should interview over there; they need an editor.'" Joe knew nothing about RVs or the vast subculture that had grown up around them, but he thought, "What the heck; I need a job. I'll go check it out."

Joe interviewed for an editor's position, but he didn't get the job. Still, that was not the end of the story. "The woman who interviewed me liked me so much that she wanted to get me in," Joe explains. "She said, 'Why don't you work in our customer service area until we have something more appropriate?' So I did that for a few months making $6 an hour answering telephones. Then I moved into a marketing position with publications, and that's what started my career here."

At that time, TL Enterprises was so named because it published a magazine called *Trailer Life*, and that was its flagship publication. But the company also put out a whole range of other publications, making TL Enterprises one of the mainstays of the entire RV industry. "That original part of the company that I came to work for was headed up by a guy named Art Rouse. He had bought a magazine called *Western Trailer Life* in the 1940s and that started it off. That became *Trailer Life*, which we still publish. He then bought another magazine called *Trailer News*." From there, Art Rouse made what proved to be a brilliant acquisition: a small magazine that also operated a small RV club called the Good Sam Club.

"Art didn't care for the club," Joe recalls:

> He thought it was cumbersome and didn't want to be bothered with it; he was more interested in the magazine. The club idea was that if you have a "Good Sam" sticker on your RV and you break down, someone else will help you—being a Good Samaritan. Art was an advertising man and he didn't know what to do with the concept. To try to kill the club he started charging people to be a member because up to then it was free. Well, lo and behold, people started sending in their money! So instead of killing it, by charging money the club actually became profitable. He said, "Wow, maybe we're onto something!"

Indeed they were. And Joe saw what happened next: "When I came to the company in 1984, the club had 380,000 members and today it has 1 million. It grew and grew, and now we're up to 1 million Good Sam customers. The company has a lot more names in the computer customer database, but the Good Sam Club is at a million." The Good Sam Club has been a powerful engine for marketing, building revenue, and providing a range of services to RV owners and for building a strong brand loyalty in the process. "One of the key benefits of the club is that you get a discount on RV camping at 1,700 places," Joe explains. "My group goes out and gets those places to participate in that discount offer. So as a revenue-generating and profit-generating operation it's a very small part of the pie, but for the company it's very strategic. Because it is the No. 1 one benefit for the club and that makes it the engine which drives this entire enterprise."

This "entire enterprise" is now named Affinity Group, Inc., an entity created initially from the merger of TL Enterprises and two other companies, and what a diverse organization it is. Affinity is a publishing giant and provides insurance products and a wide range of other support services as well. Over the past twenty-plus years, Joe's job and responsibilities have grown in tandem. "I work in a division called multimedia, which is called that because there are three big publishing divisions in this company. Two of which are RV related and one which isn't. Of the RV-related ones, I do the annual publications and database publications. I do the big directories of places to go to use your recreational vehicles. One is called *Woodall's,* and there is another one called *Trailer Life,* and they have about 15,000 listings of places where you can go and use your RV. We also publish books and CD-ROM titles specific to RVing. We publish an atlas that integrates directory information with maps from MapQuest, and we have Web sites for these publications online."

Talk about synergy. Each part of the Affinity Group cross-fertilizes others. Joe explains how it works: "Someone joins our Good Sam Club, and we immediately go in and try to market all of our things to them, including our monthly magazines, the insurance products, and the products of a select group of partners that we work with as well. We are the Microsoft when it comes to what you can and should do with your RV. We provide all the information, the services, emergency road service, insurance, and things like that. We provide locations where you can get discounts on it. There is virtually nothing we don't do."

In many ways RV owners are a tribe unto themselves, and the Affinity Group keeps its eye focused tightly on serving their needs—and protecting the RV culture. A lot of campsites across America, for instance, feature nudity on their sites, but Joe's group won't go near those. "They would love to be listed in our publications, but we don't list them because that would be offensive to our members, many of whom are salt-of-the-earth, 'greatest generation' kind of people. We're very protective of them and take our responsibility to them very seriously. I think that's one of the reasons we've been so successful. We know our base and we cater to them."

Now here comes the best part, one that I feel carries important lessons for all managers and business leaders: Joe has stayed loyal to his company for reasons that extend far beyond business or money. Joe's company and Joe's boss, president, and CEO, Mike Schneider, have actively helped Joe grow as a leader and as individual. They have empowered him and given him a wide terrain where he can be creative and where he can go to work every day with excitement and a true sense of fulfillment. He is also constantly receiving positive energy from those two great motivators: recognition and pride. Moreover, with company support Joe's personal growth over the past two decades has been guided by two empowering coaches and mentors.

His first mentor was Dale Thoreson, who was running a publications division at TL Enterprises when Joe came aboard. "Dale was very passionate about this place, and he was one of these guys who had a ton of integrity and was a dynamo," Joe says.

> He saw a lot of potential in me. I was not as confident then as I might seem now. In fact I was green. I didn't have any marketing or business background or anything—studying Shakespeare for four years doesn't prepare you for a career in publishing for RVs and campers. But he saw something and was very patient and developed me; he let my creativity come out. He nurtured that. He used to say that I was very businesslike and very methodical and logical but also very creative. He said it was really difficult to find that combination. To this day, whenever I doubt myself I think back to that and think

this was a guy I respected a lot and he saw these things in me, and I'm forever grateful for him.

What's the lesson here? Dale helped Joe grow and develop his confidence by believing in him; trusting him; encouraging, coaching, and supporting him. And that's first-rate leadership. Dale's personal mentoring and nurturing helped Joe develop a strong and lasting bond to the company. He also taught Joe, by his own example, that good managers work hard to be good teachers and coaches—and that pays demonstrable dividends for your company. A case in point: over the past twenty years Joe has had many other job opportunities, but he has always turned them down. Affinity, Joe feels, is home, it's family, it's where he belongs. "This is a very enlightened company," he says. "It gives people freedom—there are a lot of soft benefits to this place. We have rules and regulations, but if someone is sick or their kid is sick, you can work at home, things like that. This place treats the person as a whole person. It's more of a family atmosphere without being too intrusive. Just the right combination for me."

Let me step in here and offer a few reflections from a MAP point of view. As I said right in Chapter One, the best-run companies understand, in their marrow, that their most important resource is their people. They understand, therefore, the need to empower their people and help them grow. They stand by them; they support them; they care about them as individuals. Joe's company gets very high marks from me in this regard. But that is not the end of Joe's story; in many ways it is just the beginning.

LIFE COACHING

"After Dale Thoreson left the company, I was promoted and put in charge of a publications division," Joe says.

> But I realized I needed tools to manage; I still didn't have what I thought it took to be an effective manager. I had confidence issues and things like that, and I wanted some kind of system, some kind of structure. I found out about MAP through somebody who worked with me, and I took a three-day workshop. Dane Henriksen was the leader of it, and I immediately saw something both in the

system and the workshop leader that I wanted. I responded to the discipline and the structure. So I talked to Dane after the workshop was over.

At that stage Joe had no clear idea what he was seeking. He just knew that he wanted to grow as a manager and as a person, and he had some intuitive sense that MAP and Dane could bring him the knowledge and wisdom that he craved.

> I went up to Dane and I said, "I enjoyed this very much; I don't want to go back and have this be it." I really didn't understand the extent to which MAP could help. I said, "Would you be willing to work with me one on one?" and he said yes. He said he wanted to work with me because, he said, "You're a natural born leader." I'll never forget that. And I thought, "Gosh, how would he know that? I don't even know that. How does he know that?" Here's a second guy who saw some potential in me and was willing to work with me to try to pull it out. And that's how it started. We started meeting once a month, and it was quite an adventure.

Values were always central to their discussions. And Dane had the exact values that Joe wanted to better understand and cultivate.

> I can't tell you how I knew, but I knew that Dane had a lot of discipline, integrity, and energy. He was principled. I don't know where I got that from, but I picked up on it, and I wanted to be principled and have integrity and I wanted to be associated with people who did. That was what appealed to me. I wanted to be treated like a whole person. Something resonated for me with him. That's why, for the first time in my career, I came out and said, "I'm gay." He was the first person that I came across in my career that I told that to because I wanted to work with him as a whole person, not just as a client or someone saying, "I have a problem employee, what do I do about this person?" I wanted to have that kind of a relationship with him, and he was completely cool, beyond cool. He was a champion, and that's when I knew—this could be really good.

Like Joe, Dane did not see his work with Joe as only job related. For Dane this was a much deeper calling, what we at MAP call *life coaching*. Dane saw enormous potential in Joe. He knew that Joe had grown up without a father, and Dane sensed that he could help Joe enter an important new phase of growth and maturity. Dane and his wife began treating Joe like a member of their own family, as they would later do with Chris Thompson of Wexler Video. They would get together away from work and talk about everything from books to spirituality to pop music.

"Dane's just a great guy," Joe says.

> He wanted to know things about me, things I was interested in. If I casually mentioned I was interested in something, he'd go out and find books about it and bring them to me. Not even things to do with business. If I mentioned I was interested in photography, the next time I saw him he'd say, "Joe, I found these books on this photographer; I want you to take a look." Early on I told him I was a fan of Madonna, so he went out and he got a book on her and read about her, and I got him interested in her music. It's more profound, of course, than liking Madonna: he was just taking an interest in me as a person and wanting to engage in things I'm interested in and wanting me to get interested in things he is interested in.

In Dane's view—and in the view of all our best MAP coaches—this joining of business and personal coaching is one of the most important aspects of our work. For me, as for Dane, it is also one of the most rewarding and fulfilling. In earlier chapters I talked about my personal coaching of Michael Caito and Bill de la Viña. And in talking about Eric Gillberg I emphasized how he designed the entire MAP process to foster long-term relationships with our clients. Our aim, right from the beginning, has been to serve our clients as business consultants, yes, but also as trusted family advisers and life coaches. We want to help them grow in every aspect of their lives. In order to do that we first have to establish a foundation of trust, confidence, and mutual respect. We don't do that as a business strategy; we do it because we care about our clients as people. And we do it because, first and foremost, we are teachers and coaches by temperament and calling. That we have also learned many secrets about business and management only reinforces our primary instinct, which is to help. And as Joe Daquino immediately understood, the personal caring we show our clients is also a way of modeling that same behavior for the men and women we are teaching to be better leaders and managers. We stress and teach personal growth to them, and we hope that they, in turn, will stress and teach personal growth to their people. With Joe that process has worked beautifully.

"MAP helps me make sure that our people are being developed," Joe explains.

> There aren't a lot of opportunities for promotion within this department because there's not a lot of turnover and we're a mature industry. Our work comes organically—we have ideas for new products and acquisitions—but it's hard. We want people to feel that they are fulfilled and being developed. Everybody has to have two personal development goals that they accomplish every year. It doesn't have to be necessarily directly related to their job. It can't be skydiving, but someone might come to me and say, "I want to take a course on how to do presentations." Even if they don't have to do presentations in their job, I say, "Yes, go ahead and do that." That's part of what we have implemented from MAP, and I think that has been tremendous for my people. I'm so proud of them.

As I have emphasized throughout this book, one of the first obligations of a leader is to manage his or her people and help them grow. That is *exactly* what Joe is doing when he has people set two personal development goals each year (as you will see in the next section of this chapter). This is *not* touchy-feely business management either; it's enlightened leadership. The best way to grow your business is to start by growing your people. And sooner or later that kind of leadership will improve your bottom line. Just ask Joe. Since he took charge of the publications division, its revenues have gone from $6 million per year to $25 million. Now that is impressive by any standard.

BRINGING IT ALL TOGETHER

Now, how do you structure the process of personal growth? How do you align your personal growth and goals with your professional growth and goals? How do you measure your progress along the way? For Joe the answer to all of these questions was the Life Plan. And Joe has taken to heart the MAP mantra "Write it down!" His Life Plan is about two inches thick, and he keeps it in a loose-leaf binder so he can easily review it and make adjustments as he moves through life. And of course Joe's Life Plan has the same basic components that we urge companies to draft: a mission statement, a vision statement, a values statement, and a "business" plan, which reinforces another MAP mantra: "Run your life like a business. It is!"

How do you do a Life Plan? There are no hard and fast rules of course, but a good place to start is with MAP's Personal Development Plan (outlined on page 228). The Personal Development Plan is a way of helping you see where you are today in terms of your career and your personal development. It also helps you apply your MAP tools—the Vital Few, Goals and Controls, mentoring—to improving your personal life. Joe has taken the basic principles of the Personal Development Plan and added to them a mission statement, a vision statement, a values statement, and, essentially, a business plan for his life. That is a wonderful template right there for doing an effective Life Plan. (Also see the Appendix in the back of this book for a more detailed template that will help you do your own Life Plan.) But the beauty of the Life Plan is that you can adapt it to your specific needs and tastes. Like Joe, some people take a comprehensive approach and do a Life Plan that is 80 or 100 pages long, sometimes more. Other people, like my coauthor Paul Chutkow, were able to boil down their mission, vision, values, and goals—both short-term and long—into a few tight pages. Whatever form you choose, just do it! And enjoy the process. You'll be amazed at the power of this tool.

How did Joe Daquino construct his Life Plan? "I have an executive summary," Joe explains, opening a thick black binder notebook.

> Here's my mission statement, and then my vision statement. For the mission statement . . . I wrote the statement and at the bottom of it I tried to think of the handful of people that are important in my life and why. I have Dane in here. The things that I get out of Dane are that he's spiritual, moral, and wise, and I want to become more like that. So I envision myself becoming a force whom Dane thinks is spiritual, moral, and wise. I also did that for my brothers, my partner, and others. That's my mission.

Joe also drafted a five-year vision that states where he wants his life to go and what he wants to accomplish. "I broke that down into

Personal Development Plan

I. Where am I now? (Appraisal)
   A. Identify opportunities for personal growth.
   B. Identify barriers to personal growth.
   C. Identify your personal motivators: values, desires, interests.
   D. Analyze your relationship patterns (the FIRO-B assessment).
   E. Analyze your management style (the Behavioral Style Analysis).

II. Where do I want to go? (Goal setting)
   A. Identify your personal Vital Factors.
   B. Focus on the Vital Few.
   C. Write positive mission, vision, and values statements.
   D. Identify specific changes you want to make.
   E. State the rewards you want to earn, financial and other.
   F. Specify how you want to improve your relationships.
   G. Specify ways you want to stretch beyond your comfort zone.

III. Choose strategies for achieving those goals. (Strategies)
   A. Select a confidant, mentor, or coach.
   B. Select a role model you want to emulate.
   C. Leverage your strengths.
   D. Work to overcome your weaknesses.
   E. Commit to a system of accountability.
   F. Seek new experience and knowledge.
   G. Give priority to creating balance in your life.

IV. Take goal-oriented action. (Action)
   A. Implement your Personal Development Plan.
   B. Monitor your progress on a regular basis.

V. Create a system of evaluation. (Measure)
   A. Obtain outside feedback from your coach, family, and colleagues.
   B. Measure your progress in managing your Vital Factors.

VI. Take corrective actions where necessary. (Follow-up)

VII. Celebrate your successes. (Validation)

eight different areas," Joe explains. "I have career. I have personal outlook and vision. I have intellectually where I need to be. Financially, where I want to be. What I want my home environment to look like. What I want to look like spiritually and socially. That's the vision. Then I have a section titled 'Core Values and a Philosophy of Life' for each of those eight areas. I wrote a couple paragraphs for each of those and how it is that I look at these different areas."

To chart his future Joe also keeps an accurate account of previous events, which he calls "Record of My Past." "This I update every year: it's a timeline," Joe explains.

> It starts out with the present and goes back in time. I look at my jobs, where I lived, what I did for that chunk of time—it's in five-year segments—what I've accomplished, what I was doing, and what I learned. If I go back to 1989–1993, for instance, I was associate publisher of the *TL Directory*. I lived in Hollywood and West Hollywood. I was kind of a rabble-rouser in those days: I marched in Washington, I did a lot of fundraising for AIDS services, I demonstrated against Governor Pete Wilson's veto of a bill. I got my first pet, became a bodybuilder, and I have some career accomplishments. Anyway, I go back and I look at this once a year and say, "Gosh, I can't believe I was that person."

For each of those five-year segments Joe uses another MAP tool, a situational analysis that we call SWOT because it looks at strengths, weaknesses, opportunities, and threats.

From there Joe goes deeper:

> I list my *vital issues of concern,* and then I have specific goals for each of these areas. I have three sets: one-year goals, five-year goals, and ten-year goals. The five- and the ten-year goals are not set in stone. I don't think anyone knows what will happen in ten years, but what they do is they move me in a direction. One of my ten-year goals was to become a motivational speaker. I don't know if I will ever become one, but that says to me: Develop speaking skills. Continue to get opportunities to speak in front of people. Get on panels where I have to address an audience. That's why that's there. Maybe 80 percent of that will happen—that's the MAP thing, 80 percent. But at least I will be advancing in the right direction.

There's more in Joe's book too:

> In my section "Finances and Planning," I have my operating assumptions. I have all my finances, in all of my accounts. I have my goals: what I want to be worth, and what the numbers are now. I live in a house that is a historical property. When we bought it it was very run down, and we restored it. Dane said to me, "If you had

a company you'd have to have capital expenditures in your plan and facility requirements, so you should put the same stuff in your Life Plan about your home." So I have facility requirements, which are home improvements—the list has gotten much shorter—but I have capital expenditures for each year.

This might sound like a lot of work, but Joe found the process to be clarifying and empowering. Suddenly, his entire life—past, present, and future—was snapping into focus. So Joe then decided to push the process even further. "I got really crazy and I created an *advisory board* for each of these areas of my life," Joe says.

I went so far as to have a board meeting one year when I went over this stuff with my board members. People who came, they still talk about it because it was such a unique experience. The board was my partner, a brother, a couple of close friends, a doctor, and a guy who was my financial adviser at that time. We had a meeting. I didn't go through the entire thing, but I said, "This is my plan; this is how it's structured; these are the things I want to do this year. Now, what do you think I should do to accomplish these goals?"

Then Joe went a step further, a MAP step further: "I said to them, 'Go out and Team Consult,' and they did. It was at my house; I gave them lunch. Then they came back and gave me some wonderful input and advice."

Through the Life Plan process and working with his personal board of advisers, Joe was able to pinpoint and write down his *personal Vital Factors,* the key elements that were either holding him back or propelling him forward at that particular time. Once he had his personal Vital Factors identified, he designed ways to measure them. As we at MAP always say, "What gets measured gets done," and that is as true in your personal life as it is in your business. Again, just ask Joe. His board of advisers would point out areas where he needed to improve, and Joe would immediately devise an action step to address the issue. "They would say to me, 'How's your weight? What's your physical fitness like?' If I tell them I went to the doctor and he found I had high blood pressure, they'll be like, 'What's your blood pressure? They have home testing kits; you should do Vital Factors and take your blood pressure on a regular basis.' So I'd start measuring my weight and blood pressure and setting targets and deadlines to reduce them."

Dane has been a guiding influence all through this process. "That's the personal connection," Joe says. "I work with lots of people, consultants, all the time, wanting to help you, and it's not the same thing as working with MAP."

Dane sees Joe's growth and development as a glowing illustration of how the MAP process can help transform people's lives. "I couldn't be prouder of Joe," Dane says.

> Thinking back to when we first met at the MAP workshop and seeing who he is today—and how he is changing other people's lives—is very humbling for me. It makes you realize that each of us has skills and talents that haven't surfaced yet or that we haven't put to good use yet. By applying the MAP life planning process and combining it with a deep-seated commitment to the other person, wow, what can happen is astronomical. Joe isn't just a client, he is a very special person who has made a profound impact on me. This is powerful, life-changing work both for the individual and for their MAP coach. You cannot walk away from a life coaching session without being moved.

For Joe, looking back now, what has been the impact of writing his Life Plan? Joe lifts the big book up in his hands. "It's a journal of self-discovery," he says.

> I'm always finding out things about myself that I didn't know were there. That's one thing. The second thing about the Life Plan is that I've done things that I wouldn't have done without this: getting my MBA, for instance. Net worth goals that I track because of my Life Plan. Fitness and health goals that I accomplished because of this. You find out what you're capable of as a person and as a businessperson. You find out what you're made of and what you're able to do—and then MAP gives you the tools to do it. It's a process of self-discovery.

Thanks, Joe. I couldn't agree with you more. Over the years I have made the Life Plan an essential cornerstone of the life coaching I do. And I have seen how it has helped people clarify where they are in life and chart a clear course for where they want to go. I have a detailed Life Plan myself. So do all of our MAP coaches and consultants. In many cases our life partners and children have Life Plans as well. The impact of writing a Life Plan is always profound. Do it. When you finish you'll be amazed at how clear and empowered you are going to feel. It puts your personal ship on course, and it gives you a reliable compass and rudder to steer your life exactly where you want it to go. As Joe Daquino discovered, do this right and it will become the book of your life.

The Bottom Line

1. We've all had teachers or coaches who have had an important impact on our lives. Think back to them, and ask yourself, "Why were they such great teachers? Why were they so effective?" Write down your answers, and then learn from these examples.

2. Next, ask yourself this: "Am I being a good teacher with my people? Am I helping them grow? Am I giving them the *support* and *trust* they need?" Apply this measuring stick at the office and at home.

3. We all need a clear vision of where we want to go and what success is going to look like when we get there. Help your people—and your children especially—create a clear vision of where they want to go. You'll never get to where you want to go without a roadmap and a clear idea of your final destination.

4. Do a Personal Development Plan for yourself—and encourage your people to do the same. Then encourage them to find a coach or mentor to help them achieve the goals they set down in their plan.

5. The next logical step is of course to write a Life Plan. Look what it did for Joe. Do you really want to move through life *without* a plan?

CHAPTER FIFTEEN

BRINGING MAP HOME

Now you and I are going to have some fun.

You just saw how Joe Daquino brought MAP home to his personal life, and you saw all the positive changes that the Life Plan process set into motion. I hope Joe's experience inspired each of you to sit down and begin writing your own Life Plan. But there are other ways to bring MAP home, and I want to share with you a few more stories that I hope you will find equally inspiring and useful in your own life. These stories will show you how the MAP process can help transform your family business, improve your marriage, improve your health, improve your parenting, and even help you groom your successors and put a smooth succession process into place. I want to start with a young man named West Mathison, a fellow whose products you may have already brought home and served at your family table.

TRANSFORMING THE FAMILY BUSINESS

West's family has deep pioneering roots in the Pacific Northwest. "My great-great-grandfather, Thomas Kyle Mathison, came over from Scotland with his whole family, and they landed in Nova Scotia," West begins. "That same spring, at fourteen years old, he got a job as a cabin boy and sailed around South America." During the Gold Rush in 1869, Tom made his way to what would become north central Washington State, and he and his new wife settled on a 160-acre parcel of land called Stemilt Hill, not far from Wenatchee, Washington. Tom improved the land and, under the provisions of the Homestead Act, earned the deed to the property. "We have the original deed in my office," West says, "signed by President Theodore Roosevelt himself. Our family property is larger now, but it still includes that original 160 acres."

Two generations later, in the late 1950s, the Mathison family was still living and working on Stemilt Hill, growing high-quality apples and cherries for the local growers co-op to package and sell. West's grandfather, whose name was also Tom, was running the business—and it was not going well. In 1958, the Mathisons grew 100 tons of beautiful cherries, juicy and delicious, but for 100 tons of cherries, the co-op paid them only $85.00. For 100 tons! As the co-op general manager explained, the end customers were able to sell the cherries for only a few cents on the dollar. Something was terribly wrong, and West's grandfather was determined to find out what it was.

So Tom Mathison traveled to New York City and then down to Wall Street, where he knew that street vendors were selling his cherries. And there was the answer, plain as day: "The cherries looked horrible," West explains. "The stems were dry and the fruit had lost its luster. Tom thought, 'No wonder no one is picking it up. When the fruit left our farm it was beautiful, but by the time it got to the consumer, it was garbage.'"

To find out more, Tom Mathison went to California's Napa Valley, to see firsthand how the cherry growers there were taking their fruit to market. "At that point in time, there were third-generation Italians growing cherries in Napa," West says. "What Tom found was that they picked the cherries at 4:30 in the morning, finished picking around 11 in the morning, and then they would hydrocool the cherries, put them through a cold water bath. Then they packed them up, sold them, and kept them cold during delivery. And they were having much better success."

Inspired by what he found, Tom Mathison went back to the local co-op in Washington State with a plan. "Listen," he said, "we need to get up early and pick the cherries before it gets hot and then hydro-cool them." But the hydro-coolers were expensive, and the general manager of the co-op said, "Tommy, we're in the business of making money, not spending money." So Tom decided to build his own packing operation on Stemilt Hill, bringing in the most modern equipment and practices. With that, Stemilt Growers was born, a business supplying top-quality, apples, pears, and hydrocooled cherries and other fruit to quality markets across the country. Their fruit was first-rate, all the way to market, and for the growers in the region it seemed like Tom Mathison had launched a mini-revolution.

Some forty years later, however, Tom's family business faced another sort of challenge. The Mathisons were first-rate farmers, but their business practices had not kept pace with the changes in the marketplace. Their industry had moved into a phase of consolidation, and small family growers like the Mathisons were being threatened by the mammoth agricultural conglomerates. Tom wanted to bring new ideas—and greater profitability—into the company. To do that he turned to his grandson West Mathison.

Today West is leading his own mini-revolution in fruit growing and sustainable agriculture. Stemilt Growers now not only grows its own fruit but also serves as an umbrella company and joint marketing unit for a group of top-quality family farms in the region. Quality, as always, is the No. 1 priority. To that end Stemilt has worked hard to upgrade every step in its production and distribution process. It also works closely with its partner growers to improve fruit quality, from planting to harvest to market. And ever since West took over Stemilt, business has been on the rise.

"Our revenues have jumped dramatically in the last two years," West says. "We were selling and marketing around seven million cases of fruit in 2001. By 2005, we were selling seventeen million cases." Bravo, sir! That's more than double in just four years.

One reason for that dramatic jump is that West brought home to his family business a proven system for managing its operations. Through that system Stemilt and its partner growers were able to examine every aspect of their operation and pinpoint their Vital Factors, the key factors that were affecting their bottom line. They then used the new system to improve their productivity and profitability—and to effectively manage their growth. As West explains:

> Our mission statement is "Return to the land." We have to make sure that the farmer who is raising the trees, who has the investment in the dirt, is trained in sustainable living. At Stemilt all the owners are growers too, and we're all eager to create better return for our family orchards. We're farmers at heart, and out of the process of being farmers we've turned into apple packers. Then

we figured out that we needed to become marketers as well. Now when we look at where the company is going, we continually look at where the marketplace is going, and we examine how we can create sustainability for the harvesting operations.

Vital Factors. Proven system. A clear mission statement. Sustainable growth. Need I spell it out? Yes, Stemilt Growers is now powered by MAP. The management system that West brought home was ours. Craig Rhyne, a consultant in MAP's Seattle office, called West at just the right moment. Stemilt was in a rapid expansion phase, and West was having difficulty making changes fast enough.

"I'm a systems guy; I like systems," he explains.

> I needed a systematic way to manage a rapidly growing organization. I needed a system that I could hand off to my managers and directors to use and implement in their own areas. To keep up with our growth, we were basically trying to hire, manage, and organize people as quickly as possible. And it wasn't working very well. I told Craig, "I need to get a little clarity about what I need to be doing. I don't feel like I'm making any progress; all I do is put out fires all day. I don't feel like we're being very effective."

West took a three-day MAP workshop, then he brought MAP home. First, he installed the MAP system inside Stemilt and its harvesting and packing processes. Then, in keeping with MAP's mantra "Manage your supply chain as you manage your employees," West drove the MAP principles and tools all the way through his supply chain, from growers to end-sellers. The results were astounding. "In our business," West says:

> literally every order had been an exception. Every packing request was an exception. Nothing was streamlined. So we started to incorporate MAP into all our different systems. We made it a discipline. Through MAP we started to remove all the logistical problems that we had throughout our supply chain. With MAP we were able to do more with what we had. We basically created an environment where we could take on growth rapidly, and literally, our business just exploded. New business came to us just as fast as we went out to get it. A lot of the growth occurred before I went to MAP, but we are

now successfully executing it at a much higher level of efficiency. It's really driven the company.

Stemilt's explosive growth is being driven in part by America's new emphasis on eating healthier, more natural foods. Much of Stemilt's fruit goes to high-end markets like Whole Foods and other fine chains, so it's a pretty safe bet that you've already brought home and tasted some of the fruit that West and his partners have grown. "We're in all the major high-end stores across the U.S., and it's a lot of fun because we sort of like to romance the product and they do too."

There's more. By tightening up its supply chain, Stemilt has cut costs and improved efficiency, and this has given West and his team more time and energy to be creative and innovative—just like Ted Price's group at Insomniac Games. The result? West and his team have been able to create some enticing new products, some of them designed to address the growing problem of obesity in America.

"We've launched Apple Sweets, which are small containers of crisp, ready-to-eat apple slices, with complementary natural flavors melded in. Apples take on any flavor," West explains. "Think of naturally flavored caramel apple slices or a naturally flavored apple pie slice. If you put those in a lunch box or cafeteria in place of every Snickers bar and then you figure the reduction in calories, you can't have an obese child."

Great going, West! This is a revolution we can all happily embrace!

Improving Your Relationships

What Andy Cohn brought home from MAP helped his business, but it also helped him improve his marriage and his family life. Back in 1988, he and his wife, Virginia, had bought the Duncan Bolt Company, a nuts and bolts distributor located south of Los Angeles. Duncan Bolt had a good reputation, but its owner, Dave Duncan, was seventy-two years old, and he was looking to retire. Andy had this business in his veins. His father, Eric Cohn, had been a pioneer in the fastener business back in New York, and Eric had known Dave Duncan for years. So to Andy Duncan Bolt looked like a very good opportunity.

"We knew Dave through business; they were customers," Andy recalls. "I think it was my dad who said that Dave had let the business run down without letting the name run down. Everybody still knew of Duncan Bolt. When we bought the company it was doing a half a million dollars a year. Fairly quickly we took it back to a million, and that's what I needed to make a living."

Andy is in many ways a brilliant entrepreneur. He's extremely smart, quick, and personable when he wants to be, and he has a spot-on sense of humor. But business fundamentals are, shall we say, not his strong suit. They bore him. Sales, sales, sales are what drive any business, Andy believes, and as his father used to tell him, "Good sales can cover a multitude of sins." In Andy's case his sins were rather plain to see: his concept of a business plan, job descriptions, and business leadership was, let me be diplomatic, *idiosyncratic*. And Andy is the first to poke fun at himself:

"My business plan was exactly right: answer the phone, be nicer to people than Dave had been," he says, and he isn't kidding either. Beth Van Zandt, his sales manager, had a job description that was pure Andy Cohn: "Andy told me when he hired me, 'Sell a lot of bolts and don't piss me off.'"

Andy's wife worked at Duncan Bolt too, and her job description was, well, *elastic*. "When we came here, the bookkeeper was the receptionist; the accounts payable, receivable; the bookkeeper; and the billing clerk," Andy recalls. "My wife had worked in businesses like this as the lay bookkeeper, and she wound up doing all of that." On top of that of course, she was a dedicated wife and mother.

Under Andy's idiosyncratic management "system" everything ran pretty well—for awhile. "When we were at a million dollars, two million a year, I was absolutely comfortable in our business," Andy says. "I knew exactly what I was doing. I had run a business the same size before, and I could feel, smell, and taste it, and I could walk out of here at 4:30 in the afternoon, and I knew how many times the phone had rung, how business was, and what the business climate was."

Then business really started to grow, and that's when the trouble began. "We got to a certain size where, for me anyway, that feeling of comfort and familiarity disappeared." Sales went up. And right along with them, Andy's stress went up. His weight went up. His irritability went up. And his marriage went down.

The agony in a business like this is that as you grow in size, people who show up every day and do their job the best they can, well, there comes a point when they can no longer do the job. It's just too big. And too stressful. My wife is a perfect example of that. She walked in one day and sat down and said, "You know what? I don't like you here, and I don't like the way you're pressuring me here. So I think I don't want to work here anymore!" And she walked out.

Now Andy knew that he really needed help. He needed to bring some sound business practices to Duncan Bolt, and more important, he needed to bring some sound life practices to himself and to his wife and family. He knew that his marriage might be hanging in the balance. "I knew there's got to be a better way," Andy says. "I was seeking answers. I was looking for answers because things were getting totally dysfunctional."

Enter MAP.

"One day, out of the clear blue, Dave Koldstadt from MAP called me and said he'd been referred by a friend of ours in business," Andy recalls. "Could he come in and talk to me about what MAP does? If he had called on a Monday, I might have hung up on him. But he caught me in the right mood and I let him come in. And once Dave comes in, it's hard to get him out. He told me about the MAP workshop, and I thought, 'OK, I'll take the chance, make an investment, take the class myself and see whether or not it has value.'"

Andy's workshop was run by Vicki Merrill, one of our senior consultants, and she had her work cut out for her with Andy, as he is the first to admit. "I'm a tough sell; I don't do well in a student situation," Andy says. "I do great as the teacher but not well as the student. I don't know whether I was absolutely dead lucky to have Vicki Merrill as the teacher or if everybody would have been as good, but I learned a huge amount about myself and my business."

One of his most important lessons was about leading and dealing with other people: one of your first obligations as a leader is to look in the mirror and see what you're doing right with your people and, often more important, what you're doing wrong. Through MAP, Andy did just that. "There was a woman in the workshop who made a huge impression on me," Andy recalls. "She ran the communication department for the City of Pasadena, and everyone from the police dispatchers to the customer service people at the gas department—all of those people worked for her. And she didn't know any of their jobs. But she was effectively managing them as people, and, I could see, was good at it. She was managing all those people and empowering them, allowing them to be effective at what it was they did."

Now Andy saw it all, clear as day. "It was a light bulb," he says. "A lot of it was on the personal side in the sense of 'Don't be your own worst enemy. People are actually listening to what you say and looking to you for leadership, guidance.'"

After the workshop Andy brought a new style and spirit home to Duncan Bolt—and home to his wife and family. Now he delegates, he empowers, he shows his faith and trust in other people. "I joke about it at the office," Andy says. "I walk around here now and say, 'My job isn't to do anything anymore; it's just to keep roadblocks out of your way so that you guys can do your jobs.'"

On the personal side Andy has shed stress, he's shed a huge amount of weight, and thanks to his new spirit and attitudes, the humor and fun are back in his marriage. "It has improved our relations greatly—she's a better wife," Andy laughs. "I'm not saying that out loud. It might slip into print somewhere and I'd be sleeping in the garage for a year!"

IMPROVING YOUR PARENTING

In his early days as head of RQ Construction in Southern California, George Rogers was a tough, no-nonsense, results-driven, at times abrasive kind of guy. He thought quickly and made decisions quickly—and he tended to get impatient with people who were not quite as quick as he is. Still, his pile-driver approach was very effective in terms of his company's bottom line. In the year 2000, RQ was a $50 million-a-year company. In an industry as competitive as construction, that was a very good number.

But George's controlling, pile-driver approach to management often sent chips flying toward the people closest to him. Among the first who always had to duck was his younger brother, Don, a vice president and senior project manager at RQ. "My personality is that of the controller," George admits.

I'm very oriented to that style of command and control management. My brother is one of the key people here at RQ Construction. But Don and I have very different personalities. I have a personality that says, "Come on in, tell me the problem, give me your three recommended solutions, tell me which one you recommend, and then leave." My brother has a personality that is low risk, high compliance, and he likes to really think things through and is much slower to come to conclusions. Well, when he would come into my office or we would talk, after a bit I'd be tapping my foot, like, "Are we done here?" and he would take me as rude.

Well, yeah. George's wife often had to duck too. "She is an incredible woman," George says. "She puts up with my strong personality. She is the most godly woman on the face of the earth. Even when I'm a jerk, she loves me."

Then there were George's two children, Kristen and Mack. With them, George says, he had a tendency to dictate, rather than to listen patiently and understand what they were really saying. "That's very hard for me," George admits now. "I am the ultimate problem solver, and it's hard for me to listen and not respond." With his kids, as with his brother and his wife, his inclination was to listen to them briefly and then say, "OK, I've listened. Now it's your turn to listen: I've got your solution. I'll fix the problem." George, as you can see, had not learned how to delegate or how to empower his people. Nor was he aware of how poorly he was communicating or how he was violating the basic tenets of clear communication, the ones I set forth back in Chapter Seven.

Then MAP got hold of him.

In the year 2000, George went through a three-day MAP workshop, and it proved to be both unsettling and enlightening for him. The Behavioral Style Analysis made clear to him his high-D personality, meaning high Dominance, and it helped him understand why he often had trouble communicating with his brother and other people close to him. The workshop also made him see clearly how his dominating approach was disempowering his people. Right away, George realized that he had to learn how to pull back and empower his people. He had to become more patient. And perhaps above all, he had to learn how to *listen*.

After the workshop George could not claim to be an entirely new man, but he did bring home to RQ Construction a new attitude and spirit. Now he had a deeper understanding that his people were not there to serve him; he was there to serve *them,* to give them what they needed to succeed. This transition, George says, was not an easy one to make:

> We were moving from the traditional command and control mold to a more collaborative mold where we truly collaborate with each other and we elevate other people. I realized that the guy with the tattoos erecting structural steel may be as important a designer as one of the architects, because that guy can help us design the structure and save us hundreds of thousands of dollars. But no one had ever asked him his opinion or listened to him. We're learning that we have to lead with *influence* rather than with *authority.* How do you influence people to follow your lead, rather than having them follow you out of fear?

George took this same lesson home to his wife and family. "I think I am much less abrasive to my wife now," George says. "And I think I am a better husband. I'm far from perfect, but I think I'm doing better."

One of his most significant areas of growth, he says, is with his kids, Kristen and Mack.

> I have always taught my kids in our core Christian principles. The biggest difference now is that I am better able to integrate my core principles—and MAP principles—in guiding my children. They're young adults, and all of us parents need to clearly articulate our values: why you should not take drugs or alcohol, why you should abstain from sex, why you should not do all these things. It's not just a matter of saying don't do it—that's command and control. It's having the ability to teach and adapt yourself to them, so you reach to where they really understand. You have to look at your own behavior and say, "What's not working? What's not going right?" I had to adapt my behavior as a dad. I had to learn to stop lecturing them and start becoming an effective coach. That better communicated how much I care. And guess what? It turned out that they both *love* to be coached. I think all kids do.

Looking back now, George says that while he learned a lot at MAP about how to run his business, his most important lessons were about learning how to work better with people—and learning to be humble. "There are laws of the universe that apply to human behavior, and they don't stop in the office," he says. "They cover 100 percent of life. MAP puts meat and ligaments on the bones of that realization. . . . MAP helped me understand that it's my responsibility as a leader and manager to adapt to my environment—not to ask my environment to adapt to me. Another way to put that is, 'Suck up your ego and your pride and serve other people.' You serve the company and you serve other people best by meeting their needs, not by asking them to meet your needs."

Well said, George. And his words make me proud. I've personally coached him over the years, and I'm thrilled to see how George Rogers has grown and matured as a leader and as a man. Oh, one more thing. In case you're wondering if George's growth as a leader was good for his bottom line at RQ Construction, I can attest that the answer is yes. From 2000 to 2005, RQ's revenues doubled, going from $50 million to $100 million. As Eric Gillberg so wisely said right at the outset, if you want to grow your business, start by growing yourself and the people around you.

GROOMING YOUR SUCCESSORS

One of the toughest—but most necessary—jobs that any business leader faces is grooming his or her successors. And that can be especially hard in a family-owned company. The history of American business is filled with prominent examples of business dynamos who built colossal empires only to see them crumble when their children couldn't carry on with the same spirit, savvy, and effectiveness. Peter Ganahl is making sure that a similar fate does not happen to his family business, the Ganahl Lumber Company, the oldest lumberyard in California—and the oldest client in the MAP family.

The history of Ganahl Lumber is closely intertwined with the history of California itself. The landmark year was 1884. The City of Los Angeles had a population of only 22,000 people, but a boom was in the offing. The Santa Fe and the Southern Pacific Railroads had both completed laying track all the way West to California, and to spur business they were offering trips to California for the princely sum of $1.00. That same year, two immigrants from Austria, Christian Ganahl and his brother Frank, came out to Southern California from St. Louis. On a site south of Los Angeles the Ganahl brothers purchased a lumberyard, and the family business was born. Three generations later, when his father died unexpectedly in 1973, Peter took over the family business as president, at the age of only twenty-seven.

At that time Peter had experience in the company, but he was certainly not prepared for that level of responsibility. "I drove trucks, forklifts, built loads, waited on customers, put lumber in bins, sold on the counter. You can imagine all the jobs a little lumberyard does over time," Peter says. In terms of management, though, Peter was a novice, and what saved him, he says, was that Ganahl was still small. "One of the reasons I think it was possible for me to survive was that it was a small enough business that I could get my arms around it and not screw it up too badly. We had about fifty employees, and sales in 1972, the year before my father died, were $2.9 million. If it were a bigger business, I probably would have screwed it up."

Enter MAP.

Peter knew he needed to gain management experience, and in 1975 he found MAP. Peter went to one of the early MAP workshops, at a time when Eric Gillberg and his original team were still in their start-up years. Peter says that MAP proved to be a godsend: "I didn't know much, and it was really helpful to find people who knew something about this thing called business and who could impart some of their skills to me." Peter and MAP have been working together ever since. And by 2004 those sales numbers had grown just a little bit: to $250 million for the year.

Given how ill-prepared he had been to take over the company, Peter has gone to great lengths to make sure that he properly grooms his successors. He has two sons working in the business, Mark and Peter, and he has been insistent that they earn their stripes in the company just as everyone else has to. "I'll give you an example," Peter says. After Ganahl acquired another lumber company and four of its yards, Peter's son Mark threw his hat in the ring for the general manager's position at one of the newly acquired yards. He didn't get the job, and Peter says it was for one simple reason: Mark didn't have the most experience among the four candidates who applied for the job. Peter took aside the three who were passed over, including his son, and explained what they had to do to grow and be better qualified the next time around. Peter says this episode sent a clear and important message throughout Ganahl Lumber.

"The message that was sent was overwhelming: that having the right name was not entitlement to something," Peter says. "One of the things that we have worked very hard on around here is to say that this is a meritocracy, not an aristocracy. In family businesses I believe that's a vital message. As soon as the rest of the troops see a semicompetent family member doing a job that could be better done by someone else, the poison is being poured." Peter firmly believes that both Mark and Peter have the right stuff to one day run the company, but they're going to have to get there the hard way and the best way: by proving their merit.

What it comes down to, Peter says, is something that both MAP and his mentors inside the family have deeply impressed upon him: the importance of always managing your business in line with your values. In pursuit of that goal, Peter has taken a very creative step: he has instituted a series of MAP-style family meetings to plan the future, to discuss the family's values, and to achieve alignment and buy-in on the future of the family and the family business. "I have four children, two of whom are married, and three grandchildren," Peter explains. "We meet as a family and we have coaches." The process, he says, has been illuminating. One thing that the Ganahl family came to agree upon is that *money* is not the same thing as *wealth*. Real wealth, they realized, comes from values and experience, and from character and education. In line with MAP teaching, the Ganahls then turned that glowing insight into a cornerstone of a family mission statement that they drafted together.

"The mission statement said that one part of the family wealth was to run a great business," Peter says. "But when was the last time you saw money run a great business? Never happens, doesn't work that way. Real wealth has to be the sum total of the character, integrity, experiences, and education of the family members themselves. We started this process thinking about the family's financial assets and thinking that wealth had something to do with money. Then we found out that it didn't. And you know what? It was very powerful. And now we're really focusing on something else, on something much larger."

What Peter's doing in this process, of course, is coaching. He's being a good leader. He's facilitating. He's asking the big questions. He's empowering his children and his grandchildren. He's empowering them to think for themselves, to take responsibility for their own lives and their own actions, and to share with him their thoughts and ideas. In my eyes Peter has totally absorbed the MAP leadership model and MAP's guiding principles, and he has made them his own. Moreover, and thoroughly naturally, he's now modeling MAP principles and the MAP leadership model for his children and grandchildren. He's leading by example, he's managing to his values.

And there's something more. As George Rogers and Andy Cohn have learned to do, Peter is not imposing his views or his solutions. He's guiding. He's inspiring. I'm pleased and proud to see that, and I know that Eric Gillberg would be proud as well. They have all learned a leadership lesson that Robert Mondavi has expressed well, and to my mind there is no finer bottom line to each of their stories: "The best leaders don't rule; they inspire."

CHAPTER SIXTEEN

THE PROMISED LAND

We live in revolutionary times.

If you glance at the American economy, and if the only phenomenon you see is the proliferation of Home Depots, Wal-Marts, Taco Bells, and Starbucks, then you might rightly feel a little gloomy. Big conglomerates, you might conclude, rule the roost and are crushing the little guy and driving mom-and-pop businesses into the realm of endangered species. Steve Campbell put it starkly: "The big dog can eat; the little dog is going to get eaten." But that, my friends, is only a limited view.

Every single day at MAP we see a very different economic picture. We see a Ted Price taking a childhood passion and, from scratch, turning it into a computer games company with global reach and millions of dollars in sales. We see a Bill de la Viña seeking meaning and purpose in his life and then turning that humble impulse into a money-transfer business that spans this hemisphere and handles $1 billion in transfers a year. We see a Christi Wilkins determined to help at-risk kids succeed and then creating the means for those kids to do just that. And what about Peter Ganahl? How come his family-owned lumber company hasn't been eaten alive by that big dog Home Depot? Because Peter's family company has a clear mission and a faithful customer base that it serves better than Home Depot ever could: the local professionals in the building and construction industries. Let Home Depot have the amateurs and the weekend do-it-yourselfers; Peter's team serves the pros. And what about Steve Campbell? What did he do after he sold Campbell Concrete to a bigger dog? He took his windfall, created the Campbell Development Company, and poured his expertise and entrepreneurial spirit into something entirely new. Yes, this is the vibrant, exciting economic reality that we at MAP see and work with every single day. We see an economy that is in constant, self-sustaining, positive change, powered by men and women who are smart, resourceful, creative, resilient, and always ready to embrace change, growth, and new opportunities.

And there's more, much more. Back in 1848, Karl Marx and Friedrich Engels, writing the Communist Manifesto, envisioned a global revolution in which the workers would rise up and seize control of "the means of production." Well, today the world is indeed seeing that revolution, but not exactly in the way that Marx and Engels envisioned it. Today's revolution is not born from political collectivism or government fiat; it's born from the harmonious marriage of modern technology, human ingenuity, and the empowerment of the individual. Today, thanks to Bill Gates, Steve Jobs, and many other pioneers, a lone entrepreneur can sit at her home computer and run her business, manage her supply chain, pay her bills, design buildings, do scientific or medical research, or self-publish books, and via the Internet, she can promote her services, sell her products, and instantly communicate with customers and people around the globe, all this with a simple click of her mouse. With today's exciting new tools all the old walls and economic barriers are tumbling down. The free, creative entrepreneurial spirit is on the rise, even inside big corporations, and the only limits we the people have are the boundaries of our own imaginations. MAP works with that spirit every single day, and it is MAP's mission and privilege to nurture it and help it soar.

And that brings us now to the best part, the concluding part of our journey: what is the end result of the MAP process? Once you've understood how to lead and empower your people, once you've understood how to pinpoint and manage your Vital Factors, once you've brought the MAP principles and tools home for yourself and your family, what can you achieve? Where can the MAP process lead? How far can you go?

To answer those questions, I want to tell you just two more stories, the stories of Hector Orci and Ray Thurston. These men come from different backgrounds, and they followed different paths. But Hector and Ray both achieved nearly all their goals in business, and then they both set out to achieve something more.

They wanted to share what they had learned, and they both wanted to give something back. Their journeys, their paths, are filled with meaning and purpose, and as you read their stories and follow the thread of their common hopes and aspirations, I hope you will find a final measure of guidance and inspiration, a little extra boost to carry you forward and help you fulfill your own dreams and ambitions.

A Noble Mission

Hector Orci is an amazing man. He's near retirement now, living north of Los Angeles in a hacienda-style house on a hillside close to the Pacific Ocean. Hector is a calm, soft-spoken man, and right away he comes across as an Old World gentleman, a man who has lived life to the fullest and learned many important lessons along the way. Hector cherishes his family, and today his children and grandchildren remain close to Hector and his wife. In many parts of America the traditional family unit has crumbled, and more and more kids find themselves in single-parent families. But Hector and his family hold to an older, sturdier tradition, a life where your family, your friends, and your community remain reassuring anchors in a sea of social turbulence and change. Hector leads us into a den filled with photos and family mementos, then he motions his visitors from MAP to a comfortable couch and he begins to reflect back across his life and his work.

Hector explains that he was born into a proud Hispanic family living on the Mexican side of the San Diego–Tijuana border. "But I did all my schooling on the American side," he says, "and much of my boyhood was spent going back and forth." Hector went to USC, the University of Southern California, then he earned a master's degree at the prestigious Fletcher School of Law and Diplomacy in Medford, Massachusetts. From there Hector went into academia, teaching economics at the Inter American University in Puerto Rico. Soon, though, Hector decided he wanted more. He was newly married, and soon they had a baby on the way. Hector wanted to make more money, he wanted to be more creative, he wanted broader horizons, and ultimately, he wanted to make a greater difference in the world, with the Hispanic community and far beyond.

So the next stop for Hector and his young family was Cincinnati, Ohio, and the best possible training ground in advertising and marketing: Procter & Gamble, where Doug Ducey would get his start a few decades later. "It was great training," Hector says now. "In terms of advertising, it was the Great Machine." At Procter & Gamble, Hector found that he had a passion and a true flair for advertising and marketing, and there he laid the groundwork for a brilliant international career.

Hector next went to Chicago with Alberto-Culver to market that firm's lines of hair care and beauty products. Then the ad giant McCann-Erickson recruited him to go back to Puerto Rico to manage its largest account. After three years in Puerto Rico, Hector and his family moved on to Mexico City, and over the next twelve years he worked at the top of his field, first with McCann-Erickson, then with Young & Rubicam, and then with Doyle Dane Bernbach—three of the largest and most prestigious ad agencies in the world. And Hector had a wonderful added asset: his wife, Norma, had a gift for creating memorable, compelling ads. She was so talented in fact that when McCann-Erickson decided to open an office in Los Angeles, to cater to the burgeoning Hispanic community there, it recruited Hector to be general manager and Norma to be the creative director. They formed a powerful team: both of them were perfectly bilingual, both had a deep understanding of American and Hispanic cultures, and both had top-quality big agency international experience.

In Los Angeles Hector and Norma quickly built up an impressive client base for McCann-Erickson, creating Spanish-language advertising for some of the biggest brands in corporate America. After a few years, though, they both became itchy for change. "We had no freedom," Hector says. "So in 1986, we split off and created our own agency. It was October 31st, to be exact."

In creating La Agencia de Orci, Hector and Norma didn't exactly start from scratch; they took five of their clients with them, with McCann's blessing. And soon their start-up venture was one of the hottest Hispanic agencies in the country, with a client list of corporate giants like Honda, Johnson & Johnson, Verizon, and Allstate Insurance. "Hispanics are very important customers for these companies," Hector explains. "Those are very big accounts."

What's the secret to their success? Simple: Hector and Norma understand their customers and how to create ads that satisfy their needs. "Latinos prefer ads that are information and benefits oriented," Hector explains. "Latinos use ads for decision making. So in our work we don't rely on pizzazz or manipulation. We don't try to sugarcoat a manipulative message." And Hector has another secret, one that more executives and leaders would do well to emulate: he knows how to listen. "I really don't know what's in anybody's mind—until they tell me," he explains. "So we put great emphasis on what consumers tell us. We rely on direct contact and lots and lots of research."

As their client list grew, Hector found that he had a problem on his hands: "My business had grown to a point where I was having trouble managing it," he says. "It was causing me a lot of stress and strain."

Enter MAP.

Tom Hawkins, one of the executive consultants in MAP's office in Sherman Oaks, on the rim of LA, called Hector and invited him to a three-day MAP workshop. "I was interested," Hector says, "but I had no idea what it would be like or what I'd do with it." Lew Herbst, one of our best senior consultants, ran the workshop. Hector was impressed and hired Lew to bring in the MAP system and work with his team. "Lew is one of the people I value most in my business experience," Hector says. "My passion is on the creative side and on the achievements, not on the process. Lew is so good at keeping us focused on the financial side."

Like Ted Price and his team at Insomniac Games, Hector found that the MAP system actually freed him and his people to be more creative. The Vital Factors process kept their ship tightly on course and running efficiently, so Hector and his team could focus on creating better ads and bringing them in on time and on budget. The Vital Factors process also helped Hector plan better for the future and manage crises when they come. "The most important result," he says, "has been our ability to make really hard decisions on time, because of the way the Vital Factors work. The Vital Factors alert us to certain problems, and then we can move quickly to fix them."

By temperament Hector is an artist; he is *not* a confronter. But with Lew Herbst on site at least once a month to be the

Enforcer—the same role he played for Steve Campbell—Hector's operation got healthy doses of discipline and candor. "We don't sweep problems under the rug; we know Lew's coming back," he says. "With MAP, all of a sudden you find yourself running a grown-up business."

Like Ted Price, at the outset Hector worried that the MAP regimen might not sit well with his creative people. So he confronted the problem head-on by sending several of his creative people through the MAP workshop. The results surprised him: "It demystified the MAP process for them," Hector says. "It relieved their fear that it would stifle their creativity."

Now we come to the real pay-off. Now in his mid-sixties, Hector is ready to step away from the chairmanship of the ad agency he created. "It's time for me to retire," he says, "and I have a succession plan in place." The larger question, though, is this: What will Hector do next? Where will he pour his energy and talent? Now that MAP is in his veins, Hector has that carefully planned out as well.

"I'm an education junkie," he explains, relaxing comfortably in his chair. "I've known for a long time that there's a lot that I don't know." Hector has been studying one particular area of education: "the economics of underdevelopment, how people behave when their countries and communities are underdeveloped." In advertising, he says, "I sell behavior change. Now I want to change behavior on a larger scale."

More specifically, Hector has been trying to understand how Hispanic kids can be helped to do better in school—and how schools can be changed to better serve Hispanic students. Christi Wilkins, meet Hector Orci. Hector has also helped with the creation of a number of charter schools in the Los Angeles area, to serve the Hispanic community. As Hector sees it, his work in education flows naturally from his work in advertising: he wants to guide people, enlighten people, and help them make better decisions about how they lead their lives. In MAP terms he wants to empower his people, in the broadest possible sense.

Hector is excited about this new phase of his life. He's helping kids, he's helping his community, and he's finding it both meaningful and fulfilling to give something back. Now, as our conversation draws to a close, Hector wants to emphasize one more fundamental truth that he has learned along his journey. "I didn't need MBA skills," Hector says. "The theoretical is absolutely useless unless it can be applied to a real-life situation. What I've needed all along is what works, the simple and the doable. Right away with MAP I had the feeling that MAP would provide clarity and the tools by which I could accomplish much more with my life. And I was right. MAP opened horizons to what I could do, and it gave me confidence. It gave me a clear, simple, no-nonsense way to get to where I wanted to go."

Hector Orci got to where he wanted to go. He touched and influenced a lot of people along the way. And he's not finished yet. Now that he has set his sights on transforming LA schools, Hector's greatest achievements could be still to come.

ADVANCING THE REVOLUTION

Karl Marx, meet Ray Thurston.

This afternoon Ray is sitting in his low, sprawling ranch house on a quiet country road on the outskirts of Scottsdale, Arizona. He works at a huge table, in a room filled with exotic art objects from Africa and the South Pacific. Clearly, he is a man of many passions and a bit of a restless soul: when he's not traveling the world for one of his many businesses, he divides his time between Arizona and his cherished hideaway in Jackson Hole, Wyoming. Ray is an intense and very dynamic man, and once he starts telling his story it flows forth in a strong, steady torrent.

"I was born in Los Angeles in 1947," he begins. "My father was running a local delivery business called Rocket Messenger Service." Part of Rocket's business was delivering packages, scripts, and film canisters to Hollywood studios and executives. Making those deliveries quickly and reliably was hard work, as Ray learned firsthand. "When I was thirteen I learned what you do when your father has a small business: you work your butt off. Your pals are going to the beach or pretending to look for a job. In my case I was out riding a bicycle delivering packages."

Ray was not a good student, and studying foreign languages really put him against the wall. He was also in a very rough high school and that didn't help either. "In high school I was at the bottom of my graduating class," Ray recalls. "Out of 212 students, I was

209. I probably had ADHD and dyslexia; they just didn't know it at the time. When I hit the foreign languages, I got my first F. I got five A's and an F, and I just went steadily downhill after that. And I flunked Spanish."

Living in the Hollywood hills, though, Ray got a different kind of education. "There weren't a lot of kids to play with where we lived, so I'd go hunting and fishing in the lake and try to shoot rabbits, quail, and dove and actually eat them," he says. "It was like being Tom Sawyer, but going to school every day at an inner-city school. It was quite an education."

For college Ray managed to get into Utah State University, but after two years he flunked out. Then, at the height of the Vietnam War, he was drafted into the U.S. Army. When he came back from his tour of duty, Ray was far more mature and far more focused. "In high school I was the second-youngest person in my class," he says. "I often think that maybe my parents put me into school because they had their own business and that was a pretty good place for me to go." After the Army, Ray returned to Utah State and this time he did well, studying political science and animal behavior.

When he graduated Ray came back to LA and went to work for his father's messenger service. After eighteen months tragedy struck: "My dad was ill and he passed away unexpectedly. So I woke up one morning and had about eighty or ninety people working for me in San Francisco and Los Angeles, and it was right in the middle of union negotiations with the Teamsters. I was twenty-three."

Talk about a trial by fire. It took a lot of doing and a lot of personal growing, but Ray stood up to the Teamsters and negotiated a much better deal for the family company. "I think that was a pretty good accomplishment," Ray says, "for my first ninety days as the leader of the organization."

Over the next four years Ray ran the business, and though he lost four of his top five people after his father died, he put the company on a winning track. "Profits went from $25,000 a year to $25,000 a month, and our revenue tripled in three years," Ray says. With results like those Ray knew he had found his passion: "I liked running a business, being able to sell, being able to have a lot of control over the quality of the product we were selling."

At this stage his stepmother was still a partner in Rocket Messenger Service, and when she refused to accept a buyout, Ray decided to start something new. "I had saved $17,000, and with it I started a little company called SonicAir. It drained my bank account, but I wanted to see different parts of the country and the world. So I decided to get into the air courier business. I thought it would be a lot more exciting than dropping packages off locally."

This was in the days before Federal Express, and right away Ray spotted an empty niche in the air courier market—and he set out to fill it. "Back then the overnight carriers on the West Coast stopped picking up at 2:30 or 3 o'clock in the afternoon, so there was all of that time in the afternoon and late into the night for us to step in," Ray says. "We did real well. Our company would pick up late at night and deliver very early in about six or seven cities around the United States."

That was just the beginning. Ray knew that he would never stay in business delivering to only six or seven cities. So he joined forces with some partners on the East Coast: "They had agents all over the country, and they shared their agent list with us. Right away I had agents all over the country to do deliveries. We used commercial airplanes. With $17,000, you can't even buy a glider."

To build SonicAir Ray wasn't interested in delivering everyday documents or other goods of relatively low value. No, he wanted to build his business by delivering items of very high value, often requiring special handling: A kidney that had to be rushed across the country for an emergency transplant. Legal documents that had to be delivered to the Supreme Court in Washington, D.C., by the following morning. Or papers that had to be hand delivered and filed with the Federal Communications Commission by 4 P.M.—or else the lawyers handling the case would fail to meet their deadline.

Now, folks, I could write an entire book—and it would be fascinating too—about how Ray took his concept and that niche and turned SonicAir into a business colossus and a true pioneer in the air courier business. And I could chronicle for you how, when Ray's start-up venture grew too fast and hit a wall, MAP came in and helped him rescue his company from its mounting ills. By now, though, you know the outlines of that story: Ray went to a MAP workshop, then he came back and drove the Vital Factors process through every department in his company. At the same time, he totally transformed his approach to leadership, learning how to delegate and empower his people, and achieving dramatic results in the process. That's all true, but straight away let's cut deeper into the marrow of Ray Thurston's story:

"I became interested in computers back in the late 1970s," Ray says, and right away he sensed what computers were going to do: stir a revolution. Computers, he could see, were going to transform the shipping business; that was for certain. But Ray also saw that computers were going to transform the way almost all companies were doing business. Computers were going to transform the way companies developed and manufactured products, managed their inventories, did their billing, and shipped their products to market. Paper documents, Ray could see, would soon be as obsolete as the Model T; the future of documents, messages, and even financial transactions was going to be electronic and digital. To keep pace with these accelerating changes, Ray knew that he had to totally transform the way SonicAir went about its business.

"I knew we needed to start shipping things that weren't paper based," Ray says. "We had to get into the parts business, we needed to find customers that have parts that are critical for their equipment when it breaks down. And we needed to be able to get those parts to them as fast as possible. To do that I needed a nationwide network, so I bought a company called Air Couriers International, based in Arizona. It was three times my size." Ray moved his headquarters to Scottsdale, thinking that he was going to be at the forefront of the coming revolution. But it didn't turn out quite that way. To make a long story short the merger went badly—the two companies' corporate cultures were radically different—and by the early 1980s Ray's business started to tank. The crisis threatened him personally as well.

"In five to six months I lost 40 percent of the business. We were losing $50,000 a week, or maybe it was a month. Either way, it was bad," Ray recalls. "It was a highly leveraged buyout, and I was leveraged to the hilt myself: my house in California, even my car."

By this time a full-fledged price war had broken out between SonicAir and its main competitors, and Ray was so stressed that he dropped thirty pounds in thirty days. His business was a mess—and his life was a mess. Then he did something smart. "I called my wife, Amy—she was working at an ad agency—and said I want to go fly fishing. I didn't want to get on another airplane because I'd been living on one. So I bought a tent, a sleeping bag, and a bunch of gear, and we went up to the White Mountains here in Arizona."

Once they put up the tent and got settled, Ray sat Amy down—they had been married less than a year—and he shared with her a secret that he had been afraid to tell her before: "We're going broke." Ray now pauses in his story and leans back with a twinkle in his eye. "I said to her, 'Do you still love me?'

"'I do,' she laughed. 'But I'll miss you!'"

Ray laughs now too. "No, it didn't happen that way. But I do like to tell it that way. We relaxed and camped for a few days, caught fish, cooked them, and figured out what I was doing wrong. How could I have been so successful and then . . ."

Ray did figure out what he was doing wrong: he had let go of the Vital Factors process. "It had worked so well we stopped doing it," Ray says. "What I came back from that trip with was *quality:* you have to manage for quality and measure for quality. When you blow a delivery for someone who's going public, you could cost them millions of dollars. . . . And forget about it with a kidney: you can kill somebody. So I decided to go back and measure every delivery that was fifteen minutes late. I took the MAP program, and I decided to focus it on quality."

Ray also did something more dramatic. "I fired all the top management, from SonicAir and from Air Couriers International. And I promoted all of the people below them into their spots. That did two things. It got rid of all the dissension—I was no longer putting out fires created by two battling cultures—and it cut our losses significantly." In short order Ray's return to Vital Factors and business fundamentals turned the situation around, and by 1985 *Inc.* magazine had named SonicAir one of the fastest-growing companies in America, for the third year in a row. Then Ray pushed the Vital Factor process even deeper.

"I took the quality program and spread it into other departments," he explains. "I started having meetings with people, and we would decide on the Vital Factors." Candor, transparency, and value were now his touchstones: "I'd open up with, 'What do you think this company is making?' Everyone thought we were making a 50 percent profit, and here we were losing all this money. I'd say, 'I want everyone in the company to see the financials.' Then we set up financials for each department." Each department had its own Vital Factors, and its own system of incentives and bonuses to cut costs and improve productivity. In other words, Ray took SonicAir back to MAP and back to solid business fundamentals:

> We required that each department meet every week, and we went from losing $50,000 a week to making $50,000 a week. We used the MAP system, Vital Factors, and we regularly posted our results. We had a flash report. Everyone in the company got it, and it showed all of the errors, the on-time performance of each branch office, and it showed the Vital Factors for accounts receivable, for accounts payable, for information systems, accounting, payroll, everything. If I had a manager who came to me and said, "We can't find something to measure with this person," I'd say, "Fire them, because they're not adding any value to the company."

To drive this process even deeper, Ray did something else: "We sent all of the managers and supervisors through MAP, and we had a similar program that we did internally that was similar to the MAP program. We decentralized the company to put the power into the field. Everybody was accountable." Yes, and empowered.

Then Ray took another page out of the MAP handbook: he drove the MAP system and tools beyond his own company and into his vendors and customers. And this is where Ray's story becomes really exciting: Ray and his team became so expert at managing their costs, profits, logistics, and accelerating computerization—their Vital Factors—that they soon started working as consultants and coaches for their entire supply chain, helping other companies pinpoint and manage their Vital Factors. They also shared with them their emphasis on quality and finding new ways to add value.

Now, where did all this lead? Ray and his team became recognized as experts not just in shipping but in logistics, management, and mastering new technology. They weren't just highly effective business managers and leaders; they were highly effective agents of change. Computers were transforming business, the nation was at the dawn of the Internet and the Information Age, and Ray Thurston and his team were at the forefront, helping other companies grow and become more efficient, more profitable, and better equipped to manage the process of change and transformation.

Federal Express took serious notice. And so did United Parcel Service (UPS). And that led to a frantic courtship for SonicAir. In the end Ray worked out a fabulous deal to merge SonicAir with UPS. Though he made a fortune through the merger, Ray Thurston was not about to slow down. Instead UPS managers eagerly harnessed Ray and his unique talents and experience: they made him CEO of a new business, a special logistics consulting unit that helps other companies transform their operations and supply chains. In essence Ray now became both conductor and locomotive, catalyzing change and transmitting his expertise and wisdom—and MAP's—to a broad spectrum of companies across America and beyond.

"There are two things I did that really enhanced my business career," Ray says now, leaning forward across his desk:

One was joining the Young Presidents' Organization. What a tremendous resource they have been. The other was Vital Factors. Understanding our Vital Factors. Implementing a program to manage our Vital Factors. And then sticking to it. It doesn't matter if it's MAP or any other system that works. Get with something that works, stick to it, enhance it, always tweak it, continue to learn, continue to press the organization, continue to let the organization press you. All of a sudden now, we're doing first-class consulting work. People are reengineering their entire organizations because of things that we're leading them into. Part of this came from realizing what good leadership is.

Yes. In Ray's view, everything starts with the key components of enlightened leadership: Being clear in your vision. Managing to your values. Being specific and measurable in your goals. And having a strong, flexible business plan to guide you on your way. And what is the anchor of Ray's mission statement? To him, what is the essence of enlightened leadership? Simple: Empower Your People. Help them grow and develop. Set them up for success. Ray puts it this way: "Our mission is to provide a place for our people to grow personally, professionally, and financially."

Folks, that is music to my ears: it's pure MAP. It's the MAP principles, tools, wisdom, and spirit put beautifully into practice.

GIVING BACK

Ray Thurston's story does not end there. He's not yet sixty, but this man is just getting started. Ray is now developing several different companies, some of them doing important medical and scientific research. One has developed special lenses to improve people's vision. As he charges forward with these and other projects, Ray frequently meets with venture capitalists who are eager to back his projects. More than once they have examined his business plans and said, "Can we bring this to measure? What gets measured gets done." Ray just smiles quietly and says, "Why of course you can!"

Many of Ray's new initiatives come from the same impulse that is motivating Hector Orci: the desire to *give back*, to do something for his community and for the betterment of mankind. To that end Ray has given three $1 million grants to the Translational Genomics Research Institute—a nonprofit biotech research group also known as TGen—to help develop new approaches to treating breast cancer. The projects Ray is funding use the results of advanced human genome research to define a woman's specific genetic profile—her most critical medical Vital Factors—and then design the most effective cures for her, given her profile and her specific strain of cancer.

Ray is very excited about this new frontier, and he says his support for TGen is perfectly aligned with his broader aspirations: to use cutting-edge management techniques and cutting-edge technology to achieve important breakthroughs in medicine, science, and human development. That, he believes, is the proven road to progress, the proven road to creating a dynamic, positive, self-sustaining revolution.

Ray does more than just write checks to TGen: he has insisted that the group put MAP business practices into place, specifically a Vital Factors process to maximize its performance and cost effectiveness. The approach is paying off: "By having specific timelines and measurable results, TGen's leaders have cut the time it takes to do these projects by four or five months," Ray says, "and by better sharing people and resources, they have cut staff costs by $90,000." Again, computers have been key. It used to take a highly paid genetic specialist twenty dedicated days to do the necessary computerized genetic analysis that is at the heart of this research. At Ray's urging, TGen developed a software program that speeds the process and enables a lay computer technician to do the analysis—a tremendous savings in time and money. And of course Ray helped TGen push these kinds of Vital Factor processes through the entire organization. "Their approach to research is now entirely different," Ray says, "and so is their internal culture."

Ray is bringing similar changes to Conservation International (CI), a science-based organization dedicated to protecting the environment: more specifically, protecting endangered plant and animal life on land and in the sea. The group works with governments, local authorities, and the extraction industries—namely mining and fishing—to protect plant and animal life from irresponsible exploitation. To do that the group monitors at-risk regions and educates governments, industries, and in some areas indigenous peoples about sustainable extraction techniques that will safeguard plant and animal life for centuries to come. Thanks largely to Ray, CI has now made Vital Factors an integral part of its management and its mission.

"We set up a system of Vital Factors and measurements at CI headquarters to help managers improve their processes and productivity," Ray says. And that was just the beginning. CI has also set into motion 100 different projects to measure the health of the environment in different areas of the globe. "We grade on a 1 to 5 scale," Ray says, "with 5 being the best." The grades measure how well a state or a region is protecting its natural resources from rapacious mining, logging, or fishing—illegal activities involving billions of dollars' worth of these resources every year. "The Galápagos Islands, for instance, are one of the richest breeding grounds for fish on the planet," Ray says, "but that area was being overfished. Now we have built a monitoring system that enables anyone seeing illegal activity to contact the proper authorities, by drum, by smoke signal, by cell phone, or computer." By putting into place Vital Factor measurements, CI has avoided the nonprofit pitfall that Christi Wilkins refers to as "the warm, fuzzy blob problem." Now Conservation International can show its supporters and funders exactly what it is measuring—and exactly what it's getting done.

"This gives CI strategic advantage and value," Ray explains. "They can now demonstrate the cost effectiveness of their programs and how effectively they are handling their funders' money.

The new system is completely changing their culture and strategy." The result? "The revenues of CI are up 600 percent over the past six years," Ray says, beaming with pride. Just as with Christi Wilkins's group, the key was marrying MAP-style business fundamentals with a noble nonprofit mission.

Ray is pushing Vital Factors into other realms as well. "My wife, Amy, and I just gave a $1 million grant to the Phoenix YMCA over a four-year period of time, and we made them put in the Vital Factor process," Ray says. "Amy's been through MAP, and she works with them to make sure they're doing these things and learning the process. It's baby steps with them, but it's important."

It certainly is, Ray, it certainly is.

A FINAL THOUGHT OR TWO

As I reflect upon Ray's work and personal mission, I can't help but think, what a man. And what a remarkable journey his life has been. From college flunk-out to American pioneer. Indeed everyone we've written about in this book has had a remarkable journey. I think about Katherine Le, going from helpless Vietnamese boat person to the heights of American business. I think about Christi Wilkins, turning her own troubled childhood into a beacon of hope for thousands of at-risk kids. And I think about Jose Pulido, going back home to blighted San Fernando and turning it into a model of what enlightened city government can do.

These men and women didn't start out as pioneers; they started out as ordinary people eager for guidance and eager to find their way in the world. Along the way they found teachers, mentors, and coaches who believed in them, who gave them confidence, and who took them in hand and taught them the importance of mastering the fundamentals of whatever it was they chose to do. Eric Gillberg had it right: every human endeavor has its own unique set of Vital Factors, those few key elements that will either hold you back or propel you to success. Through their own life experience—and with a little help from MAP—Ray, Katherine, Christi, Jose, and the others learned how to pinpoint and manage their own unique Vital Factors, in both their businesses and their personal lives. And with a brand new roadmap in hand, they were able to go exactly where they wanted to go and achieve everything they set out to do. Vital Factors was their compass; the rest they did themselves.

As I look back now at their stories, I do so with a heavy heart, for I know that our journey together, as writer and reader, is coming to a close. And what a long, long road we've traveled together. If you start with Eric Gillberg, I think you can draw one winding yet contiguous line from Eric all the way through to Ray Thurston, a net, really, that also draws together Debra Paterson, Bill de la Viña, Michael Caito, Doug Ducey, Steve Campbell, Tammy Miller, Jose Pulido, Glenn Stearns, Katherine Le, Bob Wexler, Chris Thompson, Ted Price, Christi Wilkins, Joe Daquino, West Mathison, Andy Cohn, George Rogers, Peter Ganahl, Hector Orci, and literally thousands of other companies and individuals who have used the MAP system and its Vital Factor tools to transform their businesses and their lives. In many cases, as with Ray Thurston, individual men and women have then gone further; they have taken the Vital Factor process and radiated it out to their colleagues, families, and friends. We at MAP say great. And while we won't claim that to be a full-scale revolution, we do think it's a pretty good start.

Speaking for all of us at MAP, I just want to say one more thing, directly to the amazing men and women whom you have met in the course of our journey:

What enlightened and inspiring leaders you have become. What wonderful values you are modeling and giving back to your businesses, your families, your children, and your wider communities. Some organizations measure their success solely in terms of their bottom-line profit. But as Peter Ganahl and Christi Wilkins remind all of us, real wealth is measured in very different terms. We at MAP measure our wealth by the number of people we touch, the number of lives we improve, the number of individuals we empower, and the number of success stories that we help to create—stories we can then share with readers like you, across America and far beyond. To each of the men and women who so generously shared with us their personal stories and insights, we say thank you. What character you have. What drive. What spirit. And together, what an eloquent bow you make to the enduring power of the American Dream.

THE MAP MANAGEMENT SYSTEM'S MONDAY MORNING ACTION PLAN

MAP

Step One: Set Your Goals and Develop a Written Business Plan

A. Create and communicate a clear *vision*.
B. Define your *mission* and *values*.
C. Evaluate your past.
D. Assess your present.
E. Design your future.
F. Understand your defining passion.
G. Define the goals you want to accomplish.
H. Develop specific, measurable action steps to lead you to those goals.

Step Two: Pinpoint Your Vital Factors

A. Define your Vital Factors in four basic categories:
   1. Profit and loss
   2. Productivity
   3. Cash flow
   4. Customer satisfaction
B. Develop a spreadsheet to monitor and measure your Vital Factors.
C. Assign ownership for specific Vital Factors to specific individuals.
D. Follow the Pareto principle and focus on the Vital Few.

Step Three: Conduct Regular Vital Factor Team Meetings

A. Choose your Vital Factor Team members.
B. Meet regularly (once every 30 days at a minimum).
C. Follow this general agenda, in this order, at each meeting:
   1. Review the Vital Factor spreadsheet.
   2. Determine any corrective actions to be taken.
   3. Assign action steps to specific people, with deadlines.
   4. Review fulfillment of individual goals for the previous 30 days.
   5. Document results on an individual Goals and Controls scorecard.
   6. Set new 30-day goals.
D. Use Team Consulting as appropriate.
E. Make sure all your business goals are measurable in these areas:
   1. Output
   2. Cost
   3. Quantity
   4. Time
   5. Impact on your Vital Factors

Step Four: Focus Your Team on MAP's Six Functions of Management

A. Leading.
B. Communicating.
C. Planning.
D. Organizing.
E. Staffing.
F. Controlling.

Step Five: Go Deeper

A. Develop an organizational chart.
B. Learn how to delegate and empower your people.
C. Don't wear the Big Red "S."
D. Manage time as a valuable resource.
E. Recruit to staff your team with A players.

F. Develop 90-day training programs and goals for all new hires.
G. Develop your skills as a teacher, coach, and team leader.
H. Check your progress against MAP's 12 attributes of a leader (Chapter Three).

Step Six: Take Active Steps to Develop Yourself and Your People

A. Identify opportunities for improvement.
B. Develop positive personal growth goals.
C. Select a confidant or accountability partner.
D. Identify successful role models to emulate.
E. Develop a Life Plan (see the template at the end of this Appendix).
F. Use your Life Plan to create balance in your life.
G. Review your progress on a regular basis.

Template for Developing a Life Plan

Name: _____

Vital Elements of My Plan

- *Mission*
- *Vision*
- *Values*

- *Career*
- *Personal Growth*
- *Financial*
- *Retirement*

- *Family*
- *Health*
- *Leisure*

Step 1   **Examine the Past**
Personal history
Family history
Impact upon the family
How have you been scripted

Step 2   **Study the Present**
What's going on: personal/family life
Personal/family pressures
Personal/family enjoyments
Personal/family strengths and weaknesses
Personal/family economic needs

Step 3   **Design the Future**
Design your personal future
Personal/family security
Personal/family vision and values
Relationships and enjoyments
Resources to reach goals
Personal/family commitment to vision

Step 4   **Develop the Strategies**
Develop personal strategies
Recognize the goals
Determine the how-to's regarding marriage, children, living
     space, and so forth
Develop plans to achieve the goals
Immediate action needed

Step 5   **Assign Due Dates**
Assign dates to accomplish key goals
Create milestones/Gantt chart for visibility

Personal Situation Analysis

Strengths	Opportunities
1. _____	1. _____
2. _____	2. _____
3. _____	3. _____
4. _____	4. _____

Growth Goals

- _____
- _____

Action Steps

- _____
- _____
- _____
- _____
- _____
- _____

Barriers to My Success

Barriers	Corrective Action
• _____	• _____
• _____	• _____
• _____	• _____
• _____	• _____

Accountability System

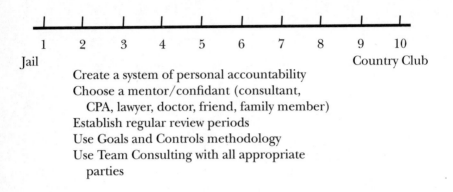

Create a system of personal accountability
Choose a mentor/confidant (consultant,
    CPA, lawyer, doctor, friend, family member)
Establish regular review periods
Use Goals and Controls methodology
Use Team Consulting with all appropriate
    parties

My coach _____

My mentor _____

My confidant _____

Career Chart

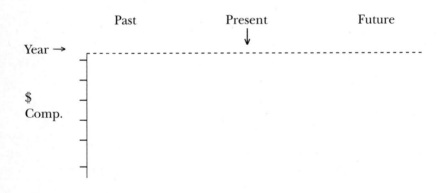

Career Goals

1 Year _____   10 Year _____

5 Year _____   Retirement _____

Strategies

- _____
- _____
- _____

Financial: Net Worth Chart

	Past	Present	Future

Year →

$

Net Worth Goals

1 Year _____   10 Year _____

5 Year _____   Retirement _____

Strategies

- _____
- _____
- _____

Mission, Vision, and Values

My mission _____

My vision _____

My values _____

Key Motivators

1. _____   2. _____   3. _____

The person who represents the kind of individual I want to be

_____

Describe the future:

My family _____

My health _____

My leisure _____

My retirement _____

My Challenge

_____

_____

_____

My Commitment

_____

_____

_____

The Authors

Lee Froschheiser is the CEO of MAP and one of the nation's most respected business consultants and coaches. He has more than three decades of experience in top-level management in both the private and public sectors. He has trained many of the top business leaders in America, and he has developed leadership and management training programs for all aspects of running a successful business.

Paul Chutkow specializes in writing about business leaders and creative pioneers. After fifteen years abroad as a foreign correspondent, he wrote *Visa: The Power of an Idea,* the story of Visa cards and the ways in which plastic money has transformed banking, consumer life, and international commerce. He co-wrote Robert Mondavi's acclaimed memoir, *Harvests of Joy,* and he is also the author of *Depardieu,* an intimate biography of the legendary French actor Gérard Depardieu.

You can reach MAP at (888) 834-3040; mapvitalfactors.com.

INDEX